Discovering t

of the

WONDERLAND TRAIL

encircling Mount Rainier

I . Clover

Bette Filley

with measurement verifications by

Beth Rossow

Cover photo: The Mountain from Indian Henrys
by Rod Barbee

Dunamis House
Issaquah, Washington 98027

Dunamis House
P. O. Box 921
Issaquah, WA 98027

Copyright 2002 by Dunamis House

ISBN 1-880405-09-1

Manufactured in the United States of America

Library of Congress Cataloging in Publication Data #91-77701
Filley, Bette E.
    Discovering the Wonders of the Wonderland Trail
        Includes Index
1.   Hiking -- Washington (State) -- Mount Rainier National Park
    Wilderness -- Guide Books.

FOREWORD

My love of Mount Rainier began the first time I ever laid eyes on it. Then I discovered it has that effect on everyone. Just seeing it produces a magnetic pull that attaches itself to your heart and draws you closer and closer into all sorts of experiences, ranging from simply basking in the beauty of it, to climbing it. And everything in between.

I should have had a clue it was going to be a part of my life. As a young wife in Ohio, I found a gorgeous photo of the magnificent Mountain in a picture book, and decided it would be pretty as an oil painting over our mantle. The paint had barely dried on my masterpiece when I found myself living in Washington. It was the inevitable outcome of having married a native Washingtonian, and putting a picture of his favorite place on earth in front of him daily.

It seems one of those giant magnets was gripping my husband too. (I've since concluded all Washingtonians are born with one in place. You may transplant them, but at the first opportunity, it snaps them back).

It wasn't long before we were bouncing up the road to Mowich Lake and in unison yelled, "there it is!" We had rounded a bend, and there was the oil painting in real life, the spot in the picture. Dog-goned if the kids weren't magnetized too!

Well that settled it. With the whole family hooked, why fight it? We just gave in and became Rainieraholics. Little would keep us away. Rain, snow or shine, every weekend we were off exploring something or other.

That adventure began in 1960. 1965 was our first trip around the Wonderland, and by 1969 this book was written. It was accepted for publication, and through no fault of my own never made it into print. I probably should have gone to another publisher, but I didn't. I put it away in a file, and went on with my life.

It probably would still be there if a decade ago I hadn't met Beth Rossow, a remarkable outdoorswoman. Beth practices what she preaches: not only low impact camping, but low impact living. She lives on the Olympic Peninsula in a very comfortable treehouse (really!) with a view of Mount Rainier. The great Mountain has her by the heart too, and when she heard about the book, nothing would do but that it be updated and published.

So that's what happened. Beth pushed the old measuring wheel again, and noted what changes there were. And guess what. There weren't that many. Even the descendents of the old bears still live in the same places. And the signs (which have been replaced many times over) still contain some discrepancies in mileages. Except for a few minor modifications, little has changed.

Beth

That shouldn't come as such a surprise, but it does. So much has happened in the world, but not at the Mountain. The quiet snows envelop the back country in a time capsule for most of the year, and recede for only a few short weeks to allow a brief glimpse of God's special treasure chest.

And what treasures there are! Of course other great mountains and beautiful places exist, but Mount Rainier is special! Film can't adequately capture the raw beauty, nor can words convey the sense of peace and contentment just being there.

Hikers of the Wonderland earn a degree of accomplishment offered by few other efforts. Don't be deterred by lack of knowledge of Northwest mountain conditions. This book was written with you in mind. It tells everything you need to know to make this trip as safely and as well prepared as possible.

Is the magnet pulling? Yield. Give in. Come discover for yourself the wonders of this Wonderland.

Bette Filley

TABLE OF CONTENTS
Part One

FIRST AID AND EMERGENCY PROCEDURES

RULES, WRITTEN AND OTHERWISE

THE TRAIL LOG
Part Two

THE WEST SIDE

THE NORTH SIDE

THE EAST SIDE

THE SOUTH SIDE

THE MOUNTAIN ENCIRCLED
by Edmond S. Meany

There lies a friendly forest path I know
Where lofty needled boughs salute the sun
And mossy mounds lift jewelled flowers
To point anew the old and gladsome way,
The upward way, to heights where all the hours
Are morning and world's new day
Reveals the Alpine heather lately won
From out the depths of slow receding snow.
I rise and all the aging years are backward flung
For soil up here and flowers and... even time are young.

Some trees are bent and winter-tempest scars
Proclaim the cruel stress of yesterday;
Yet lily-gardens, aster-strewn, and lupine pearls,
Between the snow and wind-scarped granite prongs,
Awake, as round the peak a signal whirls.
And Dawn, victorious, throws her lavish songs
On winds that set the meadowed flowers at play
Beneath the rosy blush of hiding stars.
And now, O Mountain Dawn, I own thy magic art
That stirs anew the youth, the youth still in my heart!

Above the flowers a thousand voices call.
The upward lure of wide eternal snows,
Where jagged cliffs look down on rivers swift
In brawling race, tumultuous to'rd the sea.
We climb o'er ice from rift to gleaming rift,
To crest where star and earth in kinship free
May touch the blue; transcendent glory flows
And clasps the soul of man, ecstatic thrall!
O, spare some strength of flesh and nerve, ye gnawing years,
To meet the surging call my willing spirit hears!

From park to park, the mountain splendor-chain
These precious links, embossed above the clouds
With em'rald spirit or cave of crystal ice
Or silver sheen of amethystine lake,
Give hints as of the gates of Paradise!
Ah, nevermore can earthly visions take
From me this wealth, though loud the jarring crowds
May claim lean hours among their strivings vain.
My inmost soul these mountain gems secure will hold
And eyes half closed will see the Summer-frames of gold.

-as published in **THE MOUNTAINEER**
Volume Eight, December, 1915

"To know the Artist, study His work"

When this book was first written, I had a deep reverence for the Mountain.But in the ensuing years, I have come to know the Mountain's creator, and so it is with that newfound appreciation I now marvel at the wonders of His handiwork. How good God is to have given us the ability to enjoy things! He could have made us like robots with no senses, living in a flat colorless plane. But He didn't. He made us human beings with free wills. He also gave us a beauty-filled world in which to live out our lives. And He gave us mountains.

Thank you for Mount Rainier, Father God. It is a feast for the eyes, and has been such a source of serenity, beauty and pleasure for so many people. Please be with, protect, and bless those who use this book in their exploration of this wonderful place. Reward them with revelations of your greatness, your creativity, your power and your love for them personally as they take this time apart to walk in your marvelous garden.

Thank you too for the people you have sent into my life who have encouraged me and shared the vision of bringing this long overdue project into completion.

Among those special people are Beth Rossow for re-measuring the trail and keeping measurements up to date, to Frank Heuston for his keen eye in weeding out my many typos and misspellings, and to Carl Fabiani, a park employee since 1965, and a walking goldmine of trail information and now head of all the trail crews. Thanks too to Alex Williams for his work in reformatting this new edition. Also thanks to the many kind folks who helped me track down the hundreds of obscure nuggets and tidbits of information which hopefully will give you a whole new appreciation of this wonderful lace. Among them, (retired) Stan Schlegel of the Park Service, Caroline Driedger and Kevin Scott of the U.S. Geological Survey (USGS), and Janet Tanaka, Volcanologist. It was wonderful to hear from so many readers who bought and used the previous edition, and found it useful. Your kind words are deeply appreciated, and your great suggestions are included in thisdition.

Finally, thanks to those whose photographs grace these pages: Rod Barbee, Ed Walsh, Beth Rossow, Rodney Harwood, Dick Filley, G.G. Parker, Dinni Fabiani and Dave Schnute of the Park Service. You whet my appetite to go doit again.

MOUNT RAINIER THE VOLCANO

Centered amid 378 square miles of rugged terrain on the western slope of the Cascade Mountains in Washington state, lies the object around which this book was written: Mount Rainier.

This majestic Mountain's crowning summit towers 8,000 feet above the peaks at its base, and 14,411.1 feet above sea level. At nearly three miles high, it is the tallest and most significant snow-clad volcano in the conterminous United States. It has one of the largest glacial systems radiating from a single peak anywhere in the world.

Like a lovely and serene matron whose erosion sculptured face belies her age, Rainier sits among five younger volcanic peaks overseeing all Northwest mountaineering activity. Mounts Adams, St. Helens, Hood, Baker and Glacier Peak reign the Cascades within view of each other.

Rainier, the "grande dame" of the Northwest, attained her greatest height of over 16,000 feet before the last major glaciation, which began about 25,000 years ago. Her fiery tempestuous youth behind her, she is dormant now, though evidence of her former monumental size and grandeur can still be seen in Steamboat Prow on the northeast side of the Mountain, and Little Tahoma Peak on the east.

How the former summit of the volcano disappeared is a matter of speculation, but most volcanologists today agree that fantastically large avalanches and debris flows were the cause, rather than the old theory that the top "blew" off. The debris from such a horrendous explosion would still be much in evidence throughout Puget Sound, yet such fall-out is conspicuously non-existent. The absence of it lends validity to the latter-day opinion that the old summit simply avalanched and slid away.

The material remains of the mud and debris flows offer further support of this theory themselves. The Paradise debris flow, for instance, extends all the way to the mouth of Tahoma Creek, about 4 miles below Longmire. There is also evidence that it is one of the several debris flows that left deposits in the valley as far downstream as the town of National, 13 miles below Longmire.

At about the same time, some 5,800 years ago, another even more mammoth mudflow, the Osceola flow, raveled over 45 miles down the White River Valley burying the present sites of Enumclaw and Buckley and much of the Auburn/Kent valley. It left a deposit of clay and rocks (in some areas at depths of up to 70 feet), all the way to the Puget Sound lowlands. Several of the present valley towns around Mount Rainier are built on the debris of the Osceola flow.

Between the quantity of material in just these two flows, (an estimated 500 million cubic yards in the Paradise flow, and another 1.5 billion cubic yards in the Osceola flow), it becomes increasingly convincing that the source of such a large volume may well be the missing summit of Mount Rainier.

Thus the Wonderland Trail traveler hiking the ridges and valleys of the "decapitated" volcano need not dream of climbing to the top of the Mountain to reach its summit, for remnants of the original summit may indeed lie beneath his feet.

Yet the very bedrock of the Mountain is still vulnerable to constant attack, witness the milky appearance of the rivers. Volcanic rock "flour" from high on the sides of the Mountain is carried away first by the mighty glaciers, then to still lower elevations by the cold churning river waters.

Water has always been a particularly devastating force upon the Mountain. The Kautz Creek flow of October 2, 1947, for example, moved 50,000,000 cubic yards of rock debris downstream in a matter of a few hours. And many times during his or her course around the Mountain, the Wonderland hiker will see many examples of the devastation water can produce with its tremendous energy.

Every large valley originating on the Mountain shows evidence that it has experienced floods and mudflows.

Active volcanoes are especially prone to mudflows, for these phenomenon materialize in two ways: **Hot volcanic oriented flows** are steam-melted snow, which in turn floods and picks up loose rock debris. This accumulated mass then becomes a mudflow. **Cold mudflows** are those initiated by landslides. These may be triggered by volcanic explosion or earthquake.

The Wonderland Trail traveler will get a good first hand look at the results of such mudflows: first in the "minor" flow which inundated Tahoma Creek on the west side. That one buried the former Tahoma Creek Campground in August, 1967, and again in October, 1988. Then six floods occurred in one week in 1989. An even more massive flow created Reflection Lakes on the south side of the Mountain between 5,000 and 6,000 years ago.

Another rockfall, possibly initiated by a steam explosion, which the hiker won't get to see without a side trip, will be the 4-billion cubic feet of rock-avalanche debris from high on Little Tahoma Peak. This "dry" slide finally came to rest just 2,000 feet short of the White River Campground after a fast 4-1/2 mile slide down the Emmons Glacier one clear December Sunday morning in 1965.

The hypothesis on how it got this far instead of landing in a heap at the base of the glacier goes as follows: The force was so great, and the rock was moving so fast (100-300 miles per hour) that a cushion of compressed air formed beneath it, and thus it literally flew down the valley, finally crashing almost two miles down the bed of the White River. Rock debris up to 100-feet thick (including rocks as big as box cars) still blankets the valley floor. Skiers atop nearby Crystal Mountain heard an "explosion", saw "smoke" (probably either steam or dust), and watched that one go.

The Wonderland traveler will also be getting at least 3 mountains for the price of one. Those nice sandy trails are actually pumice deposits of airborne souvenirs from other volcanic eruptions in the Cascades. As you take your self-guided peripatetic geological tour around the mountain, watch for the color clues of the various pumice layers. Therein lies the key to their age and source.

COLOR	SOURCE	AGE OR YEARS AGO	DEPTH	WHERE FOUND
Olive Gray	Rainier	100 - 150	1"	NE > E
White	St. Helens	450	Sand	All over
Brown	Rainier	2,150 – 2,500	1/4 – 8"	N-NE-E
Yellow	St. Helens	3,250 – 4,000	Sand	All over
Brown	Rainier	5,800 – 6,600	1/4 – 6"	E > SE
Brown	Rainier	5,800 – 6,600	1/4 – 2"	SE
Yellowish-Orange	Mount Mazama	About 6,600	1 – 3"	All over
Red-Brown	Rainier	8,750 – 11,000	1/4 – 1"	NNE > SSE

data courtesy Dr. R. Mullineaux USGS

The Mountain

THAR SHE BLOWS

Mount Rainier tops that list, notes the astute hiker, remembering the 1980 eruption of nearby Mount St. Helens. Could Rainier go again?

Captain John Fremont, while exploring the Oregon Territory, recorded that Mount Rainier erupted in November 1843. In fact between 1820 and 1894, observers reported at least 14 eruptions. Most were probably just steam, because the most recent tell-tale pumice is found between Burroughs Mountain and Indian Bar and is found only up to a distance of 6 miles from the crater.

Slumbering Mount Rainier is akin to the fable about the old woman in the cabin: just because there's snow on the roof, doesn't mean there isn't fire in the stove. There is indeed fire in her stove, and yes, she could stir the pot at any time. The steam caves, sulfur emissions and warm ground at the summit, plus the steam vents which show up periodically, all give evidence of the life within.

As volcanologists are quick to point out, "dormant" does not mean "dead." Several agencies, including the U.S. Geological Survey (USGS), the U.S. Coast Guard's Geodetic Survey Earthquake and Crustal Studies Branch, the University of Washington and the National Park Service all pay close attention to the Mountain's slightest quiver. And although there is considerable seismic activity, (800 small earthquakes in the past 20 years) none of the experts feel there is any significant change in the mountain's behavior to indicate that an eruption is imminent.

Besides, next-door neighbor Mount St. Helens gave plenty of warning before she let out with her now famous burp.

THE GLACIERS

Glaciers are fascinating! Though they appear to be still and silent, just the reverse is true. Mount Rainier, with more glaciers on her slopes than any other peak in the conterminous United States, is the home of 28 named glaciers. Six of these, — the Nisqually, Tahoma, Kautz, Ingraham, Emmons and Winthrop, are born at the Mountain's summit. All told, about 40 distinguishable bodies of ice mantle the Mountain; however, only those, which move and crevasse are considered glaciers. The combined icy masses (156 billion cubic feet of ice and snow) cover a total surface area of nearly 37 square miles year-round within the park.

Day and night, summer and winter, the ancient glaciers methodically wend their way down the Mountain. As the untold billions of tons of ice move over the contours of the Mountain's bedrock surfaces, huge crevasses yawn open and expand, only to close again, ever in slow motion. The continuing driving pressure of its own weight on the steep slopes moves the mass along. Crevasses cross and criss-cross, frequently creating seemingly bottomless abysses, towering seracs and steep crumbling cliffs of ice, beautiful and awesome at the same time.

The ever-descending icy masses continue to eat away at the Mountain, which sustains them, carrying off each crumb of rock scoured or wrested from the ever-diminishing peak.

That the glaciers have been active during the last century is evidenced by the fact that the snout of the Nisqually Glacier had receded over a mile by 1991 from where it stood in 1857, the year Lt. A. V. Kautz attempted the first ascent of the Mountain.

In the mid-1940's a very interesting thing happened. The glaciers stopped receding and the majority of them began to advance and grow in bulk again. The Nisqually, for instance, advanced 100 feet in 1964 and 125 feet in 1966. The Kautz Glacier also advanced about 500 feet in 1966 after having been in retreat the first half of the century. Then after about a decade of advance, the Nisqually retreated briefly, then again advanced down valley beyond its potion of the 1960's. Since 1983 the Nisqually Glacier has again been thinning and retreating, reflecting the drier Pacific Northwest climate which has had warmer summers and drier winters since 1977.

Currently, all but one of the glaciers is again retreating at varying rates. The Cowlitz appeared to be the exception, since it advanced 21 feet between 1985-1990, however that advance slowed or stopped in 1991. The Carbon is very stable by comparison to other Rainier glaciers. It retreated only 8 feet between 1985-1990, while the South Tahoma retreated 975 feet during that same time. The changing glacial picture on Mount Rainier is well worth watching!

It is interesting to imagine, in nearing the glaciers, and crossing the long moraine ridges far beyond their present snouts, what the former termination points must have looked like. They are now far from the safe footpaths and bridges, but several times during the ice ages, these glaciers advanced many miles beyond the present park boundaries.

High on the Mountain, the glaciers are clean and mantled with fresh snow, but near the toe, they tend to be dirty, darkened with rock and debris collected during the long journey down the Mountain.

It is at the snout, however, we are most apt to realize the true size and scope of a glacier. The high final walls of ice, dwarfing everything in sight, instill an awe and curious admiration of the sheer volume and weight of that which is above the viewer. No wonder the crevasses on the upper slopes seembottomless, when from the snout, the glacier itself seems almost topless.

This snout is a good area of which to be wary if venturing near the glacier, for what appears to be solid rock and grit underfoot may actually be just a superficial deposit on the final tailings of ice. Snouts are also notoriously dangerous rockfall areas, and are best avoided and viewed from a distance.

A word to the wise regarding travel ON the glaciers: DON'T! Glacier travel should never be attempted without proper training and equipment, nor without proper back-up rescue gear and know-how at hand. Aside from being prohibited by park regulations, it is an invitation to a tragic death for the unsuspecting.

While originally researching this book, the author watched a Boy Scout troop work its way, unroped, up the Ohanapecosh Glacier. Their leader, the first one back in camp, left the boys on the glacier to find their way back to camp over the next few hours. He explained that they just wanted to "play in the snow." It was his contention that the glacier was "up higher."

The closest rescue gear was nearly a day's travel time away. Even if there had been ropes in the shelter (there weren't), it takes a team of at least six experienced people to effect a rescue and haul somebody out of a crevasse, assuming the person in the freezer isn't injured.

Fortunately no one was injured in this risky "play," but it could have ended in tragedy.

PERMANENT SNOWFIELDS

The Wonderland traveler will cross many permanent snowfields during the northern and eastern legs of the trip. Snowfields can be expected when crossing from Spray Park to Seattle Park, and again between Summerland and Indian Bar, especially crossing Panhandle Gap, where it gets icy and steep near the top. Early in the season you will also probably find them on the north slope of Klapatche Ridge, Skyscraper Pass and Emerald Ridge, all of which are also often icy. All are steep with rocks below.

Coming upon snowfields should be no cause for alarm, for though frequently impressive to look at, those along the Wonderland can be navigated without too much concern — although a couple will be memorable! The difference between a glacier and a permanent snowfield is that a glacier moves and forms crevasses, whereas the permanent snowfield does not. If the conditions are such (i.e. an increasingly heavier snowpack, causing the mass to begin to move and creep over the slope), the snowfield is then classified as a glacier. This is the reason for the inconsistency in the number of glaciers credited to Mount Rainier and the Mount Rainier National Park, for the number of them changes almost annually. Beware of steep snow slopes above rocks.

Be sure to put on sunglasses or goggles for crossing snowfields. It doesn't take long to get nasty sunburn or snowblindness from reflected light on snow, even on overcast days. Also use sunscreen, lip protection and some kind of hat or head covering.

Before August and after September, an ice axe would be a welcome implement on some of the steeper snowslopes, provided the hiker knows how to use and carry it. Without that knowledge, an ice axe is a dangerous instrument.A number of lives have been lost over the years by people impaling themselves on their ice axes. But if properly used, in addition to its basic use as an aid to arrest a fall on steep snow or ice, the versatile ice axe will be put to constant use in such functions as providing

3-point suspension when crossing streams, as a tent or tarp anchor, clearing weeds off the trail, chopping steps in snow, digging holes, and on rare occasions, even defending oneself. Many mountaineers are reluctant to even go on an ocean beach hike without theirs. Why? They're also great for opening clams!

WATER, WATER, EVERYWHERE!

Former Park Chief Naturalist Bill Dengler once noted "some believe Mount Rainier should be pronounced Mount 'Rainy-er,' and Longmire split to become 'Long-mire.' He added, "in 1983, the total precipitation (rain and melted snow) recorded at Longmire was 86.96 inches, at Paradise 130.11 inches. There are 272.42 cubic inches in one gallon, so we calculate that 45.14 gallons of water fell for each square foot of Longmire during 1983, and at Paradise, each square foot of ground received 67.54 gallons. No wonder the level of Alder Lake (west of MRNP) can rise and fall so dramatically in such a short period of time!"

Little else takes on more importance to the Wonderland Trail hiker, for seldom is one far from a decision regarding water. It must continually be drunk, crossed, searched for, taken cover from, and protected. One may even swim in it, either deliberately or accidentally. In any event, the hiker will emerge at trail's end with greater respect for it.

WATER: CROSSING IT

Though the trail log denotes countless "dry" streams, "dry' runoff gullies, and "dry" riverbeds, the hiker may begin to wonder if this book was written about the same mountain that he or she is backpacking. Early in the season or during a "wet" year, one may wish for a dry streambed or two, for a considerable amount of time and thought will be spent in crossing water, or even worse, mud. Crossing stretches of mud will give an opportunity to practice low impact techniques. Circumventing mud creates new trails, begins erosion and destroys groundcover. Instead, try crossing via roots and rocks.

A normally dry stream in late August may be a raging torrent in early July. The same beautiful tumbling glacial rivers seen safely from the roads around the park as the snows melt, are busy upstream in the vicinity of the Wonderland Trail working to loosen the bridges in their paths as their melt-swollen waters course down the Mountain. And the placid waters crossed in late summer give little hint of the true size and might they represent.

Mount Rainier is drained by five major river systems. Clockwise, they are The Puyallup and Carbon River systems on the northwest, the White River on the northeast, the Cowlitz on the southeast, and the Nisqually on the southwest. Except for the Cowlitz, which is a tributary of the Columbia River, the other rivers all drain into Puget Sound.

The Mountain

Even after the early season fury passes, there is no constant to riverflow. It fluctuates throughout the day in almost direct relation to the temperature. The higher the temperature, the greater the melt, — and the higher the water! Thus, the best time to ford a river is early morning or as early in the day as possible. (However park officials make every effort to maintain safe bridges over all water courses along the trail, and it is hoped no river fordingwill be necessary.)

One final important thought to keep in mind regarding crossing glacial rivers: **RESPECT THEM!**

Take time to search out the best possible crossing. Ripples generally indicate shallow water. Find a sturdy stick for a depth probe and for three-point suspension against the swift water. Plant the stick downstream so each step is supported, and cross diagonally at an angle to the flow. Whenever crossing without a bridge, it's a good idea to unfasten pack waist straps, so you can get out of it fast if necessary, and so your water-logged pack won't drag you underwater if you fall in. If you have a rope, use it.

In 1967, nobody expected unpretentious little Tahoma Creek to deliver its surprise of August 29. In a matter of minutes, the river flooded to a highwater mark of 15 feet in the vicinity of the Wonderland Trail bridge crossing,and 25-feet deep farther up the mountain. That 1967 flow marked the beginning of a new period of activity on Tahoma Creek. In the past 35 years, over 25 flows have coursed down Tahoma Creek. Between October 1986 and September 1987 alone, five floods flushed down the valley.

Greg Gilbert - Seattle Times Photo

**A Souvenir of the November 1986 Tahoma Creek Flow
left at the Tahoma Creek Campground**

"There are boulders as big as the Entrance Booth bouncing down the creekbed in a river of mud," a breathless wide-eyed tourist told the ranger at the Nisqually entrance one Sunday afternoon in 1986. She was lucky to be alive to report the South Tahoma mudflow. Mud lines were up to 12 feet high on the trees. In 1987, a work crew narrowly escaped injury by running uphill during a similar event. Later that same season, a hiker was covered to above his knees by the concrete-like mud, but managed to extricate himself without injury. In the Park's history, there have been over a dozen witnessed mudflows with no fatalities.

LAHARS (Mudflows)

October 1926	NISQUALLY
October 1932	NISQUALLY
October 1934	NISQUALLY
October 1947	KAUTZ
October 1949	NISQUALLY
October 1955	KAUTZ
August 1967	SOUTH TAHOMA
August 1970	SOUTH TAHOMA
July 1985	KAUTZ
June 1986	NISQUALLY
October 1986	SOUTH TAHOMA
August 1987 (2)	SOUTH TAHOMA
September 1987	SOUTH TAHOMA
July 1988	SOUTH TAHOMA
Sept/Nov 1989	SOUTH TAHOMA
August/Oct 1990	SOUTH TAHOMA
Novmber 1991	SOUTH TAHOMA
September 1992 (2)	SOUTH TAHOMA

C.L. Driedger, U.S.G.S

Kautz Creek had delivered a similar cataclysm in 1947, and the chances of it happening again are well within the realm of possibility at any glacial-oriented river. Debris flows are known to have occurred in recent times from four glaciers on Mount Rainier: the Nisqually, Kautz, South Tahoma and Winthrop glaciers. At least three others, - the Carbon, South Mowich and Emmons - are suspect. Man can't prevent the happening, but he can exercise caution in the area of the rivers, and be ready to move fast if necessary.

A "lahar" the technical name for a volcanic mudflow, is the most devastating (and most likely) hazard at Mount Rainier. The debris flows (lahars) occur when water from high rates of melt or rainfall, or glacial outburst floods, mobilize loose rock into a churning slurry of boulders, mud, water, tree and plant debris. They leave in their wake destroyed forests, splintered and uprooted trees, buried campgrounds and damaged roads. They occur about once every three to ten years. South Tahoma Glacier has been trying to increase that average with four flows down Tahoma Creek in 1989 alone.

The Mountain

The Wonderland Trail now crosses Tahoma Creek via a high suspension bridge about 2 miles upstream from the destroyed picnic area, but the crossing area bears a scar of its own which tells an interesting story. Erosion by passing debris has deepened the gorge beneath the bridge from 30 feet to well over 80 feet since 1986.

The U.S.G.S scientists who study the Mount Rainier flows now know of some interesting factors: The flows tend to occur in late summer or fall. The mean date of the known flows is September 7.

Warning signs of an oncoming mudflow are: a mighty blast of air rushing down the canyon, thick dust clouds, violent ground vibrations, the pungent smell of freshly killed vegetation, rapidly rising waters, a surge of oncoming debris or a sound like a rushing freight train. Most lahars occur in the late afternoon or evening. If any warning signs are present, move out of the streambed and as far uphill as fast as your terrified little legs will carry you.

Hikers who have witnessed debris flows at Mount Rainier say that only 1-2 minutes passed between the time they first heard the rushing sound, and the time the flow roared past. Scientists studying the phenomenon estimate the flows travel down the valleys at speeds of 10 -20 miles per hour.

WATER: DRINKING IT

Stream and Lake Water: When this book was originally written, just about any moving water was safe to drink. Today only water obtained from piped water systems in the park can be assumed safe to drink. All other water must be treated either by boiling, filtering or chemical purifying.

The culprit is a parasitic microorganism called Giardia Lamblia (Giardiasis) but more commonly known as "beaver fever." Beavers aren't the only culprits responsible for it though. It's also been found in the fecal material of people and both domestic and wild animals. If an animal or human with it defecates too near a lake or stream, the organisms find their way into the water and can spread over a wide area miles from the source.

Symptoms of the resulting major gastro-intestinal disorder include chronic diarrhea, severe abdominal cramps, vomiting, bloating, fatigue, and needless to say, loss of appetite and your pep for the trail. In short, it can ruin a good trip. (It takes medical treatment to get rid of it.) Fortunately, preventative measures aren't too difficult. The safest method (and that which is recommended by the NPS) is to boil all water 5 minutes plus 1 additional minute for every additional 1000' elevation gain. (7 minutes at a rolling boil is safe for anywhere on the Wonderland trail.) After allowing the water to cool, it can be made more palatable by adding a pinch of salt and pouring it back and forth from one clean container to another several times.

Other hikers prefer to carry purification filters which are available at most outdoor equipment stores. They filter out the smallest microbes and Giardia cysts. A filter is lighter in weight than the extra fuel, which would be required to bo drinking water. It also means less water must be carried if sources are available along the trail. Filters are great for virtually all water from glacial river water to when "mud puddles" are the only water source available. One word of caution about filters however. This is no place to go for the bargain basement brand. Your health (for months and perhaps years to come) depends on your choice. Get the best one you can afford!

Also keep in mind that glacial silt will quickly clog most filters. Bring an extra cartridge as well as iodine or chlorine for emergencies if planning an extended trip.

For those who don't want to boil or filter, the EPA recommends the following chemical disinfectants (dosage listed is per quart of water): Chlorine tablets (five tablets), household bleach (four drops), iodine tablets (two tablets) and two percent tincture of iodine (10 drops). After adding most of the above, you need to let the mixture stand for 30 to 60 minutes before drinking.

"Watering holes" are located about one to four hiking hours apart, and because of the necessity to purify all water, a good practice is to each evening boil or prepare a big pot of water for the following day's drinking needs. *Don't forget to use purified water for cleaning teeth too. Also remember to bring extra stove fuel for all that boiling if not using a filter.*

The NPS also recommends that hikers be especially wary of lake water. Also particularly risky are streams that flow through campgrounds, or down a series of switchbacks. Be safe. Treat **ALL** water!

Glacial River Water: Though milky with minute particles of ground rock (called rock flour), *in a **DIRE** emergency* glacial river water is consumable **if filtered.** Permitting a container of it to sit a while will settle out most of the grit. (However it leaves A LOT to be desired as a drink). It too can contain giardia.

Melted Snow: A process which should be unnecessary below timberline, but which does provide an *emergency* source of water, ...again **only** if filtered. (Those beavers sure get around!)

The primary reason for not drinking snow or glacier water is because it has been up on the mountain for months or even years accumulating crud and pollution from the air and isn't a pure water source. (Not to mention that it would take a lot of snow, fuel and time to get a cup of water from melted snow).

WATER: TAKING COVER FROM IT

To head down the Wonderland Trail without adequate rain gear is an invitation to disaster. But the degree of adequacy depends on how long travel in the rain might be necessary. A simple hooded plastic jacket might suffice for a one-day trip, but would surely disintegrate if used daily on a two-week trip.

Basically, all rain gear eventually gets wet inside and out. If the rain doesn't get you, the condensation from sweat will. Even the 'wonder' materials like Gore-Tex™ can only do so much in a sustained downpour. The best raingear is that which dries out quickly! Buy the best rain gear you can afford.

The decision of rain jacket versus poncho must be made. Our choice is a poncho, which also covers the pack. It provides comfort, ventilation so you don't get too hot while hiking, dries quickly when stretched out in a breeze, and doubles as a tarp. It is the most functional lightweight rain gear. A pair of gaiters will complete the rain gear requirements. (They're also handy early in the morning when trailside weeds and flowers are heavy with dew).

Gore-Tex™ coats and pants are warmer, and if hiking in extremely cold rainy weather, should be considered. Their drawbacks are that they will get wet, are heavier, and are clammy to put on. If choosing the coat and pant combination, one will also need a brimmed rain hat or head cover and a pack cover (more extra weight.) In a real pinch, a large garbage can liner makes a super raincoat and another makes a pack cover.

Time spent in packing individual items in plastic bags will be repaid daily in dry food and clothing. Make up one bag of items used on the trail: toilet paper, medicines, trail journal, etc. Lining your sleeping bag stuff sack with a plastic garbage bag will make it more waterproof, especially if you carry it on the outside of your pack. And an evening spent waterproofing boots will pay innumerable dividends on the trail.

Dry sleeping shelter is equally important, as is the means of keeping the pack itself dry. A waterproof tarp of heavy gauge plastic or coated nylon will be perfectly adequate, provided the hiker knows a combination of shelters he or she can rig to suit all conditions. (Practice setting it up at home first). Remember too to waterproof all tent or tarp *seams*!

One of the new super-absorbent cellulose towels would be handy too.

Pack several extra empty plastic bags (bread or bun bags do nicely) for such things as wet tarps and groundcloths. And *in a pinch*, a bread bag slipped over the foot as a liner between two pairs of wool socks will insure dry feet regardless of how wet the boots and outer socks may get.

WATER: SWIMMING IN IT

For those who like swimming in ice water, they can go for it at Mirror Lakes, St. Andrews Lake, Mowich Lake, Mystic Lake and Shadow Lake. Swimming is not allowed in Reflection Lakes.

WATERFALLS AND LAKES

Mount Rainier National Park contains 34 waterfalls, a few of which are visible from the Wonderland Trail. The Trail passes by Spray Falls (side trip), Ipsut Falls,

Martha Falls, Garda Falls, Sylvia Falls, Narada Falls, Carter Falls, Madcap Falls and Wauhaukaupauken Falls. One which is noteworthy, but which will not be seen since it is totally inaccessible, is Fairy Falls. It plunges 700 feet at the head of Stevens Canyon. It is fed by the tiny Williwakas Glacier. Not only is it the highest waterfall in the state, but *World Book of Facts, 1992* lists it as the fifth highest waterfall in the nation (the first four are in California). It's about 3 rugged miles off the Wonderland and it would be too damaging to the fragile groundcover to have people scrambling cross-country in search of it, thus we ask that hikers not attempt to find it.

127 lakes and tarns of various sizes also lie within the park boundaries. Of these, about 40 are by or within sight of the Wonderland Trail. A tarn is a small shallow lake in a glacier-carved basin. Mirror Lakes at Indian Henrys, and Shadow Lake at Sunrise are examples of tarns.

WATER: PROTECTING IT

Unfortunately, today many of the pristine lakes and streams of the back country are polluted, however that is no reason to contribute to the problem. The following precautions are a guide to keeping them from getting even worse:

Never wash dishes or dispose of leftover food in a lake or stream. Wash dishes with biodegradable soap, (not detergent), and dump the wash water at least 150' from the river or lake. Attend to personal functions and hygiene as far as possible from any water (at least 200'). Keep horses and pack animals away from human "watering holes" and quarter them as remotely as possible from the water source. Water livestock downstream from the trail or campsite or in designated areas.

WHAT'S IN ITS NAME?

One final interesting tidbit about the mountain's watercourses is their inconsistent geographic nomenclature. It's true the Carbon Glacier feeds the Carbon River, but the Tahoma Glacier is the source of the South Puyallup River, and the Tahoma Creek comes mostly from the South Tahoma Glacier. Similarly, the Paradise Glacier now feeds Steven's Creek, not the Paradise River. The Winthrop and Emmons glaciers both feed forks of the White River, though it takes 30 miles for the branches to merge.

WILDLIFE

If from time to time the hiker gets the sensation there are "eyes upon him", he's probably right, for one is never alone in the forest.

It's probably possible, if noisy enough, to do the entire trail without seeing a single animal. But under normal circumstances, the Wonderland hiker will probably exchange glances with a few of the park's estimated 300 black-tail or white-tail deer, 100 bears and 350 goats (all figures are one-time Ranger estimates). At just about every rock pile, it is usually possible to stare down a marmot or cony (pika). And the hiker can count on becoming intimate friends with countless chipmunks and ground squirrels. For good reason! They'll all be eating out of the same pack.

The Mountain

(Note: About 20 years ago the Park Service stopped conducting inventories of animals native to the park. Most of these figures were from a count done by Park Rangers in 1969. They've been updated as best possible.)

Large animals to look for are mountain goats, or perhaps some of the more than 1,000 elk that graze in the park's East Side each summer. (Although elk are occasionally seen elsewhere around the Mountain, everywhere from Summerland and Klapatche Park to along the Nisqually River near Kautz Creek.)

Those nice fresh "cat" prints that are encountered were just a cougar (otherwise known as panther, puma, catamount or mountain lion) or a passing bobcat, (Lynx Rufus) or Lynx (Lynx Canadensis) out looking over the season's crop of backpackers. A few years ago there were 12 sightings of cougar in the West Side backcountry and several more sightings in the Carbon River area. Others have been sighted at Ohanapecosh, the highway west of the Kautz Creek flood area and in the vicinity of Longmire.

In 1992, a Wonderlander left his camera in camp at Dick Creek. Upon discovering the loss near Moraine Park, he doubled back to retrieve it. 50 feet after turning around, there were *big* fresh cat prints. He followed them all the way back down to Dick Creek. Like their domesticated little cousins, big cats are curious too. They like to follow what interests them. You're more apt to see the tracks than their maker though. However mountain lion (cougar) sightings do seem to be on the increase in Washington. This shouldn't be too unusual considering there are an estimated 2,000 - 4,000 of them in the state. (Not counting those who live around Pullman!)

In case you've forgotten Mountain Lion 101, the average male cougar ranges from five feet to nine feet long (nose to tip of tail), the females average six feet. Males weigh 150-200 pounds, but are strong. Females weigh between 95-110 pounds. It's said that an adult lion can carry off a full-grown deer, or jump a 6' fence with a calf in its mouth. A mature lion varies in color from tan to grey to reddish brown. and has tracks about 3" x 3". Their really distinctive feature, if the preceding isn't attention grabbing, is their l-o-n-g-g-g tail. They usually patrol about a 20 x 30 mile territory. They have no natural enemies. They hunt both on the ground and by dropping from trees on their prey. Just to set your mind at ease, we found **no** stories of human encounters (other than sightings) in the Mount Rainier files, however more have occurred elsewhere in Washington State and in British Columbia lately. Nationwide there is more and more concern about Mountain Lion confrontations. Try to stay calm if one actually approaches. If you run, it may trigger his predatory instincts.

"Dog" prints, on the other hand, are probably from some of the many coyotes in the park. Coyotes, elsewhere called 'Prairie wolves' are the most commonly seen predators at Mount Rainier. They're about the size of a collie and are brownish-grey in color. Coyotes could be anywhere and probably are because they roam large territories. Other clues their tracks give: a coyote or dog meanders whereas a fox walks in a straight line. Their toenails leave imprints, and the imprint of the front paws is larger and of a different shape than the rear paws. Their tails drag and leave an impression too.

It's highly unlikely, but if you see a "dog" print (with 5 toes) it could be from an extremely rare visit of a wolverine. In 1926, 10 timber wolves (now called grey wolves) were observed in the park. The most unusual sighting was of one just below Camp Muir in 1933. Grey wolf sightings are on the increase in Washington State, especially in the North Cascades. Human "Howling Brigades" from Wolf Haven (a non-profit wolf sanctuary) evoked a response from a single wolf east of the park one night in 1993.

And many of those interesting little holes by the side of the trail (perfect for breaking a leg) are home sweet home to many of the park's smaller inhabitants.

Approximately 50 species of mammals are permanent residents of the wilderness wonderland. Among them are 6 species of shrews (four-legged), 3 species of moles, 3 myotis, plus 2 other bats, 2 weasels, 3 squirrels (ground squirrel, red squirrel and flying squirrel), 5 voles, 2 species of mice, and one each of raccoon, beaver, mountain beaver, marten, fisher, mink, ermine, red fox, porcupine, pika, snowshoe hare, and — the not to be ignored — little spotted skunk.

Birds common to the Mountain are the mountain bluebird, Clark's nutcracker, varied thrush, kinglet, chickadee, nuthatch, ptarmigan, grouse, finch, grosbeak, gray jay, Steller's jay. Far less common is the northern spotted owl. (Report any sightings of the latter.) Both Bald and Golden eagles are known to pass through the Park. Look for them in Stevens Canyon, at Sunrise, and along the Nisqually River.

THE BEAR FACTS

Black bears, (Ursus americanus), the only bear species that will be met at Mount Rainier, top out at 3 feet high at the shoulder, and can be as large as 6 feet long. They can weigh up to 300 lbs., of which 120 are muscle. The *average* Mount Rainier bear, however, is 59.6 inches long, and weights 188.1 pounds! Their weight varies widely from spring to late fall. The black bear can actually be black, brown, rusty cinnamon, blue-black or gun-metal. Whatever the primary color, the muzzle is always medium brown. One interesting fact to keep in mind when in bear territory, is that a bear's hind legs are longer than his front legs, thus he prefers to escape *uphill* if startled. (Uphill running is easier for him.) Bears running down steep terrain frequently get rump heavy, and go tumbling tail over tincups down the hill. Remember during berry season, bears scrounge for food twenty hours a day to fatten up for winter.

There used to be a "Don't molest the bears" sign that stood just inside the Nisqually entrance. It always brought humorous visions of a lecherous old man hiding behind a tree waiting for a sweet young bruinesse to trip by, but the fact is, people really do molest bears.

The Mountain

One gang of 30 young people the author met on the trail one year had just finished playing ring-around-the-rosy around a bear! The frantic bear finally charged through and escaped, but imagine his reaction to the next humans after an experience like that. Here's hoping it made him into a hermit!

The expression "hungry as a bear" truly describes old Bruin, for he really does eat at every opportunity. This is nature's way of building up the thick fat layer off of which he must live all winter. But feeding the animals, and treating them as if they were in a zoo, can prove disastrous to all concerned. There are no "tame" bears at Mount Rainier, only bears which have lost their fear of humans through repeated contact. Bears have been known to bite the hands that feed them, and a few that haven't fed them, too.

A garbage can or backpacker-handout fed bear is soon a sickly animal. He is a wild creature whose metabolism is geared to a berry, fish, bug, egg and fresh food diet, not the candy, cookie and leftovers fed by (or taken from) humans. There are also regulations prohibiting feeding, teasing, touching or molesting the animals, and though the animals may not be unhappy over disregard for the rules, the rangers will be.

Bears could be encountered anywhere along the Wonderland Trail, however some places are more likely "meeting spots" than others. A bear's life really revolves around his stomach. In the spring, bruin is likely to be in open areas looking for tasty new shoots and grasses. In summer and fall, he'll likely be in the berry patches and around lakes and rivers containing fish. Known haunts along the Wonderland are marked in the Trail Log.

Normally, wild animals will keep their distance, and are as anxious to avoid humans as vice versa. Black bears, will generally attack only if provoked or if a hiker inadvertently gets between a she-bear and her cubs (another good reason for not sneaking through the berry patches!) Bears have notoriously poor eyesight, and must depend on their keen senses of smell and hearing to compensate for this natural failing. Thus to handle close encounters of the carnivorous kind, head downhill, and look and sound big and imposing. (Personally, I prefer to practice the Anvil Chorus on my cook pot when crossing known bear hangouts. Beth takes the opposite tack. She removes her pack and slowly moves her arms and legs to look large and human.

A bear in the camp is worth at least two in the bush! At night, a light shined in a bear's eyes will usually stop him in his tracks or get him out of camp. When in known bear country, the practice of putting the flashlight in or by the sleeping bag might come in handy. Hanging packs or food supplies and doing cooking away from the sleeping area may reduce the possibility of a visit. Bears can (and do) climb trees to reach packs. Some Wonderland camps have lines already strung for suspending your food out of reach of bears. Practice throwing a line for the bear bag. Remember to hang your garbage bags you're carrying out too. Otherwise you may be sporting a well-ventilated pack!

Finally, to paraphrase humorist Dave Barry, these aren't plain old civilian bears. They're *federal* bears! That means they can behave any way they want to, because they're protected by the same union as postal clerks. They can help themselves to your food or your pack and there isn't a darned thing you can do about it. If you attempt to prosecute, they'll just get a slick, fast-talking raccoon lawyer and be back out in the woods within hours.

DEAR DEER

With a little luck, some morning the party may awaken to find a beautiful brown-eyed lady and her equally charming offspring making themselves right at home in their camp.

Being chosen by Bambi and his mother to share their breakfast field and welcome the morning is to discover a new delight in life. The distinguished hostess may linger a little longer if things are quiet and peaceful and there are no fast moves or loud noises.

What deer are really looking for when they nuzzle packs and boots is salt, so don't kill them with kindness by feeding them. (Deer and rodents will also eat towels and cotton socks, while pack rats prefer wool socks). Deer digestive systems are not adapted to anything but vegetation, so to feed them "people food" is to sign their death warrant. They either become weakened and diseased, (frequently causing the doe to lose her fawns), or they become dependent on hand feeding and starve to death when winter comes.

Resist too, the temptation to touch fawns which appear to be abandoned. Mother is always close by. Because fawns cannot outrun an attacker, they instinctively "freeze," lie motionless and rely on their camouflage until mother's return. A human scent may cause her to abandon them. A deer may also surprise you with a good swift kick if you corner her or get too close.

GETTING YOUR GOAT

Goat herds (known as "bands") are comprised of nannies, kids, and the previous year's offspring. Mature billies are usually solitary. Where hunting is not allowed (such as a national park), the size of the herd is controlled by nature through predation and disease, and by locale, since any area can support only so much wildlife of a given type.

These rugged and interesting residents of the precipitous slopes are actually relatives of the antelope family. Their fine white coats are more like wool than hair, and their feet are unique in that their soles are soft and spongy, rather than hard, as are most other animal hoofs. It is the traction provided by these pads, which enables the goat to negotiate the precipitous slopes with such ease and abandon.

The Mountain

Goats spend their summers in the highest and most inaccessible places they can find. Thus the best chance humans stand to view these "loners" of the animal kingdom, is to find a comfortable rock overlooking a known goat hangout and scan the area with binoculars.

They'll soon be spotted cooling themselves in a patch of snow, or working their way around the rocks in search of some tasty moss or other tiny plants to eat. Although they graze all day long, late evening or early mornings are especially good times to see the goats moving about their windswept domain.

Known herds within sight of the Wonderland Trail inhabit Packtrain (Scyscraper) Ridge, the Cowlitz Chimneys, Goat Island Mountain (south of Yakima Park), Klapatche Park, Emerald Ridge and the Colonnade on the West Side of the Mountain.

Wonderland Trailers may also find tufts of goat "wool" entangled in brush and on tree trunks at lower elevations where the goats occasionally come to scratch and scrape against anything sharp enough to help them discard some of their thick coats, and find relief from the heat of them. The author once found some in the woods just a few feet out of Longmire.

CREEPY CRAWLIES (and things that go bump in the night)

One of the joys of living in western Washington is the freedom from worry about poisonous critters. This generally holds true for Mount Rainier National Park as well. Your chances of seeing a bear are probably better than seeing a snake. The only snakes at the park are garter snakes and an occasional rubber boa, neither of which is poisonous.

Ticks are another matter. Ticks have been found at two places in the northern part of the park: Immediately under the Northern Crags on the Northern Loop Trail, and along the short stretch of trail between the Suspension Bridge and the Dick Creek Camp. Those found at Mount Rainier were large wood ticks, though, not the Ixodes tick, better known as the small deer tick which carries Lyme Disease and Rocky Mountain Spotted Fever. There has never been a case of either disease attributed to Mount Rainier National Park, but Lyme Disease is getting closer.

It has now occurred in the Cascades (in King, Pierce and Whatcom counties), and increasingly throughout Washington state (77 cases through 1990). However, report all "tick sightings" just for the record. Also just to be on the safe side check yourself frequently for ticks *everywhere* around the Mountain. If you find one, it should be removed by carefully grasping the tick with tweezers as close to the head as possible, and pulling firmly but gently away from the skin. Burning them out frequently leaves (infectuous) mouth parts in the skin.

Another thing to keep an eye out for is yellowjackets. These winged tormentors prefer to nest in dry forest duff, usually along forest trails. There are some hair-raising tales about yellowjacket incidents in the Park's annals. The variety found at Mount Rainier is particularly sensitive to vibrations such as those caused by footsteps. It seems the first person walking past a nest doesn't get stung as often as the second person going by. Their stings can be quite painful. Covering the sting with mud will usually provide a little relief. Even better is to carry hydrocortisone otherwise known as "anti-itch cream" for relief from insect bites and stings. Also note, once a yellowjacket is squashed, a scent marker is released, which acts as a signal for other yellowjackets to attack.

Yellowjackets do not leave their stinger! They are capable of multiple stings.

THE ONES THAT WON'T BE SEEN (The Emperor's Revenge)

Predators barred by law from the park's foot paths are those noisy maimers of trails, nerves and tranquility, ORV's, ATV's, "tote-goats", motor bikes, motorcycles, and wheeled motorized vehicles of every type. Latter day additions to the list, though not motorized, are mountain bikes, skate boards, roller skates and roller blades or in-line skates.

THE FORESTS

The magnificent dense coniferous forests of Mount Rainier deserve a book of their own. The Wonderland Trail passes through the all the major life zones in the park, from lowland forests of Old-growth Douglas Fir, western red cedar and western hemlock, up to sub-alpine flower meadows.

The lowest tree zone, the Western Hemlock Zone (*Tsuga Heterophylla*) lies between 2,000-3,000 feet in elevation. Its dense old growth forests are composed of trees with diameters of 80-100 inches at chest height, and towering 250 feet or more. Other trees in this zone are the Pacific Yew, (whose bark is now famous as a source of the anti-cancer drug Taxol), vine maple and such understory plants as salal, Oregon grape, huckleberry and blackberry.

The Pacific Silver Fir Zone (*Abies Amalelis*) is the most extensive forest zone at Mount Rainier. Extending from 3,000 to 4,500 feet, it is comprised of Pacific silver fir, noble fir, western hemlock, western white pine, and douglas fir.

The Mountain Hemlock (*Tsuga Mertensiana*) zone is divided into the lower (forest) subzone, and the upper (parkland) subzone. The forest subzone, beginning at about 4,500 feet, is dominated by mountain hemlock, Pacific silver fir, subalpine fir and Alaska cedar. The parkland subzone between 5,200 and 6,500 feet is basically treeless, and has mostly flowering plants. These are the ridgetop flower gardens.

Treeline on the Mountain extends to about 5,250' elevation on the western side of the Mountain, and to about 6,000' on the northeastern slopes. Windswept tree islands, meadows and parklands extend the upper limits of vegetation 1,000' higher to the margin of perpetual snow here and there around the Mountain.

The Mountain

Dense forests cover about 60% (or 200 square miles) of the park's landscape, but there are only 17 species of trees.

Several small pockets of large trees over 1,000 years old exist within the park. Such patriarchs exist along the Cowlitz, Ohanapecosh, Nisqually and Carbon drainages where they have been protected from fire, flood and lightning. The oldest tree in the park is an Alaska Cedar, which you will pass by on the Wonderland Trail between Mowich Lake and the Carbon River if you go via Ipsut Pass. (page 123).

THE FOREST HOSPITAL

It won't take much hiking through the forest to see the trees in various stages of their life cycle. Amid the millions of huge healthy robust trees, note too the dead and dying, the broken and the injured. Decaying trees are returned to soil by fungi, insects, and bacteria.

One term we use as an occasional identifier is "nurse log." A nurse log is a rotting log on the forest floor with young trees growing on it. The decaying wood absorbs and retains water, which nourishes the seedlings and helps provide the nutrients they need to grow.

For another fascinating forest phenomenon, when you come upon an uprooted giant take time to study the root system. It's amazing that such colossal trees can have such shallow roots. Yet not only do the small roots gather the water and nutrients from the earth necessary to sustain them, they anchor the giants (for centuries!) through drought, an occasional flood, tons of snowpack, and weather extremes ranging from roasting to sub-zero. Their vulnerability is to wind!

AND *IN* THE TREES...

Even the trees hold some secrets. You may be fortunate enough to find one of the old blazes, tin trail markers, or even an old insulator. What would an insulator be doing out in nowhere, you wonder? A telephone line used to completely encircle the mountain, connecting all the fire lookouts and ranger stations with park headquarters. It was a constant struggle to try to keep it working as the winter storms and heavy snows would bring the lines down every winter, and crews would work all summer putting them back up.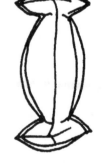

With the advent of radio communications following World War II, the telephone system was gratefully abandoned. The job of taking down the wire and old ceramic porcelain insulators went on for years, however an occasional insulator or bit of old telephone line still may be found high in an old tree (and much of it will still be found as hand wires on bridges and as lines for hanging packs in camp). Some of the old insulators have been put to ingenious uses too, as you will see on your trip around the Mountain.

Also very high in the older trees, particularly on the east and south sides, were small triangular metal trail markers. These served as winter route markers for winter wilderness travelers. Hardy old timers used to plod into the rugged backcountry with much more frequency than people do today.

The very oldest route markers were blazes, marks cut into the tree bark with an ax. These are mostly found on the East Side, and the design to look for looks vaguely like the shape of a bone as illustrated on the previous page.

THE TRAIL-LESS WONDERLAND

God has a wonderful sense of humor. If you don't believe it, look down occasionally, and discover the miniature wonderland beneath your feet.

For every gigantic marvel, stands an equally wondrous creation an inch or so high. Incredible beauty lies in the rocks, roots, mosses, lichens, fungi, molds, baby trees, plants, seeds, cones, flowers, ferns, pumice, bugs, spores and mushrooms. I once discovered an exquisite little flower garden with the tiny plants only 1/4 inch tall, and the intricate little flowers about 1/16 in diameter. Everything in the setting was in perfect proportion. I felt like Gulliver in the Lilliputian Paradise of Mount Rainier.

MINING

With the 1860's discovery of coal near Wilkeson, hundreds of prospectors descended on the Mountain to see what other bounty the area might contain. They came looking for gold, silver and other precious metals, but found only a few small deposits of copper.

By 1908 approximately 300 mining claims were located within the park, most of them in the west and northeast sections. Old Park records state that few of the prospectors were serious in their attempt to extract ore, and most digs proved unprofitable. One old-time observer noted that most claimants stayed long enough each summer to construct unsightly cabins, cut timber indiscriminately and hunt game freely. Most of the claims were soon abandoned.

There were three notable exceptions, all of which had a great deal of work and money put into them. The first was the 1903 "Adula Claim" which lies south of the confluence of the Paradise and Nisqually Rivers on the north side of Eagle Peak. In 1906 the Paradise Claim was staked beside it, and the two claims totaled 41.32 acres. In 1908, the Eagle Peak Copper Mining Company was formed and acquired both claims. As of that same year, new mining claims were no longer allowed within the park by act of Congress, however existing claims were not affected.

Between 1914 and 1930 several tunnels were driven, numerous prospector pits dug, buildings erected, and of most interest to hikers, an 800-foot flume was built from upstream on the Paradise River to a powerhouse at the confluence of the Paradise and Nisqually Rivers. You will see the remains of the old wooden flume beside the trail. The now cemented-over openings of the 'Eagle Rock' mines are visible high on Eagle Peak. They can be seen as soon as you cross the Nisqually River from the highway and Cougar Rock Campground. Look back across the river for the best view.

The former mill site is just to the left of the trail, immediately after crossing the river. In the 1960's, we used to eat lunch here, between the road and the river, while sitting on the rusting running boards of quaint old trucks still parked there amid jumble of old mining equipment. Thick cables up to the mines still crossed the river. When operational, two cars rode the cables counterbalancing each other, so the weight of the rock coming down would pull the empty bucket back up. Today nature has reclaimed the mill site, and only those who know to look up for the old mine entrance have a clue of what was once here.

Early in the century, once there was power enough to dig through the rock, 1,100 feet of tunnels, drifts and cross-cuts were made inside Eagle Peak. But when the ore was finally shipped to the Tacoma smelter, one load showed a profit of only $9.00, a second shipment realized just $115.00 profit. As late as 1955, the company was still proposing developmental plans and insisting Eagle Rock was a valuable copper claim, but by then the government wanted no further development in the park. It wanted the mines closed. But it took until 1976 for it to realize this goal and close the chapter on mining in the Park.

By 1898, on the other side of the Mountain, men were prospecting and working claims in Glacier Basin. Within ten years, 41 claims were filed. When the dust finally settled, one firm, the Mount Rainier Mining Company, emerged with the Starbo Mine. Between 1914 and 1930, several tunnels were driven, numerous prospector pits dug, many buildings (including a large hotel) were put up and a road and a power plant built. Small amounts of ore were taken out, containing mostly copper. In 1924, patents were granted on eight claims, the rest were relinquished. The total area under claim was 164.8 acres.

In 1928, stockholders filed complaints against the company for using the mails to defraud in their stock selling operations. This resulted in two men serving time at the Federal Penitentiary on McNeil Island in nearby Puget Sound. In 1932, the claims were sold at a Sheriff's sale for $500. Then in 1946, a new Mount Rainier Mining Company was organized and more stock sold. In 1948 forty-seven tons of ore were shipped and again, little money was realized. In 1950, stockholders valued the claims at two and one half million dollars, while the government valued them at between $500 to $6,000.

The third large operation was "the North Mowich Glacier Mine" at the base of Eagle Cliff in the Northwest corner. It was perhaps the most ambitious, since tons of heavy equipment had to be brought in for miles by sled from Orting over incredibly rugged terrain. This mine is detailed on page 133. One final note regarding all old mines. There is virtually nothing left to see, and it is unwise to go exploring since unknown open shafts may still exist. The Park would prefer that you let by-gones be gone-bys.

Mount Rainier National Park Photo
The last days of the old prospector's hotel at Glacier Basin

THE WONDERLAND TRAIL

IN THE BEGINNING

By the time Mount Rainier became the nation's fifth national park in 1899, many miles of trail already laced the ridges and hills around the Mountain's flanks.

Most were game or Indian trails leading to favored hunting grounds and berry patches. About 1854, James Longmire, an early pioneer from Indiana who had homesteaded near Yelm in the Nisqually Valley, and his friend Billy Packwood searched for a new route over the Cascades south of the Mountain. They first followed the Nisqually River and ultimately discovered "Cowlitz Pass". It never developed into a route of travel, but in 1861, Longmire blazed a packhorse trail between Yelm and Bear Prairie near the southwest corner of the present park. From there, he began to explore the surrounding terrain.

But it wasn't until 1883, at the age of 63, that Longmire finally climbed the Mountain. It was after returning from the climb, and finding his horses had strayed from their camp by the Nisqually River, that he discovered the soda and iron springs in the nearby meadow, which now bear his name.

Seeing an opportunity to develop a business, the early entrepreneur soon built a crude log hotel and proclaimed the medicinal values of the mineral baths to a populace already intrigued by the mountain. When not busy building cedar bathtubs, furniture and more lodging, he and his son Elcaine, and young grandsons Leonard and Ben, (Elcaine's sons) surveyed and built many of the early trails around his bustling little early-day health spa.

Still, the various trails were not connected, and there was no way to completely encircle the Mountain as one can do it today. This didn't stop the adventuresome members of the then newly organized (1906) Seattle Mountaineers from journeying to the Mountain for their early annual outings to pursue their avowed goals of "exploration and study of the mountains, forests and water courses of the Northwest."

It was, in fact, these early Mountaineers who pioneered and blazed the "missing link" portions of the trail when in 1915, over 100 members undertook the first major expedition around the Mountain. (In anticipation of the Mountaineers' trip, work on connecting east and West Side trails was begun in 1914. A crash trail-building program was resumed as the snows melted in 1915; however the trail over Panhandle Gap was roughed out by the traversing Mountaineers, using alpenstocks and their own brawn.) (Picture on page 138).

Thus it was in 1915 that one of the finest wilderness trails in America came into being, although the first mention of the "Wonderland Trail" by that name doesn't show up in Park Service records until 1921.

THE WONDERLAND TODAY

ITS UPS AND DOWNS

Encircling Mount Rainier by hiking the Wonderland Trail is like walking the crimped edge of an immense pie crust. The many glaciers radiating off the Mountain have carved deep valleys separated by high ridges. The Wonderland travels up and down these ridges, crossing the rivers and valley floors at the bottom, before going up and over the next ridge, to repeat the process again and again. The high spot on the trail is Panhandle Gap at 6,901', and the lowest is the Ipsut Creek Campground Trailhead at 2,320'.

The tremendous elevation gains and losses of the Wonderland Trail usually surprise people not familiar with Mount Rainier, or those coming from out of state. Climbing and descending over 3,500 feet a day is not unusual. More than once, the hiker will conclude that the only flat spots are the "parks" on the ridge-tops and the riverbeds at the bottom. There is little else level in between, with the exception of an occasional square foot or two of trail that accidentally got flattened.

It is also for this reason that campsites are preselected. Because they're so few and far between, the only real choice comes where there are two or three possible camps within a day's travel. Then the hiker must decide in advance whether to take it easy and stop at the first camp, or make a longer day of it, and continue on to the second or third.

Should one bite off too much and get caught on the trail at night, the weary traveler will find himself with a high angle problem about bedding down. The closest thing to "flat" will probably be the trail itself, but that will lead to another problem. While in broad daylight, the trail belongs to the hiker, at night its primary users come out. After dark, the trail becomes a virtual freeway for the park wildlife. Back and forth come the animals, large and small, and finding a sleeping-bagged body in the middle of "their" highway would make an interesting night for all concerned.

The trail log points out the locations of all approved camps in a manner enabling the reader to estimate his exact distance to them from wherever he might be.

However before making ANY decision, take time to consider all the facts and take into account such questions as:

- Would it be best to turn back before dark and return to the last known campsite?
- Is it advisable to move at all? (In a "white-out", snowstorm, an extremely dark night, or without adequate light, the trail could be a death trap.)
- If staying put in poor visibility situations, exercise EXTREME caution in stepping off the trail. There are places on the Wonderland where that first step could be your last one.

The BEST decision, of course, would be to do the trail in the conventional manner, and travel from campsite to campsite in daylight, with adequate time to reach each destination.

WHERE TO START, — AND HOW

This trip is actually begun the day the decision is made to do it, or maybe even before that, when the idea begins to kindle the imagination. The reading, pondering, packing and preparation are all a part of the adventure. Putting on the boots and pack are simply the middle part, for once completed, having hiked the Wonderland is an adventure which will be enjoyed over and over again in memory. Viewed in this perspective, where to actually set foot on the trail seems of minor consequence, but it *is* important to get the trip off to a good start.

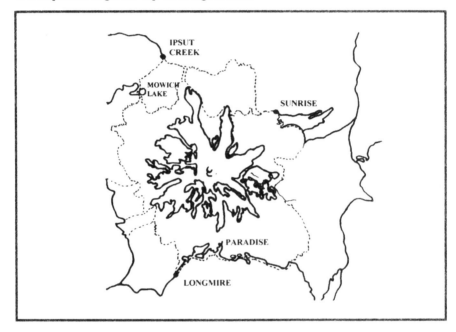

There are eight principal starting points accessible by car: Longmire, Mowich Lake, Ipsut Creek, Sunrise, White River Campground, White River Highway, Box Canyon and Reflection Lakes. In addition, *if* the West Side Highway ever opens again, there are four more access trails, each about 2-1/2 miles in length.

Selection of the starting point should be determined by one thing: the physical condition of the hiker.

If he's out of shape and has done nothing to remedy the situation, the trip can still made reasonably enjoyable and the hiker whipped into shape en route, by taking one of the three easiest starts: Mowich Lake, the White River Highway, or Reflection

Lakes (though the second and third days are fairly hard on the latter.) If up to tackling something a little more difficult, start from Sunrise. Or if backpacking is duck soup, don't worry about difficulty, and start from Ipsut Creek, Box Canyon or Longmire.

Longmire, (elevation 2,761') is the traditional jumping off point. It has the advantage of being home to the Wilderness Information Center where backpackers can get the latest information on trails, the backcountry and permits. It's also close to Cougar Rock and Sunshine Point Campgrounds, where hikers can stay the night before starting. But tradition and convenience aside, Longmire is not necessarily the easiest choice. It begins the trip with very tough first, second and third days, and no time to even think of relaxing until the fourth or fifth day.

Furthermore, it's the worst possible concluding point. The 5-mile uphill stretch between Box Canyon and Reflection Lakes, followed by the long descent to Longmire, is the straw that breaks the proverbial camel's (hiker's) back for an unfortunately large number of people. They either call it quits somewhere from Box Canyon on, or they finish, but between their haste to get it over with and their frame of mind, miss much of the beauty and enjoyment the south side has to offer. (Although when done as another part of the trip, this is a most enjoyable segment.)

Starting at Mowich Lake, (elevation 4,929') on the other hand, has none of these disadvantages. It gets the trip off to an easy relaxed start, and ends it with a pleasant and mildly exciting concluding day. The "hard" parts come in mid-trip after the hiker is in prime condition. Obtaining the Hiker Registration Permit and trip planning information on the north side of the mountain is now far easier thanks to the new Wilderness Information Center located on the highway in downtown Wilkeson. (360) 829-5127.

If intending to do the whole trip at once, a lot of thought should be put into getting the right start. The Wonderland will offer plenty of challenge without handicaps!

TIME AND DIRECTION

WHICH WAY TO GO

Like their watches, Wonderland hikers who want to make the best time and go the easiest direction, go clockwise. While there may be an occasional segment which would be more easily done counter-clockwise, the trip as a whole is best done clockwise.

Up-to-the minute trail conditions may be learned by contacting the Longmire Wilderness Information Center. Phone (360) 569-HIKE. If you're on-line, you can also check out the park's nifty new website showing every trail section at http://www.nps.gov/mora/trail/tr_cnd.htm It tells how much snow is on the trail, where the bears are, and any current trail revisions.

HOW LONG TO TAKE

It all depends on how long the hiker wants to take (or can spend.) In 1991 two power runners did the entire trail in 27 hours and 56 minutes. Then in 1993, two separate parties, one from Germany, and another group of 3 reporters from the Tacoma News Tribune, each did the trail in 4 days. (The latter in 93 hours total elapsed time.) We're presuming those reading this book have slightly longer vacations. Seriously, don't construe those times to imply that this trail is easy, **It is not!** In fact if there is one thing that those who have done the Wonderland would wish to convey to future hikers, it is to be prepared psychologically. It's a *tough* trail!

The trip can be completed (with no layovers) in as few as 8 BIG days, or by traveling a little more leisurely, taking smaller "bites" and/or adding a layover day or two, it can take up to two weeks. The ideal would be 10-12 days.

Finding things to do to fill the time will be no problem. Fishing and unscheduled exploration could easily take several days, so prepare to allow for some leisure time. It's always possible to come out sooner, but life can get mighty difficult trying to keep up with a too-demanding schedule. It's also nice to have a spare day to "hole up" if bad weather hits.

Most of the following suggested plans do not allow for layover days, so if a mid-trip rest is desired, add an extra day to the chosen plan.

Total mileages differ because of variations in route such as going by way of Spray Park instead of Ipsut Pass, or via Lake James instead of Mystic Lake.

PLANNING SUGGESTIONS

(These first two trips are exceptionally hard, and are only recommended for very strong and well conditioned hikers)

8-Day Trip

1st day	Longmire to Devils Dream
2nd day	Devils Dream to North Puyallup
3rd day	North Puyallup to South Mowich River (or Mowich Lake)
4th day	Mowich River or Mowich Lake to Dick Creek via Spray Park
5th day	Dick Creek to Granite Creek
6th day	Granite Creek to Summerland
7th day	Summerland to Nickel Creek
8th day	Nickel Creek to Longmire

9-Day Trip

1st day	Longmire to Devils Dream
2nd day	Devils Dream to Klapatche

3rd day	Klapatche to Golden Lakes
4th day	Golden Lakes to Mowich Lake
5th day	Mowich Lake (via Ipsut Pass) to Mystic Lake
6th day	Mystic Lake to White River
7th day	White River to Indian Bar
8th day	Indian Bar to Maple Creek
9th day	Maple Creek to Longmire

10-Day Trip

1st day	Longmire to Devils Dream
2nd day	Devils Dream to Klapatche
3rd day	Klapatche to Golden Lakes
4th day	Golden Lakes to Mowich Lake
5th day	Mowich Lake to a Carbon River camp (via Ipsut Pass)
6th day	Carbon River camp to Mystic Lake
7th day	Mystic Lake to Sunrise
8th day	Sunrise to Summerland
9th day	Summerland to Nickel Creek
10th day	Nickel Creek to Longmire

11-Day Trip

1st day	Longmire to Devils Dream
2nd day	Devils Dream to Klapatche
3rd day	Klapatche Park to Golden Lake
4th day	Golden Lakes to Mowich Lake
5th day	Mowich Lake to a Carbon River camp (via Ipsut Pass)
6th day	Carbon River camp to Mystic Lake
7th day	Mystic Lake to Sunrise
8th day	Sunrise to Summerland
9th day	Summerland to Indian Bar
10th day	Indian Bar to Nickel Creek
11th day	Nickel Creek to Longmire

12-Day Trip

1st day	Longmire to Devils Dream
2nd day	Devils Dream to South Puyallup
3rd day	South Puyallup to Klapatche
4th day	Klapatche to Golden Lakes
5th day	Golden Lakes to Mowich Lake
6th day	Mowich Lake (via Spray Park) to a Carbon River camp
7th day	Carbon River camp to Mystic Lake
8th day	Mystic Lake to Sunrise
9th day	Sunrise to Summerland
10th day	Summerland to Indian Bar
11th day	Indian Bar to Nickel Creek
12th day	Nickel Creek to Longmire

The Wonderland Trail

13-Day Trip

1st day	Longmire to Devils Dream
2nd day	Devils Dream to South Puyallup
3rd day	South Puyallup to Klapatche
4th day	Klapatche to Golden Lakes
5th day	Golden Lakes to Mowich Lake
6th day	Mowich Lake to Cataract Valley via Spray Park
7th day	Cataract Valley to Mystic Lake
8th day	Layover day at Mystic Lake (or lay over later elsewhere)
9th day	Mystic Lake to Sunrise
10th day	Sunrise to Summerland
11th day	Summerland to Indian Bar
12th day	Indian Bar to Maple Creek or Paradise River
13th day	Maple Creek or Paradise River to Longmire

14-Day Trip

1st day	Longmire to Devils Dream
2nd day	Devils Dream to South Puyallup
3rd day	South Puyallup to Klapatche
4th day	Klapatche to Golden Lakes
5th day	Golden Lakes to North Mowich River
6th day	North Mowich River to Mowich Lake
7th day	Mowich Lake via Spray Parkto one of the Carbon River camps
8th day	Carbon River camp to Mystic Lake
9th day	Layover day at either Mystic Lake, or later at Summerland or Indian Bar
10th day	Mystic Lake to Sunrise
11th day	Sunrise to Summerland
12th day	Summerland to Indian Bar
13th day	Indian Bar to Nickel Creek, Maple Creek or Paradise River
14th day	Maple Creek or Paradise River to Longmire

ALL AT ONCE OR WEEKEND WONDERING

Fortunately for a great many people who can't get late summer vacations,those who don't feel up to doing the entire trip at once, or those who want to do EVERY section by the easiest route, the Wonderland Trail is also ideally done in weekend segments (except for the West Side, now that the West Side Road is closed). The entire trip can be done piecemeal in 6 or 7 weekends of hiking. Of those, a coupleare one-day hikes which can be accomplished with just day packs, allowing the hiker to sleep in a campground (or at home.)

There will be other weekends where the mileage will be a little more than might be preferred for a two-day trip, but there is consolation in the fact that there are five days in which to rest up before it's time to shoulder the pack again. The "long-haul" weekends are Longmire to Mowich Lake, Ipsut to Sunrise, and from the White River Highway to Box Canyon.

Of these, one weekend-long trip can be eliminated by turning it into three one-day hikes, *(again, this is possible only IF the West Side Highway is open, or if you can bike up the West Side Road and then hike a loop.)* The Indian Henry-Klapatche segment can be done as day trips via the Klapatche Loop trip, the Emerald Ridge Loop trip, and by taking the South Tahoma Creek Trail to Indian Henrys and out the same day to Longmire.

These access trails will add extra mileage, (and some fine scenery), but offer another means to the end, if the goal is ease or even shorter segments. (But this same entire southwest corner segment can be done easily as a weekend trip by doing it COUNTER-clockwise, and should be done in this manner in preference to making a big production of it, if at all possible.) Call the backcountry desk at (360) 569-2211 to see if the West Side Highway is open or if a shuttle is running up there yet.

DAY HIKES ON THE WONDERLAND
(A Little Taste of Heaven)

Everyone involved in mountaineering had to start somewhere. What better place to sample the joys of the wilderness experience than a day trip on the Wonderland. Great day hikes would be:

Spray Park to see the flowers and the panorama
(page 132 to page 136 and back.)

A look at the big tree
(page 127 to page 130 and back.)

See a glacier close up
(Carbon River loop, page 149 to page 151 and back.)

A spectacular view of Sunrise [Frozen Lake],
(counterclockwise page 164 to 162 and back.)

Just a nice easy mile in pretty woods.
[paralleling Sunrise Road, page 181 to page 182.)

See a real trail camp [Nickel Creek],
(counterclockwise page 197 to page 194 and back.)

Downhill all the way...provided somebody picks you up at the bottom.
(Steven Canyon - pages 200 to 197.)

Reflection Lakes to the base of Narada Falls (page 204 to page 205.)

Mowich Lake to Ipsut Creek Campground (page 127 to page 131.)

RECOMMENDED WEEKEND SEGMENTS

SEGMENT		TRAVEL TIME		WHERE	EASIEST
From	To	Days	O'night	To Stay	DIRECTION
Longmire to N. Puyallup River		3	0 or 3	- - - - - - -	clockwise

(This is based on the West Side Road being open, and doing this as three one-day
trips using the access trails off the W. Side Rd.
If the West Side Road is not open, it would be a 4-6 day trip to Mowich Lake.)

SEGMENT		TRAVEL TIME		WHERE	EASIEST
N. Puyallup to Mowich Lake		2	1	Golden L.	clockwise
Mowich Lake to Ipsut Creek		1	0	- - - - - - -	clockwise
Ipsut Campground to Sunrise		2	1	Mystic	counter-clock
Sunrise to Fryingpan Creek		1	0	- - - - - - -	clockwise
Fryingpan Creek. to Box Canyon		2	1	Indian Bar	clockwise
Box Canyon to Reflection Lake		1	0	- - - - - - -	counter-clock
Reflection Lake to Longmire		1	0	- - - - - - -	clockwise

One Day Trips

Mowich Lake to Ipsut Creek (Clockwise)
Sunrise to Frying Pan Creek at Sunrise Highway (Clockwise)
Reflection Lakes to Box Canyon (Counter-clockwise)
Reflection Lakes to Longmire (Clockwise)

SUGGESTED WEEKENDS

Two one-day trips

Day 1: Reflection Lakes to Box Canyon (Counter-clockwise)
Day 2: Reflection Lakes to Longmire (Clockwise)

Two one-day trips

Mowich Lake to Ipsut Creek (then drive to Sunrise, hike to Sunrise Camp,
camp there, then the following day, hike from Sunrise to
Frying Pan Creek Bridge (Clockwise)

Weekend-long trips necessitating overnight stays

Sunrise to Ipsut Creek (Counter-clockwise)
Fryingpan Creek to Box Canyon (Clockwise

WHAT TO DO ABOUT THE WEST SIDE

Until the West Side Road reopens,
the entire west side will have to be hiked as one long stretch
It's more easily done clockwise.

OH FOR THE WINGS OF AN ANGEL

Of considerably more difficulty than the backpacking, will be arranging transportation. On most of these weekend trips, the hiker ends up an impossible distance from his or her car. The real wonder of the Wonderland may be getting the backpacker back to his car or getting his car back to him.

The solutions are rather limited:

1. (The BEST choice). Be dropped off by a non-hiker who then drives to the exit point at the appropriate time and picks the party up there.

2. Arrange with a fellow hiker to hike the same section at the same time, but from the opposite end. When meeting in the middle, switch car keys, then meet again on the way home and swap vehicles. (Or better still, do the car swapping *before* hiking so each ends up back at his own car.)

3. Post a notice on mountaineer bulletin boards or put ads in publications hikers are likely to read, (such as the Mountaineer Bulletin, Signpost Magazine or Pack and Paddle) to round up other hikers with cars.

The Mountaineer, 300 Third Ave. West, Seattle, WA 98119. $.80 a word for non-members.

Signpost, Washington Trails Association, 1305 Fourth Ave., #512, Seattle, WA 98101, Free ad for subscribers.

Pack & Paddle, PO Box 1063, Port Orchard, WA 98366, Free ad for subscribers. $.50 a word for non-subscribers.

4. Unfortunately, the simplest solution is illegal and very dangerous: - hitchhiking. (It is prohibited by Park regulations.) However there's no law against making friends on the trail and accepting a ride with these new friends provided they happen to be heading the right direction. But don't bank on a ride half way around the Mountain. That's a pretty heavy strain on even an old friendship.

(Trail friendships may also prove very valuable in solving future transportation problems if both parties have some of the same segments left to do. Most people doing the trail in weekend sections are faced with the same problems, so speak up, and do everyone a favor.)

FOR THOSE WHO FLY FIRST, HIKE LATER

For those flying in from other parts of the country, the closest commercial airport is Seattle-Tacoma International Airport (Sea-Tac). The Mountain is about a 2 - 2½ -hour drive away. Fortunately for backpackers, there's now "the Rainier Shuttle" which picks Rainier-bound backpackers and climbers up at Sea-Tac and drops them off at Longmire, Cougar Rock Campground, or Paradise. The shuttle runs from May 15 to mid-October, and runs $37.00 one-way or $46.00 round trip. It makes pickups at Sea-Tac (Island 2) at 9 a.m., 1 p.m. and 8 p.m. Make arrangements for pickup by calling 360-569-2331.

Accommodations at Longmire are available year-round, but at Paradise during the summer only. Write to Mount Rainier Guest Services at 55106 Kernahan Road East, Ashford, WA 98304, or call (360) 569-2275. The nearby towns of Ashford and Elbe have several nice motels and Bed and Breakfasts ranging from charming to elegant. There's even a tree house you can rent. (But none except Whittaker's Bunkhouse that have shuttles to Longmire). Send a #10 SASE to Dunamis House, Box 321, Issaquah, WA 98027 and we'll send you an up to date accommodations list.

SHIPPING YOUR BACKPACK AS LUGGAGE

The biggest problem with backpacks on airlines is the possibility that buckles or straps might get caught and torn or destroyed. Seasoned hikers who frequently ship packs suggest tightening and tucking in (or taping down) all straps so they don't hang loose. Don't strap anything to the outside of the pack, and some even cover the pack with a pack cover. This will keep it safe from theft and keep stuff in outside pockets secure. Others put theirs in a big pack-size box to ship as luggage.

If going right to the park to hike, change into your hiking clothes at Sea-Tac and put your "civilian clothes" in a locker at the airport along with other luggage and anything else you don't need at the Mountain. There are no storage lockers at the park. Remember you can no no longer ship knives on carry-one baggage.

Should you find yourself with anything you want to mail home once off the trail, there's a U.S. Post Office in the Inn at Longmire, but you may have to scrounge a box off the folks at the store. They may not have a box big enough for your pack, however, if you want to ship that home while you continue traveling on elsewhere.

MILEAGE

THE GOSPEL ACCORDING TO THE MEASURING WHEEL

All it takes to complete the Wonderland Trail is to put one foot in front of the other for 486,667 feet or 92.2 miles. This book was born of curiosity over that very figure. Researching the subject for the first time, turned up seven major sources of authority on the trail. No two of them agreed on much of anything. But the main bone of contention was the mileage.

What was it REALLY? There was only one way to get the truth. Measure the trail!

The device used, commonly known as a measuring wheel, is the same kind used by foresters and surveyors everywhere. As it rolls along it measures every foot of the trail by counting revolutions of the wheel. It is like a giant rolling tape measure.

The mileage in this book is computed from the precise number of feet between points. It is then converted to the closest tenth of a mile. If the number of feet is more than one tenth, but less than 264 feet, it is shown as the tenth plus (+). If it is over 265 feet or more than half the distance to the next tenth, it is shown as minus (-) the next tenth.

For example, 2,364 feet would be shown as 0.4+ miles, but 2,384 feet would be shown as 0.5- miles.

Don't be surprised when you emerge from the final segment of trail with legs of steel. Not only will you have hiked the equivalent of over a hundred miles, you will have *climbed* 22,786 feet going up all those ridges, (plus descended another 22,786' coming down them!) Climbing to the summit of Mount Rainier requires ascending 9,051 feet if going up from Paradise, thus **Wonderland Trail hikers will have done enough climbing to have climbed the Mountain 2-1/2 times!** A neat little formula shown in the Longmire Hiker Center suggests you add one mile of extra mileage for each 1,000 feet of elevation gained, and one-half mile for every 1,000 feet of elevation loss. Using this formula, hiking the Wonderland Trail is equal to hiking 126.2 flat miles.

MILEAGE

Longmire to Devil's Dream	5.9+
Devil's Dream to South Puyallup River	6.6+
South Puyallup River to Klapatche Park	3.6-
Klapatche Park to North Puyallup River	2.8-
North Puyallup River to Golden Lakes	4.9-
Golden Lakes to North Mowich River	6.3+
North Mowich River to Mowich Lake	3.7-
Mowich Lake to Carbon River	
(Ipsut Creek Campground)	
via Ipsut Pass	5.4+
via Spray Park (Alternate Route)	11.9+
Ipsut Campground to	
Carbon River Loop Corner C	3.3-
Carbon River to Sunrise	
via Mystic Lake	
Ipsut Creek to Mystic Lake	7.4+
Mystic Lake to Granite Creek Camp	4.1+
Granite Creek Camp to Sunrise	4.7+
via Lake James (alternate Route)	
Ipsut Creek to Yellowstone Camp	5.0
Yellowstone Camp to Lake James	3.4
Lake James to Fire Creek Camp	5.0-
Fire Creek Camp to Berkeley Camp	3.5+
Berkeley Camp to Sunrise	3.8+
Sunrise to White River Campground	3.1+
White River Campground to Summerland	6.6+
Summerland to Indian Bar	4.5-
Indian Bar to Nickel Creek	6.8-
Nickel Creek to Maple Creek Camp	3.1-
Maple Creek Camp to Paradise River	6.8-
Paradise River to Longmire	3.4-

MOUNTAIN WEATHER

A former Park Service employee was once quoted as saying, "There's no summer up here, only ten months of winter and two of late fall."

Not only are 37 square miles of Mount Rainier covered year-round by glaciers, the entire park is snow covered much of the year. Above 6,500-7,000 feet, more than 50 feet of snow falls each winter. Some of the greatest annual snowpacks in the world have been recorded at Mount Rainier. Between July, 1971 and July, 1972, a record 1122 inches of snow (93.5 feet) fell at Paradise. This snowfall still holds the record at the Mountain.

Thus it wasn't too long ago that the flower-bedecked trail you're standing on was under 15 feet of snow. But in 'normal' years, by mid-to-late July, the last lingering snows usually have melted off the Wonderland in all but areas of the perpetual snowfields. Occasionally, snow in the higher elevations may last into August. In the event of a **really** horrendous winter, a few segments of the trail may remain snowbound the entire following summer.

But summer weather is generally beautiful and clear, with "warm" meaning a daytime temperature of anywhere from 60°- 80°, and evening temperatures ranging from freezing on up. Mount Rainier's fickle summer storms may dish up a smorgasbord of elements, including rain, snow, whiteouts, blizzards, hail, violent winds, lightning and thunderstorms. Annual precipitation varies within the park, ranging from 60 to 85 inches per year at elevations below 3,000 feet, to 90 to 110 inches annually at higher elevations. The need for good rain gear can't be overstated, because any kind of weather can be encountered (and usually is) at Mount Rainier, even in summer.

An "Indian Summer" (a brief return of summer-like weather) frequently extends the hiking season well into October, - a favorite time for many hikers who save the Mount Rainier trails until then so they can see the old Mountain resplendent in her autumn colors. The trails are in their best condition, many of the bugs are gone, and the meadows are at their prime. Patches of scarlet foliage signal the location of the low-growing delicious blueberry and give a feast to the eye as well as the tummy. The National Park is also a bulletproof sanctuary when "outside" trails are unsafe for man and beast due to the advent of Washington state's hunting season.

WALKING ON THE WINTER WONDERLAND

Postholing would probably be a more accurate description of winter travel on the Wonderland if one isn't skiing or snowshoeing. We include this brief discussion only because so many people have asked if it is possible to do the trail in winter, not because we recommend it.

Take all the hardships and difficulties of a summer expedition, and multiply by 3 or 4. Starting with the worst first, is the ever-present danger of avalanches coming off the many ridges always above, below and beside you on the Wonderland. The steep climbs and descents on slick ice or deep snow instead of solid footing will greatly increase normal travel time, as will finding water, crossing rivers with bridges out, disorientation because familiar landmarks are gone, and virtually all the normal creature comforts obliterated. Add to that piercing icy winds howling down off the Mountain bringing an unbelievable wind-chill factor, plus snow, snow, and more snow. Then there are the short bitter cold days and long nights, hungry animals, extra weight added by additional clothing, food and fuel, (plus skis or snowshoes). Of course there will be no food caches, no easy access trails, longer hikes in and out, no emergency help at hand and the possibility of frozen equipment, hypothermia, frostbite or snow blindnes. Last but not least, will be the death-defying crossing of the South Tahoma River via swami belt on the cable because the slats on the bridge will have been removed for winter. At least there won't be bugs!

Winter day and weekend hikes by *experienced* outdoorsmen are fairly commonplace in the Northwest. However unless those contemplating a winter Wonderland trip are in the expert survivalist category, it shouldn't even be considered. Access to the Park backcountry in winter is restricted to via the Nisqually entrance on the south, and some long hikes into the Park on the north. The Carbon River road will be most likely be closed at the Carbon Entrance, or sooner. Likewise, the Mowich Lake Road will probably be closed at the Paul Peak gate, one mile inside the Park boundary, and 4.5 miles from the lake, if it isn't blocked by snow even farther down. Highway 410 is normally closed at the North Park Arch, just beyond the Crystal Mountain turnoff.

MAPS

A good topographical map is essential! Our top choice for use on the trail is Earthwalk Press's waterproof "Hiking Map & Guide - Mt. Rainier National Park". The fact that it won't disintegrate in the rain puts this map in a class by itself for trail use.

In addition to a good topographical map for trail use, we recommend Dee Molenaar's classic pictorial map for use in trip planning. It gives an oblique bird's eye view of the entire trail, and provides a realistic picture of whether the terrain is open, wooded, steep, etc. It's also beautiful framed on your "Mount Rainier wall" and as an aid in pointing out the location of your trail exploits in a visual way that helps "flat land touristers" get the picture. Both maps are available as indicated on page 218.

"THAT FUNNY-LOOKING CLOUD"

Whether seen from afar or viewed from her ridges, a lenticular cloud over the mountain is a novel sight. These caps form when warm, moist air from the Pacific Ocean on the west meets the cold air over the mountain. The ensuing condensation forms into a lens shaped cloud of fog, ice particles or snow. The unique cloud-cap may be an early warning of a possible change of weather, and usually indicates that weather on the summit may not be as sunny and serene as that being enjoyed by its viewers a few miles below.

Climbers have reported winds of over 100 MPH within a lenticular cloud, while below, lower elevations haven't even a breeze.

Lenticular clouds generally blow leeward (to the east) and it isn't unusual to see several of them come off the summit in a line looking like space ships taking off in formation.

FOGS, WHITEOUTS AND CLOUDS

Most backpackers don't really care what the white stuff around them is, for whatever it is, they can't see. If it's fog or a low-hanging cloud, finding the trail ahead may be difficult. If it's a "whiteout", finding even their *feet* may be downright impossible! On snow in a whiteout, it becomes difficult to even tell up from down.

A whiteout is a phenomenon in which moisture, be it from fog, mist or a cloud, is so dense that all perspective is lost due to the complete jumbling of the visible light spectrum. There is no horizon; atmosphere and snow run together into a uniform whitish-gray. There is no distinguishing whether the gradient ahead is up, down or level. A hiker can not only lose his sense of direction and can't tell ground from air, he cannot see the hand at the end of his arm. It has been described as being instantly blind. Being in one is a truly frightening experience!

Fortunately, whiteouts at Wonderland Trail elevations are relatively rare. Whiteouts usually occur higher on the Mountain. If caught in one, **stop in your tracks and take shelter right where you are.** If aware one is coming, try to find a tree or large rock for partial shelter, and prepare to stay there for the duration. Do not get separated from your pack or your companions for any reason. Above all, maintain body heat. Get and stay warm and dry. Get in your sleeping bag inside your tent, even if it isn't possible to set the tent up properly. Most deaths during whiteouts come from hypothermia. Whiteouts can hit with paralyzing swiftness, but fortunately, most leave the same way.

Fogs differ from whiteouts in that fogs still allow limited visibility and aren't as disorienting. Most mountain fogs are brief and are actually harbingers of good weather to follow. Dreary morning fogs are usually "burned off" as soon as the sun climbs over the surrounding Cascade peaks.

NUTS AND BOLTS (Hikers and Lightning)

Few experiences produce white hair quite like waking up from a sound sleep in what appears to be the epicenter of an electrical storm.

Lightning prefers peaks to valleys, lone trees to grassy meadows, and tall timber to flattened sleeping-bagged hikers, but being reminded of this brings little consolation in the backcountry. It is generally then that the hiker remembers he's on a knoll, with his tarp tied to the tallest solitary tree in sight, anchored on the other end by his shiny new metal ice axe, and with his feet elevated from the stream under him by his metal pack frame.

Separating oneself expediently from such conductors, timber and prominent points is usually the backcountry traveler's only recourse until the storm dispels itself. Frequently within an hour or so the sun or stars will be back out as if nothing had happened. The trembling usually subsides shortly thereafter.

STEP BACK IN TIME

Everywhere about you are examples of the powerful forces of nature at work. The very ground you're walking on has been formed by one cataclysmic event or another. Such events are volcanic, glacial, erosion, fluvial (stream action), fire, (which has occurred in approximately 90% of the park's forests), snow and rock avalanches, mudflows, floods, wind and blowdown. Every so often another violent event comes along to continue to reshape it.

The Columbus Day windstorm of 1962 wreaked extensive havoc and destroyed untold thousands of trees as it cut a swath through the Cascades just north of the Mountain. Wind, of even far less velocity, is a worthy adversary at the Mountain. It can toss giant trees around like matchsticks.

If a serious windstorm comes up unexpectedly, seek shelter beside a boulder big enough to stop a tree from falling on you.

.....AND THINGS THAT GO BUMP IN THE NIGHT

Hikers having experienced middle of the night sonic booms while in some remote corner of the backcountry seldom ever complain about city booms again. At least there they know what they are.

True to their tradition for precision and detail, the Air Force usually waits until every last hiker is snug in his bag and sound asleep before cutting loose with the boom. True to THEIR tradition, the then-deafened hikers usually vault with equal precision from their warm bags into the icy night screaming, "Is the Mountain erupting? Is the Mountain erupting?"

When, after a respectable time, no lava or mudflow runs through the camp, the realization dawns that civilization has sent a brain-rattling reminder to the hikers that it is still alive. Considering what effect such a jolt might have on the mountain, most hikers re-retire grateful that the old Mountain didn't respond with a reminder that she is alive too!

SO YOU WANT TO CLIMB MOUNT RAINIER TOO

If climbing Mount Rainier is one of your life goals, there will never be a better time to do it than immediately after finishing the Wonderland Trail. You'll discover firm muscles your legs never knew they had. You'll be acclimated and ready to leap tall mountains in spring-loaded bounds.

Unless those considering this feat are trained and experienced climbers, a guide service should be used. Mount Rainier has claimed the lives of many climbers over the years, with more added to the sad statistics nearly every year. Going up with a professional guide service is the way to do it!

There are two guide services operating at Mount Rainier. In 1891, Leonard Longmire set himself up as the first professional guide. His fee was $1.00 per person for the trip to the top. 100+ years later, there has been a price change.

PERMISSION TO DO THE TRAIL (Wilderness Permits)

Long gone are the days when you can just sign in at a trail register and hit the trail. The National Park's Wilderness Management Plan is designed to minimize impacts on the vegetation, soil, water and wildlife. It is achieving this by controlling backcountry usage and encouraging low impact camping. A backcountry use permit is required (year round) for any overnight travel in the wilderness.

Two types of overnight trail camps exist: trailside and cross-country camps.

There are 20 trailside camps along the Wonderland Trail at distances of three to seven miles apart. Each of the camps has from 1-10 "individual" sites for 1-5 persons. Group sites for 6-12 persons are available at several of the camps.

Each camp has cleared tent sites, a toilet and a nearby water source. (You still must treat or boil all camp water before drinking.)

Advance reservations for campsites are now accepted up to two months in advance. Forms are available on-line or in the back of this book. For those coming from out of state, try to arrange the trip to start between Sunday and Thursday to avoid the crush of maximum usage on weekends. Even more important, to avoid the disappointment of traveling all the way to Washington State only to find that sites are full at your first choice starting point, be prepared to make alternate arrangements.

These could include waiting an extra day to start until your preferred site opens up, starting at a different point, or going a different direction. (Once you're allotted the first couple sites, or cross-country permit for the first night, reservations will be committed for your entire trip.)

If all assigned campsites are full, a limited number of Cross-Country permits are also available. Cross-country camping in designated Cross-Country zones allows

50

backpackers to decide on their own place to camp, using minimum impact camping techniques. The camps must be at least 1/4 mile away from the trail. Camp on unvegetated ground so as to not damage meadows, and make no "improvements" to the camp (trenches, leveling, tables, etc.) Leave the campsite in a natural state, and remove all traces of your stay. The permit is good for one night at a time, and only in specific zones. (Even cross-country camping is not a casual arrangement, advance planning is essential.) Party size is limited to five people or one immediate family, and permits are only issued to those with proven backcountry experience.

It is possible to change reservations, but in order to do so, you must first find a ranger with a computer terminal and then find a campsite with room. The chance of this happening would be highly unlikely on a Friday or Saturday.

The free permits may be obtained at the Hiker's Information Centers at Longmire, Wilkeson, or White River Entrance or at other visitor centers or entrancestations. The permit issuing stations are all connected by computer, so the Park Service has an up-to-the-minute picture of exactly who is in the backcountry.

TRAIL CAMPS

	INDIVIDUAL SITES	GROUP SITES	ELEVATION FEET
Berkeley Park	4	-	5600
Carbon River	4	-	3100
Cataract Valley	7	1	4700
Devils Dream	7	1	5000
Dick Creek	2	-	4320
Eagle's Roost	7	1	4700
Fire Creek	3	1	4600
Golden Lakes	5	1	5000
Granite Creek	2	1	5732
Indian Bar	3	1	5100
Klapatche Park	4	-	5400
Maple Camp	4	1	2800
Mowich River*	4	1	2600
Mystic Lake	7	2	5620
Nickel Creek	3	1	3350
N. Puyallup R.*	3	1	3600
Paradise River	3	1	3950
Pyramid Creek	2	-	3760
S. Puyallup R.	4	1	4000
Summerland	5	1	5900
Sunrise	8	2	6300
Yellowstone Camp	2	2	5100

WONDERLAND TRAVELERS

THE CALL OF THE WILD

In 1910, a Tacoma author, John Williams, eloquently described the Mount Rainier backcountry: "Stupendous scenes await the adventurer who penetrates the harder trails and climbs the greater glaciers of the North and East slopes. No book will ever be large enough to tell the whole story. That must be learned by summers of severe though profitable toil."

When Mr. Williams wrote those words, the Wonderland Trail was still a dream, five years away from becoming a reality. Those early adventurers would no doubt marvel in disbelief at the relative ease with which we can encircle the Mountain today, compared with the hardships they endured to accomplish the same end. It was a major expedition just to get to the Mountain.

Time has brought many improvements in access, trail and equipment, but it hasn't changed the beauty of the Mountain, or the rewards heaped on those who venture to the high and remote corners of this great park. Theirs is still a special treasure.

The Wonderland Trail today is one of America's finest wilderness pathways. (It was the #1 choice of a reader's poll of Backpacker Magazine in December 2000.) The Trail, and the magnificent park through which it passes, is the property of the more than two hundred seventy-five million citizens of the United States. Their taxes protect and maintain it for all to use and enjoy.

Surprisingly, more people hiked the entire trail in the early days when traveling it was harder, than hike it today. The last couple decades have seen only about 200-250 people a year hike the *entire* trail. A few hundred more, do sections or use it for short hikes each summer. Thousands more annually trek to lookout or scenic points near the trailheads touching the roads. But how tragic that of the roughly two million visitors to the park each year, so few ever get to really know the Mountain backcountry! It also means that with the U.S. population currently being over 275,000,000, *you are one in a million if you are one of the few who complete the entire trail.*

WHO ANSWERS?

This trail is a great equalizer. Your trail companions may be lawyers, psychologists, janitors, military people, homemakers, truck drivers, and every profession in between. But all will share the same hardships, weather, tough trail, bugs, sweat and toil, and the kinship and mutual respect that comes from participating in this special adventure. The key to success lies not in physical prowess, but simple desire. Anyone in reasonably good shape can hike the Wonderland if inclined to be inclined on the ever-sloping trail.

Contrary to the perfect-bodied specimens shown in the equipment catlogs, genuine backpackers come in every imaginable shape, size and age. Over the years the trail has been done by everyone from toddlers to 80-year old grandmothers. The common bond shared by those who travel the backcountry is their mutual love of the great outdoors, and their understanding of the values and rewards to be found on the high trails. Backpackers are that self-sustaining independent breed whose freedom rings from every mountain side!

WOMEN

Since 1890, when Fay Fuller of Tacoma made history as the first woman to reach the summit of Mount Rainier, countless women have participated in every sport and adventure the ountain has to offer.

Accepting the challenge of the Wonderland Trail has been no exception. Since its 1915 inception, the Wonderland has felt the step of many hundreds of women who count the completion of it among their more rewarding of life's achievements.

KIDS

Many a Northwest child took his first hike on a Wonderland section or access trail. The favorite "beginning trail" for little children, was probably the West Side access trail to Klapatche Park, however that trail's future is now in limbo. The next best choices for young children are Mowich Lake to Spray Park, (and return) or from Ipsut Creek Campground up to the Carbon Glacier. The latter trail is gentle, and the glacier is educational and exciting to be so near. The suspension bridge will make this first hike an especially memorable starter hike for kids. There's no law saying you must go all the way once you start, so if it turns out to be too long or too strenuous for little ones, turn around and go back while there's still enough energy reserve to make the return trip. The objective should not be reaching a destination at all costs, but making the family hike a pleasurable experience.

The age at which a child could successfully endure the rigors of the entire Wonderland would depend on the child. Some eight year olds have successfully done it, and there have been twelve year olds who could not. As with adults, children need to get in condition for a hike of this magnitude.

Key factors to keep in mind are finding a little pack and frame that fits the child, and keeping the child's pack weight low. Remember to watch out for their basic needs: plenty of water, adequate raingear and not "burning out" by overdoing it. (VERY important!)

Since children are not usually motivated by the same goals as adults when hiking, an extra helping of "encouragement skills" will be needed by the parents. Patience will be the key to success. It helps to make the trip into an adventure, by organizing sort of a scavenger hunt, and giving "points" for finding certain objects or sightings: (the first peek of the Mountain, layers of "color" in a hillside, hearing a marmot whistle, finding a red "rock", etc.). It also helps to include special surprise treats, such as their own camera, their own poly water bottle, or fruit leather snacks.

Basic ground rules, which should be established, understood and agreed to in advance are: 1. No running on the trail. 2. No "running off": into the woods or running ahead out of sight. 3. No screaming or unnecessary noise. 4. A buddy must go along on all off-trail trips, even including potty breaks. 5. No touching, chasing or frightening animals. 6. No throwing or rolling rocks or sticks. 7. No cutting across switchbacks or taking shortcuts. No littering or making and leaving messes. 8. No carving or writing on trees, bridges, signs, buildings, etc. 9. ALWAYS keep the party together! Additional rules can be added as appropriate.☺

A WORD ABOUT HIKING COMPANIONS

Put a lot of thought into the selection of whom you pick to hike with. The rigors of this trail bring out both the best and the worst in people. The ideal party would be friends of equal ability, temperament and interests. We've heard more than one sad tale of people who did the trail in perfect weather, glorious hiking conditions and missed it all because they daily grew to hate their hiking partner. Fortunately for every breakup or divorce, there are many more lifelong friendships and commitments and bonds that have come off the trail.

Check out little things like basic hiking philosophy. Is this going to be a marathon, or a leisurely 'take time to smell the flowers and check out every little interesting tidbit' adventure? Are you going to hike together, or will the faster hiker take off and leave the other to cross rivers alone? Or the reverse. Is one hiker such a slow starter that many hours are lost before the slowpoke can be coaxed and cajoled to get going? Is one person a "borrower" who expects others to supply what he forgot or didn't care to carry? What will the cooking setup be? Will everybody do his own, or will the cooking and chores be shared? If you have any idiosyncrasies, fess up beforehand. One person we heard from spent the entire trip in silence except for a few quick words with passing hikers. Her companion, (found through an ad), announced shortly after getting on the trail, that she didn't like idle conversation, so she didn't talk for the next two weeks.

Just the reverse can happen too. A trip with horrid conditions, shared hardships, and a good scare or two, but balanced with good laughs, great companions and good times amid mutual adversity can fuse bonds for life. A good attitude is all important, and if you suspect there may be differences, talk out the trip in advance, and perhaps lay out some ground rules on 'do's and don'ts, will's and won'ts.' Interpersonal relationships will play a major role in the success of the trip. Know ahead of time there could be stress. Try to minimize it.

NATIVE AMERICANS

The first users of the entire park area were the various Indian tribes living in proximity to the mountain. These included the Muckleshoot, Klickatat, Puyallup,

Nisqually, Upper Cowlitz, and Yakima Nations. They came to the park seasonally for get-togethers to hunt, play games, and pick berries.

In 1885 or '86, a party of six or seven Yakima Indians along with a Mr. Allison Brown climbed the mountain via the Cowlitz Divide, then the Whitman and Ingraham Glaciers. This was an unusual event, because the Indians of the day all thought the white men were crazy for wanting to go to the summit. The Indians did not worship the Mountain, as many have stated, but were fearful of the area above snowline. Also contrary to popular opinion, Tacoma is not an Indian word, although many of the area names in the park are legacies left by the early Indian users.

According to park records of 1906, Cowlitz Indians were still making occasional hunting expeditions up Cowlitz Divide from Ohanapecosh to Indian Bar and Summerland. The Cowlitz Divide section of today's Wonderland Trail is the same old Indian Trail.

By 1920, the Indians were coming to the Park by car.

HORSE SENSE

Horse or stock use on the Wonderland is now virtually non-existent. It is due in part to practicability, and partly to the fact that only a few sections of trail are accessible to stock. (27.1 miles or roughly 1/3 of the trail). Pack or saddle stock is defined as horses, mules, burros, or llamas. Stock parties are limited to a maximum of 5 animals on the authorized Wonderland Trail segments.

While riding may be easier on the traveler (and that is a question open to debate), it can be tough on the horse. Only horses in prime physical condition, and experienced on steep mountain trails should be considered for use on Park trails.

Greater distances can be traveled than by foot, however the decision is generally made by the endurance of the seat rather than the feet. A horse can travel 18-20 miles a day, but horse travelers who have put in such mileage on the Wonderland, strongly recommend about half that distance, or about the same mileage segments as traveled by the hiker.

Since grazing is not permitted anywhere within the park, *all food must be carried for the animals.* Hay pellets or cubes and grain are the normal stock feed preference. Water is readily available, but be sure to water animals **downstream** so they don't further pollute upstream water.

A horse can carry from 150-200 pounds, depending on his weight and size. Some horseback parties bring spare pack animals to carry supplies.

Glacial rivers must be forded since horses aren't allowed on the bridges, and by mid-day in summer such rivers may be raging torrents with tumbling boulders (big enough to break a horse's leg).

Horses have one attribute people don't have — horse sense! They're fairly surefooted animals, and are pretty particular about where they'll set foot and the route they take. Generally they don't take chances. Even at that, horses have been known to slip and fall, usually in situations where, if the rider had the horse's sense, he would dismount and walk.

Crossing snowfields with horses is accomplished simply and safely by switchbacking the steep snow, rather than attempting to go straight up or down.

Horses and bears don't mix. It's generally a matter of which sees or smells the other and bolts first. A rider on his own horse, or a horse he knows, can better predict his mount than a new horseman on a rented animal.

The horse's "first aid kit" is far simpler than his master's is. Old Paint's consists of (LOTS of) bug repellent, disinfectant for wounds, bandages, a curry comb, a hoof pick, a horse brush, and a sharp knife as a last resort should he break a leg. (Then be prepared to pay to helicopter him out.)

Horses have the right of way on a trail, and backpackers should get off the trail for a mounted party, stepping BELOW the trail. They should remain reasonably quiet until the horses pass to avoid spooking them.

Park rules specify that horses may not be kept in campgrounds or within 100 yards of a trail campsite or shelter. They should be tethered to hitching rails or away from the root zones of trees.

Stock parties are bound by the same requirements and rules as backpackers, and must also obtain backcountry permits.

The following are the sections of the Wonderland Trail (plus Wonderland access trails) open to stock use:

WEST SIDE

Wonderland Trail from Ipsut Creek Campground
to North Puyallup horse camp
(dismount and lead along the road shoulder at Mowich Lake)

North Puyallup Trail from North Puyallup Horse
Camp to Klapatche Point at the north end of the Westside Road

Westside Road (gravel, auto traffic)
from Klapatche Point south to Dry Creek (road barricade)

Paul Peak Trail from the Mowich Road
to the Wonderland Trail
near the North Mowich River Horse Camp

SOUTH SIDE

Wonderland Trail from Longmire to Box Canyon
(along the road shoulder past Reflection Lakes
Rampart Ridge Loop Trail from Longmire and back

EAST SIDE
Stock no longer allowed on East Side Wonderland Sections

LLAMAS LOVE TRAILS TOO

They don't call them "the freight train of the Andes" for nothing.

An even more interesting beast of burden to lighten your load, would be the lovely llama. They come under the same rules as horses, but because of their soft padded feet, they're easier on trails than human beings. They need far less in the way of feed and equipment, however they also carry far less. An average full-grown male llama can carry a pack weight of about 60 pounds. A rented pack llama will come complete with packs for your gear and his own food supplied.

Besides having a loyal companion, you'll find you also have a "watchdog" in the llama. Nothing escapes his attention, and he will be aware of all wildlife and activity around you long before you are.

THE CARE AND FEEDING OF RANGERS AND PARK PERSONNEL

With a little luck, you may also come across some of the unsung heroes of the park, - a trail crew. Not only are they the trail experts, several of the permanent crew have worked the park's trails for years. They're the hard-working men who maintain the trails and bridges, and know every square inch of the ground you're walking on. Give them a tip of the sun visor and a word of appreciation for a job well done. Ask about the trail ahead, but don't get too gabby. They have a lot of work to do, and precious few days in which to do it.

JUNIOR RANGERS

When in the backcountry, realize that you can greatly assist the rangers and staff by reporting anything unusual, particularly interesting, or dangerous. Very detailed records are kept of all the animal goings-on and natural phenomenon, and the naturalists will really appreciate reports of what you've seen out there. (Send us copies too so we can include the best ones in future books.)

On the criminal side, be alert for vandalism, natural resource violations, arson, poaching and safety hazards. If you observe criminal activity, do not take action yourself, but note the location, description of the people involved and their license number (if at a trailhead). Report it to a ranger or call (360) 569-2211 or (360) 569-2809. Put a lot of thought into protecting the belongings you leave in your car while you're hiking. Unfortunately thieves and vandals enjoy going to the Mountain too, and many have had profitable vacations at Mount Rainier. Don't leave valuables in sight!

EQUIPMENT

WHAT TO TAKE

The temperature may be over 90 degrees when packing day arrives, but keep in mind the ice that may be on the water pot a few mornings hence. Those beautiful picturesque ridge-top campsites have unobstructed views of beloved old Mount Rainier, but they're also in the direct course of the wind and weather as it blows down off her icy slopes.

The elements not withstanding, mountain weather is just naturally colder, the reason being that temperature drops about 3 degrees for every thousand-foot gain in elevation. Thus when it's 80 degrees in Seattle, it will likely be 65 degrees at Summerland — which is at 5,000 feet. The wind chill factor will make it even colder, and nighttime temperatures drop still more.

The wise backpacker will select the clothing for the trip with this in mind, regardless of the distracting or misleading circumstances under which he may be packing.

Of all the tragedies which have occurred at Mount Rainier over the years, the number one killer has been hypothermia. This is a physiological condition, which occurs when the human body loses heat faster than it, can produce and retain heat. If the body's inner core temperature drops below 78°, the heart and brain cease to function. It begins when a person gets cold and/or wet, usually "soaked to the skin."

Wet clothing can extract heat from a body 240 times faster than dry clothing.

This is why it is *essential* that clothing taken into the backcountry must be capable of keeping the wearer **warm, dry** and **protected from the wind.** It seldom just rains at Mount Rainier; rain is invariably accompanied by a driving wind, thus you get the wind-chill factor.

PACK WEIGHT

In 1897 a party of Portland Mazamas arrived at the Mountain with 2 beef steers, 7 milk cows, 45 tents and 4 tons of supplies. You can do the trail with considerably less stuff. Still, the total weight of his final selection of food and equipment will come to be quite close to the heart of the backpacker, only about three inches away, in fact. He won't be on the trail very long at all before beginning to have serious reservations about the selection and wisdom of some of his decisions.

There will inevitably be items which should have been taken, and those which should have been left at home, but the more thought that goes into the planning and preparation, the fewer of these wishes there will be.

Equipment

The pack on your back contains your home for the next two weeks. It is your bedroom, your bed, your clothes closet, medicine chest, and a complete kitchen and pantry. The trick lies in getting it all into a pack weighing 25-40 pounds (more than that and your enjoyment of the trip diminishes in direct proportion to weight carried). That amount will be reduced considerably by the time the mid-point cache is reached, only to go up again temporarily. The more the pile grows as trip time approaches, the more unlikely this statement sounds, but some ruthless elimination will eventually get the poundage down to the prescribed limits.

A second consideration soon evident is sheer volume. The weight may be right, but getting the bulk of the gear to fit into the pack may be like trying to pour three quarts of water into a two-quart jug. And that's only the beginning of the bulk problem. Wait until the first morning on the trail when the process must be repeated in shades of blue indigo and with numb fingers packing wet gear.

The answer lies in *packaging* the food and supplies, and packaged it must be if everything is to fit (and be fit to use upon arrival in camp.) Now is the time to haul out your collection of too-good-to-throw-out plastic bags, and hope you have a good supply of bread bags and Zip-Lock ™ bags.

Casting aside "citified" disdain for wrinkles and rumples, roll and pack each item as tightly as possible into its most condensed or compressed form. Want to vacuum seal your gear, but you don't have an expensive suction machine? Pack the stuff in baggies, and suck the air out with a straw. Works great!

WHAT TO TAKE

THE TEN ESSENTIALS (plus some)

First Aid Kit	Extra Food *and* extra water
Extra Clothing	Sunglasses/sunscreen
Compass	Fire starter
Firestarter/lighter	Knife
Flashlight/extra Flashlight bulbs & batteries	Topographical map of Mt. Rainier showing the Wonderland Trail
Poncho/Rain gear Broad brimmed hat	Ensolite™ or closed-cell foam ground insulation
Whistle	Mylar Space (Survival) Blanket

Equipment

The addition of these few basic items to the pack provides everything necessary to handle just about any emergency, which might arise in the mountains. With them, the wilderness hiker can travel secure in the knowledge that he is well prepared for any eventuality. These items should remain with him at all times, particularly on little side expeditions. (Those seem to be the times people are most apt to get disoriented, lost or injured.)

Disaster in the mountains generally is swift and unexpected, so don't invite it by becoming separated from these survival essentials or your companions. Take the short side trips leaving the pack in camp or by side of the trail, but put the "terrific ten+" in a fanny-pack or plastic bag and carry them like a lunch sack or tied to the belt. Many a person is alive today because he did, and countless more made evening news because they didn't.

THE PACK AND FRAME

The means of carrying the load rates second only to footwear as the most important factor in personal comfort.

Presuming you're not letting a llama lug the load, get the lightest weight pack and frame combination that you can afford to buy or rent. Since space age engineering techniques have now been applied to the design of packs, treat yourself to an engineered body-contoured frame that rides perfectly and is a relative joy to carry.

Be sure to get a pack with a waist strap. The strap serves the dual purpose of holding the pack in the position in which it was designed to be worn, and provides a means of shifting the weight occasionally. It also stops the pack from bouncing during a jarring descent.

Most packs come with shoulder pads. Additional padding for sore or rubbing spots can be made using socks or a corner of an Ensolite™ pad.

WHAT TO WEAR

FOOTWEAR

While it's true that the Wonderland Trail has been done in tennis shoes and thongs, it's also true that Mount Hood has been climbed in high heels. Some people just have no respect for their feet.

With all the hiker expects of his feet during this trip, the least he can do is treat them well. Comfortable footwear is a necessity, not a luxury when hiking well over a hundred miles. (And that's a modest estimate considering all the extra walking which will be done around camp and on side trips.) Remember that steep uphill and downhill travel requires extra toe room, so if your toes touch the end of your boots, the boots are too small. (We know of several Wonderland hikers who lost their toenails from boots that were too tight.)

Boots today incorporate modern technology. Most now are made of tough lightweight fabrics and feature soothing air cushions, soft synthetic padding, and high-tech water repellant liners, all at about half the weight of the old leather boots. An added bonus is their easy and brief break-in. Whichever boot you select, get some with lug soles, and good ankle support.

Some hikers like an extra pair of shoes or slippers for use in camp and for crossing streams. A light pair of 'aqua-socks might come in handy here. Remember, sneakers are hard to dry and weigh like rocks when wet. It all comes down to weight. How much do you want to carry all the way around the Mountain?

One last word to the wise. *Break new boots in before hitting the trail.*

SOCKS

Adequate socks are another essential, and that adequacy includes quality as well as quantity. Boots should be large enough to allow room for at least two pairs of socks. Both the added cushion and warmth they offer will be welcomed on the trail. Wool is the most durable fiber for several reasons. It "breathes" and allows perspiration to escape, and it is the only material that provides warmth even soaking wet, (although polypropylene is good too.) The ideal combination is thin Polypro socks under wool socks.

Four pairs of socks (wear two, carry two) should be the minimum number considered, five or more if space and weight permit. If caching supplies, put the extra pairs in the cache for the second half of the trip. A pair of gaiters will be a welcome addition for keeping socks dry and legs protected when passing through wet morning meadows with tall grasses and flowers hanging over the trail.

CLOTHING

Long pants should be lightweight wool. The wool will retain warmth even if wet. Big pockets sewn on the front of each leg will be much used and appreciated on the trail for carrying such frequently used items as the collapsible cup, map, pencil, the log portion of this book, etc., and will save countless stops to take off the pack and dig. Short pants should also have lots of pockets.

Blouses, shirts and pullovers should be an assortment of long and short sleeves. An ideal combination would be one short-sleeved and one long-sleeved cotton, and one light-weight wool shirt. Any with Gor-Tex^{TM} would also be welcome additions. A wool sweater will get a lot of use here too. The layer system has never been topped as the way to dress in the mountains, so use it. When overheated, take off a layer, when cold, put one on.

Equipment

The (waterproof or Gor-Tex™) jacket should be light in weight, but as warm as possible. Roll and compress it in a plastic bread bag before putting it as ballast in the bottom of the pack.

Gone are the days when you could do a load of laundry in a stream or lake, so remember adequate underwear too. Be creative. Clothes can be washed in a cook-pot, or even a Zip-Lock™ or trash bag. Beth can even take a trail bath in a Zip-Lock™ bag.

One final note about clothing. Recent studies have shown that mosquitoes are attracted to dark-color clothing.

OPTIONALS

Even in summer, ice-cold winds sweeping off the mountain are the norm, so if prone to wind-caused earaches, take preventative measures in advance by carrying and using a (wool) hat or headscarf or earmuffs. A bandana large enough to double as a triangular bandage, sling or dishtowel would do nicely. This trail is no place for an earache or to have equilibrium off kilter.

Mornings on the Mountain can be so bitter cold, even on days that later turn out to be scorchers, that fingers will hardly function to strike a match. A pair of light-weight wool, fingerless gloves or plastic-coated garden gloves should be added to the pack to remedy just such chilly mornings and evenings.

JUST A BITE TO REMEMBER YOU BY

As each new hiker sets foot on the trail, the Bug Eyewitness News takes to the air to spread the good news that a delectable dinner (you) will soon be by. All chiggers, black flies, horse flies, deer flies, no-see-ums, mosquitoes, and other assorted winged critters with long noses and sharp biters race to the trail, waiting for you to trip by.

Seriously, hungry little critters can nearly eat you alive on the trail and ruin an otherwise wonderful trip. *A **good** repellant is an absolute necessity!* **DEET** is the vital ingredient for repelling mosquitoes, but isn't too effective on flies. The best solution is carry a variety of "terminators" to combat this invading army. The stuff comes in sprays, creams, liquids, lotions, potions, wipes, swipes, bottles and tubes. Buy one of each! (Beth says make that a gallon of each). At least marinate their seasonal delicacy (you) in terminal tenderizer.

August on Mount Rainier is springtime for the insects, and unfortunately, some of the most beautiful areas have the hungriest bug populations. Without good repellant, you'll feel like that cartoon character with the little black cloud over his head, only the black cloud will be after you to eat you!

If it isn't too hot, some hikers find that wearing their rain-pants in camp or while hiking, to be effective barriers against the bugs.

LET THERE BE LIGHT

A votive candle will be a small, lightweight, long-burning addition to the junk bag, besides providing a second source of light or fire starter. A Cyalume™ light stick or two might be nice for camp use.

Go for a good Halogen or Zenon flashlight and don't forget spare batteries. REI headlamps are great, no hands needed to carry them, and the light is always aimed where the head is turned. So are plumber's headlamps. If a conventional flashlight is used, at least get one with a belt loop or ring.

Remember too to reverse the back battery in the flashlight when it isn't in use. It prevents the light from accidentally getting turned on and burning out in the pack. Carry the spare batteries side by side, securely held by a rubber band in a plastic baggie.

Fire starter can be a lighter or stick matches, (not book matches), and plenty of them, placed in various locations throughout the pack. Don't waste time or money on any that aren't waterproofed, and be sure the container is too. The best choice is a butane or Bic™ lighter, left in its plastic wrap until you need it. Pack a spare in the 10+ essentials.

EVERY OUNCE COUNTS

WHAT *NOT* TO TAKE

The list of strange things people take backpacking could fill a volume, but there are a few things worth mentioning, which should not be carried.

Don't carry FULL tubes of anything if a whole tube isn't absolutely needed. As trip time approaches, stash away the last few days' supply of toothpaste left in the tube for the trip. The same can be said of toilet tissue. Allow extra for the diarrhetic effects of huckleberries, and carry just what you'll need. Remove the cardboard core and put the flattened roll in a baggie.

Avoid the "everything but the kitchen sink" variety of pocket knife, and carry one with a minimum of junk (and weight!) Also worth looking over is the selection of small, thin-bladed, belt-sheathed knives, if only a one-blader is wanted. But unless you drive to the park, knives can no longer be shipped as carry-one baggage.

The latest addition to make this list, is the cellular phone. Yes, it will work from the line-of-sight high ridges, and it's only a local call to Seattle. But how would you like to be awakened with a call about getting your carpets cleaned as you're executing the great escape from carpets and civilization?

EQUIPMENT CHECK LIST

OPTIONAL SURVIVAL GEAR
(in addition to the Ten+ Essentials listed on page 59)

Mylar 'survival blanker'
Electrolyte balanced drink mixes
Twine, wire, plastic tape, fishing line, adhesive tale

CLOTHING WORN OR CARRIED

GOOD RAIN GEAR (Jacket/rain pants/hat & pack cover or poncho)

Boots (waterproofed)	Sweater (wool) Heavy weight
Shirts (3 short sleeved)	Sweater (wool) Medium wt.
Shirts (2 long sleeved)	Socks (2 polypropylene)
Parka/jacket	Socks (3 pair wool)
Long wool pants	Shorts or hiking pants
Underwear	Bandana
Wristwatch	Hankie(s)
Gaiters	Gloves (Polypro or wool)
Toe warmers	Poly/Woolen hat/face mask
Brimmed or visor hat	or skier-type headband

OPTIONAL CLOTHING

Rain pants	Down vest
Camp slippers/thongs	l boot insoles
Belt	Longjohns
Swimsuit	Sweatpants

THE PACK

Pack and frame	Quick-release waist strap
Shoulder pads	Bungee cords or straps

SHELTER

Tarp or tent (+poles-stakes)	Lines or cord (50 yards)
Plastic ground cover	Visclamps (if tarping)
Fly cover for tent (opt.)	Mosquito netting (opt.)

SLEEPING GEAR

Sleeping bag	Waterproof stuff sack
Ensolite pad or Air mattress	

PERSONAL ITEMS

Water Bottle (1 Qt. Min)
Toothbrush and paste
Biodegradeable Soap
Comb
Good sunglasses

Sunscreen (#15 or higher)
Toilet tissue (in baggie)
Towel/washcloth/pack towel
Any required Medications, vitamins
or personal products

OPTIONAL PERSONAL ITEMS

Chapstick
Shaving gear
(not recommended)

Extra prescription glasses
(only if you can't find home
without them)

JUNK BAG CONTENTS

Safety pins/Wire
Tiny mirror
Extra shoelaces
Needle/thread/buttons in
35mm film container
change for phone call and shower

A foot or two of Duct Tape
Pen and small notebook
Tiny magnifying glass
Hamburger & Coke money for
Sunrise and Longmire

TECHNICAL EQUIPMENT (All optional)

Ice ax with wrist strap
Binoculars/monocular

Camera and film
Thermometer/altimeter

CAMP SUPPLIES

Water filter or purification tablets
Extra filter cartridge
Fishhook/line or gear
2 clamp-type clothes pins
Bear bag and line for hanging food

Spare plastic bags
Insect repellent (LOTS!)
Litter bag & spare plastic bags
Carabiner
Cyalume™ Light Sticks

COOKWEAR

Cook stove and *adequate fuel* (in at least medium-size fuel bottles)
Water bottle wrapped w/tape
Cup & plate
Pot gripper/pot holder
Can opener if needed
Scouring pad

Billie (nesting) cookpots
Cutlery: knife/fork/spoon
Soap (biodegradeable)
Wire hanging hook (S-shaped)
Nylon dunk bag

Butane or Bic™ lighter left sealed in plastic factory pack or more
matches (waterproofed by dipping in wax)

FOOD

Water
2-1/2 lbs per person/per day (bag daily meals separately)
Snack bag full of goodies
More cord for hanging food at night
Salt, Pepper, Oleomargarine, or any needed "makings"

MISCELLANEOUS OPTIONAL

Plastic map case	Heavy aluminum foil
This book	Anti-fog for glasses
Extra sheet of heavy plastic for covering packs/gear	
2 Hefty™ garbage sacks	small collapsible umbrella

The most important thing to not take, is anything that doesn't work or fit. *Test, taste and try on everything before leaving home.* Finding out that your stove doesn't work once you're in camp means cold meals. You can't expect fellow campers to loan or give away their meager supplies.

SHELTER: THEIRS AND PROVIDING YOUR OWN

The ultimate experience is sleeping under the stars. No tent, no tarp, just the hiker is all God's glory. Falling asleep watching the stars play over the Mountain, and wondering whether the Milky Way will clear Columbia Crest is an experience one can never forget. Waking up in a sudden summer storm with no shelter overhead is another unforgettable experience. So sleep under the stars if the weather looks predictable, but have a tarp or tent at least ready to roll up in if the rains come. (A heavy wet mist or dew usually rolls in at night on the Mountain, so you may wake up wet even if it didn't rain.)

SHELTER CABINS

Depending on personal opinions of shelters, they're either the ultimate in comfort, or a good place in which not to be caught dead! Whichever one's leaning, there will be the opportunity to look forward to, or distain them, only five times during the trip around the Mountain, for that's all the shelters there are left on the Wonderland.

Spacing of the shelters is either feast or famine, with three of them on the east side, two on the northwest and none on the north or south. Wonderland Trail shelters are located at Summerland, Indian Bar, Nickel Creek, and both North and South Mowich Rivers.

Most are three-sided log cabins with the exception of Summerland and Indian Bar, both of which are beautiful stone structures. Indian Bar is considered the most "plush" shelter due to its real bunk beds and indoor fireplace (now filled with rocks.) The North Mowich shelter is the newest one, but the South Mowich is in very poor condition with holes in the roof and floor.

Don't make the mistake of planning on staying in shelters, or the even more dangerous error of DEPENDING on such a wistful gamble. Shelters are the designated group sites, so the shelter is the group's if they want it.

With any luck, there MAY be an empty shelter two, three or even four nights of the trip, but finding space in one should not be looked upon as something to which one is entitled. Some note with tongue in cheek that rodents are the real shelter residents and the real question is whether they'll share the place with you.

Assuming no group is using the shelter, use is on a first-come, first-served basis until the shelter is full. Hikers have neither the right to monopolize a shelter and keep others out of any available spaces, nor the right to make themselves obnoxious if a shelter is full. In the event of a bad storm, there will likely be midnight dashes and some interesting makeshift arrangements made, but under normal circumstances, conscience and the Golden Rule should dictate shelter etiquette.

Then there are people like Beth. You probably couldn't pay her to sleep in a shelter. Her sleeping preference is a hammock covered with a tarp.

TENTS OR TARPS

The type of shelter carried affects the backpacker in more ways than just being the covering over his head. While he's hiking, it's also a considerable portion of the weight on his back.

Aside from the privacy a tent offers, a tarp can be rigged to do everything a tent can do, at far less weight, more ease in rigging, and fewer technical problems. (The exception is a "tube tent" which is essentially a tarp sealed on two sides to form a "pup tent" with a built-in bottom.)

A good coated nylon tarp, used in conjunction with a heavy gauge plastic ground cloth (or another coated nylon tarp as a groundcloth), should provide adequate shelter for anywhere along the Wonderland Trail. The only additional weight needed will be for several visclamps and about 20-25 yards of strong nylon line to be used in pitching it.

The handy tube tent requires nothing more than a line run through the top, and strung between two trees to hold it up. If made of heavy plastic, it requires no additional ground cloth, and is thus the lightest weight possibility and possibly the easiest shelter to set up.

Equipment

SLEEPING TIGHT

Not only can a heavy sleeping bag be backbreaking to haul around the Mountain, if the design and contents are inadequate, it will prove to be worthless in fulfilling it's purpose of providing a warm sleep. Down bags are wonderful as long as they're dry, but down is not warm when wet. Some of the synthetics are actually better to use in the Northwest.

If you don't already have one, check with your local Mountaineering or sporting goods store, and buy the best one you can afford.

The addition of an air mattress, Ensolite™ or Thermarest™ pad isn't necessarily a luxury either. Beside the obvious comfort provided, they all furnish valuable insulating barriers between the cold, cold ground, and warm, warm you. Without one, the night could easily be spent trying to warm up a 2-foot wide and 6-foot long patch of Mount Rainier, an unachievable task. A 3/4 length or "shortie" mattress is nice, since it provides exactly the support needed for the torso and no more. The legs can be supported by the pack frame, boots or anything handy at no discomfort to the sleeper.

FOOD

THE WATCHED POT

The trail meal should be lightweight, high in energy, nutritious, filling, reasonably priced, easy to prepare and delicious. With a little planning and forethought, there's no reason why it shouldn't be.

The fact is, these days such foods are readily available in the corner grocery store.

Backpacking is one time calories are friends, not enemies. Calories are the fuel for the body's engine. Backpacking burns them up at the rate of about 4,000 to 6,000 per day, (depending on weather and terrain), and it takes about 2 1/4 to 2 1/2 pounds of low water food per man/day to supply 3,500 calories.

The amount of available energy will be determined by what is eaten, and when it is eaten. Foods eaten at night furnish tomorrow morning's energy. Those eaten for breakfast give the drive to get up that late afternoon ridge, and lunch helps keep the camper warm as he sleeps. Sweets and sugary foods offer ready energy on the trail.

Weight being the critical factor it is, every item should be scrutinized for its water content. Better to reconstitute or rehydrate foods at the campsite than to carry water-laden food mile after mile.

Bulky foods should also be avoided, and all foods should be repackaged or condensed to their smallest or most compact form. (Remember to include cooking directions and to identify what's in the package.)

Nutrition isn't as critical on a two-week trip as it would be on a longer expedition, and a fairly well-balanced diet will probably result by following natural cravings to cook the dinner that is most appealing at the moment. If still in doubt, carry high-potency vitamin pills to supplement meals.

BREAKFAST: IT'S IN THE BAG!

For those who believe the ideal breakfast is one prepared without leaving the sleeping bag, try this one: it's easy, filling and nutritious. It's fixed spoon ready at home and needs only the addition of water at the campsite.

Into a *sturdy-seamed* zip-lock plastic bag, combine a serving of concentrated breakfast cereal (such as Granola, Grapenuts™, or Familia™), sweetener to taste, and a spoon each of powdered cream concentrate and *granular* dried milk (the type that pours like salt), then close securely. The later addition of water (poured slowly right into the bag) produces a delicious breakfast without even dirtying a bowl. Eat it c-a-r-e-f-u-l-l-y right out of the bag. There are also instant breakfast and cereal bars that are small and fairly filling. Many individual serving packages of instant hot cereal are now on the grocery shelves as well, and all produce a tasty warm breakfast once hot water is added.

For early birds who don't care for conventional breakfast fare, cut-throat or rainbow trout make a nice breakfast, and go well with that bowl of fresh picked huckleberries. That's a real Wonderland breakfast, although perhaps not a realistic one since the lakes are no longer stocked.

LUNCH

Lunch is the biggest headache to some people, and the most fun meal to others. It all depends on what's stashed away in the old nosebag. Lunch is generally a cold meal unless it's a particularly cold day. Then it might be nice to fire up the stove for a hot drink or cup of soup to help thaw the bones as well as warm the victuals.

The best lunch is simple, filling and yet not heavy. An assortment of the following should provide enough variety to keep one well fed and happy.

Cheese	Cup of Noodles	Dried Beef
Salami	Cookies	Sardines
Beef Jerky	Fruit Newtons	Smoked Fish
Kippered Herring	Logan Bread	Summer Sausage
Raisins	Candy	Nuts
Rye Krisp	Bagels	Rice Cakes
Crackers	Peanut Butter	Granola Bars
Drink Mixes	Cheese-its	Cereal

Cup-a-soup with potato flakes mixed in to thicken
Dried fruits: dates, apricots, apples, banana chips, prunes
High carbohydrate bars: Granola, Power Bars, Breakfast bars, etc.
Sneak in an apple or orange for a mid-trip surprise, or if caching, put some in the mid-week cache.

DINNER

Trail dinners will be as diverse as the cooks preparing them. Some will be elaborate feasts, while others will be the epitome of simplicity. Possibilities range from one-pot meals through the variety of pre-packaged dehydrated, dried or freeze-dried full course dinners. The list of such dinners is almost endless with more being added each year. One important tip: buy one or two of the pre-packaged dinners and try them at home first to see how many those "two-servings" really serve.

Get dinner underway as soon as possible after getting into camp, because it will take at least twice as long to cook as it would at sea level. At 5,000 feet, cooking time doubles, and don't forget that cooking water will be ice cold and will take longer to heat too.

Dessert possibilities include stewed or dried fruit, candy, gelatin or instant pudding. Those made with artificial sweetner weigh only an ounce or so.

DRINKS

Gene Fear has a great line in his book *Surviving the Unexpected Wilderness Emergency*, "it's the water in your body that saves your life, - not the water in your canteen." Your water requirements are much more vital than your food requirements. You could live off your body fat for weeks, but die within hours from dehydration.

Drink *at least* two quarts of water a day when backpacking (in addition to water used in cooking.) You'll be losing it from perspiration, respiration and urination. Thirst does not always accompany the body's need for fluids, so don't wait until you're parched to drink. ***Dehydration actually reduces the body's blood volume supply and promotes heat exhaustion.***

The first warning sign your body gives you is the color of your urine. A dark yellow indicates your body is short on water. Listen to your body. Drink water frequently. Other early signs of dehydration are loss of appetite, drowsiness, general discomfort and lack of desire to move muscles. Secondary warnings are headache, dizziness, dry mouth, rubbery legs, and slurred speech. The third stage is collapse and spasms. All stages can be treated with water, salt and shade. While the cool fresh water from a rushing stream may look incredibly refreshing, don't drink it without treating.

That same treated water will leave something to be desired after a few hours in the water bottle. Add one of the new powdered ERH (Electrolyte Replacement with Glucose) mixes for more oomph in getting up those hills. One of the grocery store drink mixes such as Gatorade, Crystal Light, Tang, Kool-Aid or Instant Iced Tea renders water more thirst quenching too. Include at least one packet of drink mix per day (plus several extras depending on personal 'thirsts.')

Hot drinks will really hit the spot and revive the spirit, and warm the heart! Bring an assortment of coffee, teas, spiced cider, cocoa, soups, powdered broths and bouillon.

DON'T FOOL WITH FUEL

If flying to Washington to do the Wonderland, you have to solve your stove fuel problems after landing and before going to the Mountain. You cannot carry fuel on board a commercial aircraft. It's dangerous and illegal, so it must be purchased after arrival.

Food

The closest place to the Mountain to get fuel is the store at Longmire (although they may be out). If you have a car, stove fuel can also be purchased on the way to the Mountain at:.

The Elbe Mall, 541st St. E and the Mountain Highway,
Elbe (360) 569-2611

Summit Haus
Mountain Highway
Ashford, 98304, (360) 569-2142

Suvers Country Store, Mountain Highway,
Ashford 98304
(206) 569-2373

Speaking of fuel, consider using fire paste or ribbon to prime the stove. Many hikers consider this part of their "essentials." Also, consider replacing all of the "o" rings in your pump before doing the Wonderland. A well-maintained stove uses less fuel.

CARRYING LESS AND ENJOYING IT MORE

FOOD CACHES: Lighten the pack and save the back

Caching food and supplies at various points around the Mountain is the easiest way to cut down the pack weight. The number of caches is limited only by the number of bundles the hiker makes up, and his means of getting them to the pick-up points.

Some people make an advance trip to deposit the goodies, while others have someone **dependable** bring the extra supplies at a pre-arranged date, either leaving them with a ranger, or meeting the hikers.

You can also ship your cache ahead to the park, via U.S. Mail or UPS, provided you have made prior arrangements with the rangers. If shipping it, be sure it is clearly marked as *FOOD CACHE*, with your name, date of pickup and location where the pickup will be made. Be sure to mail or ship early enough! Especially if the destination is Mowich Lake. If it arrives during the ranger's days off, it will sit at Carbon River till he gets back.

Caches at Longmire are stored in the (former) jail cell in the basement of the Hiker Center.

While rangers try to accommodate backpacker's needs, they cannot make special trips to pick up or deliver packages. Arrangements for cache drop-offs and pick-ups must be made by phoning (206) 569-2211 or writing one of the following stations:

Mount Rainier National Park
Longmire Hiker Center
General Delivery
Longmire, WA 98397

Mount Rainier National Park
White River or Sunrise Ranger Station
Star Route, Box 194
Enumclaw, WA 98022

Mount Rainier National Park
Ohanapecosh Ranger Station
P. O. Box 249
Packwood, WA 98361

Mount Rainier National Park
Church Street
Wilkeson Ranger Station
Wilkeson, WA 98396

The latter is the address for Mowich Lake caches too. The Mowich Lake cache is outside the Ranger Station in a metal garbage can.

Actually, one cache should suffice if it picked up in mid-trip. If starting at Longmire, stash a cache at Sunrise. If starting at Mowich Lake, many hikers want to have one at Sunrise (3 or so days away) and Longmire with their provisions for the West Side and the final 4-6 days of the trip. The Carbon River Entrance Station is 5 miles from the Ipsut Creek campground, - too far to run down to pick up the cache, and rangers don't deliver. The Ipsut Creek cache is a barrel behind the Ranger station.

The Sunrise Ranger Station also has a hiker to hiker emergency food supply. Hikers can drop off any extra food for emergency use by other hikers. Those in need can see what's in the pot, (Grubbing food off other hikers or tourists is called "Yogy-ing" as in Yogi Bear.)

Other things to consider putting in the mid-point cache are part of the film supply, dry socks, extra matches, and any other food or clothing, (or extra supplies) which are not needed during the first part of the trip. Stove fuel cannot be stored in the cache.

Put your cache in a plastic or metal, mouse-proof container *with your name and address clearly visible as well as the approximate date of pickup.* (Many people use lidded 5-gallon buckets.)

One final note on shipping caches. Some UPS offices, and some neighborhood shipping franchises will accept plastic buckets for shipping, and others insist you pack the bucket in a box. If they so insist on a box, find your own. Many hikers have reported they were charged more for the box than they were for the shipping.

Food

LIVING OFF THE LAND (The Berry Best)

Nature's bounty is for people to use (within reasonable limits) and enjoy in the national park. Edible berries and mushrooms *can* be picked for personal consumption, the only restriction being against taking of them for commercial purposes or for profit. For those looking forward to sharing some berries with the bears, the very best berry patches are near Golden Lakes, in the areas that were burned many years ago. The berries get ripe in mid to late August. there are several varieties of huckleberries at the part, including the large black, the low blue with bloom, and the low tiny red. All are good to eat.

Mushrooms abound throughout the park, but unless you're an expert, this is not the time to sample the bounty. While most varieties are edible, some are not. There is no foolproof rule of thumb for determining which are the deadly ones, so don't play this Washington State lottery.

FISHING

Hoping to catch a breakfast or dinner trout or two during the trip is a reasonable desire, but since the Park's lakes are no longer stocked, better bring the instant oatmeal, just in case.

Fishable lakes and rivers adjoining the Wonderland Trail are Mowich Lake (overcrowded and over-fished by "drive-in" fishermen), Carbon River, Mystic Lake, White River, Louise Lake, Paradise River, Nisqually River, Mirror Lakes (just east of Indian Henrys) and Golden Lakes.

The alternate Northern Loop Trail takes the hiker to some of the best fishing in the park at Lake James (page 170) and the chain of upland lakes to the north of it. (Lakes Ethel, Marjorie, Oliver and Adelaide). It also intersects a two-mile trail to Lake Eleanor (page 174) which reportedly still has some fine fishing.

Lakes are open to fishing between July 4 and October 31. The season for stream fishing conforms to that of the State of Washington, and changes from year to year.

Lakes *closed* to fishing along the Wonderland are Reflection Lake on the south side, and Frozen Lake and Shadow Lake, both in the vicinity of Sunrise. Ipsut Creek above the campground water intake is also closed to fishing.

No license is required for fishing in the park. Anglers may expect to find four species of trout (cutthroat, rainbow, Montana blackspotted, and brown trout), plus two charr (eastern brook trout and Dolly Varden) within the park. A run of Kokanee (landlocked sockeye salmon) introduced above the Alder dam, spawn in the Nisqually River.

There is no minimum length, limits are six pounds and one fish per day, and possession of more than one daily limit is prohibited. Successful fishermen are requested to assist park fisheries management by submitting a completed Creel Census form for each day of fishing. Anglers are encouraged to use barbless hooks and to release uninjured fish.

FISHING GEAR

This is not the time to tote the usual lure-packed tackle box or the expensive fishing gear. Again, the accent is on saving the shoulders and using the brain. Brain-food in the lakes has been caught using just a line (carried wrapped around the hat or a spool) and a hook.

In fact, (say the rules) forget about possession or use of any live or dead bait fish, amphibians, non-preserved fish eggs or roe, chumming or placing any substance (fish eggs, food, drugs, etc.) in waters for the purpose of attracting or feeding fish. Also forget about fishing with nets, seines, traps or other drugs or explosives, or any means other than hook and line with the rod or line being closely attended. You may also not dig for bait.

Streams are not stocked with fish. Because they are so often filled with milky glacier flour fed by the active glaciers, they are not optimum trout waters except at lower elevations. There have been reports of Coho or silver salmon in the Carbon and White Rivers but none recently. The Chinook is native to the White River, and some probably occur within the park. In the past there have been trout in the Carbon River in the vicinity of the Wonderland Trail and Ipsut Creek Campground. In the White River, good fishing begins at elevations below the Wonderland Trail. The Paradise River will occasionally yield rainbow, cutthroat and Dolly Varden (or as one fisherman noted on his creel census report, he caught a Dolly Parton).

PROCEDURES
FOR MAKING LIFE COMFORTABLE

THE FIRST FEW DAYS: Know What's Coming

There's no denying it. This trail is tough! The first day you'll think you're going to die. The second day, you'll wish you would. Your leg muscles will beg for mercy. The third or fourth day you'll notice a wonderful change. The painful mincing steps of the first couple days will change into long strong strides. This leg strength just gets better and better as the trip goes on. By trail's end, you'll have what we call "legs of steel." You'll have so much spring in your step you'll feel like you could leap small buildings in a single bound.

We were amused to find that Hazard Stevens noted this phenomenon in his journal over 100 years ago. He wrote, "For days afterward, in walking along the smooth and level pavements, we felt the strong impulse to step high, as though still striding over innumerable fallen logs or boughs of the forest, and for weeks our appetites were the source of astonishment to our friends, and somewhat mortifying to ourselves."

CONDITIONING: Pay now, Fly later

Just about any leg exercise will help defray the "agonies" of the first two or three days on the trail. Half knee bends, sit-ups, push-ups, leg raises and jumping rope will all help. Another dandy is an evening trek up the highest hill around, or climbing a zillion flights of stairs wearing a full pack. Don't worry about speed. Concentrate more on practicing the rest step, coordinating breathing, and toning up some leg muscles.

PACE: The Tortoises and the Hares

Old time mountaineers had a philosophy regarding speed and destinations which many of today's wilderness travelers would do well to heed: Man does not climb to get somewhere, he climbs to be on the way. **In other words, take time to discover the wonders of the Wonderland Trail!**

At least once during the trip around the Mountain, the party will round a turn and come upon a pleasant looking, puffing, overweight man on the verge of a heart attack or stroke.

About a mile or more ahead, setting the pace, will be the two or three fiendish devisers of this sadistic virility test. Scattered in between, will be a number of visibly suffering young hikers, desperate in their efforts to meet and keep the impossible pace. They usually attempt to do this by what has come to be known as the "charge and drop" system. This consists of going full bore until simply unable to go any further, then dropping in a state of exhaustion on or beside the trail. Upon recovery, the process is repeated until camp is finally reached.

Given enough time and mileage, the tortoises will overtake the hares. The chargers can eventually be overtaken by a party doing the rest step knowing the real secret of making haste lies in not wasting valuable energy. With a comfortable pace, plenty of water, and adequate rest stops, the miles rhythmically dissolve beneath the heels, and the scenery rolls by at an enjoyable speed.

The ideal pace is the one which can be sustained without huffing and puffing. It is established by starting out at about the same speed at which the hiker expects to finish. Once the body gets in gear and warms up, the hiker can adjust to the changing demands of the slope much as a truck gears up or down on hills.

When the second wind comes, coordinating breathing and walking is easier still, and the hiker slips naturally into the rest step (a steady, breathing-coordinated pace). This allows the lungs to discharge carbon dioxide, and causes the lactic acid and other waste products of energy use to be flushed from the muscles by the blood. Don't let anybody tell you rest stops are a waste of time. A 15-minute break will allow approximately 50% of the by-products of energy production to be discharged from the muscles. Several short breaks are better than one long one. Lethargy and muscle stiffness sets in if breaks are too long.

Two final notes on speed: Have the slowest person set the hiking pace. (Psychologically, being the "leader" usually speeds them up.) Secondly, be particularly careful descending. Most sprains, strains, slips, slides and falls happen on descents. Descending on wet pumice can be like slalom skiing without skis and going downhill on those little round glacially polished rocks can make you into a figure skater, sans skates. Try stepping down heel first, rather than flat-footed on steep terrain. This is called "the plunge step."

A common problem is having your knees give out, "lock up," or develop a condition known as "treadle foot" or "sewing machine leg." (Muscle spasms, causing the leg to mimic the action of operating an old-fashioned treadle sewing machine.) It is generally caused by holding back a little too much on downhills, sending the rebelling knee ligament into painful spasms. Once started, it's hard to stop.

Try using a walking stick or ski pole to help hold yourself back with the stick, rather than your knees. You might also try electrolyte drinks, muscles relaxants (Ibuprofen for the duration of the trip will help keep swelling down), salt tablets (if you don't have high blood pressure), and if it's really bad, a layover day or two to let things settle down and heal. Once getting to camp, keep the bum leg elevated and "iced up" with a baggie of that near-freezing river water on it. If need be, get in your sleeping bag and prop your legs up, bag and all.

THE ART OF MAKING CAMP

A good campsite will reward its occupant with many dividends beside the material ones. A tent or tarp pitched where it will get the morning sun will begin drying out as soon as the sun comes up. It will also enable its lucky inhabitant to be

Procedures

awakened by the warm sun on his face, and with his sleeping bag deliciously warmed and toasted by its rays. Sleeping under the trees is a pleasure of a different sort. Watching the changing patterns and hearing the music of the breeze in the branches, the teasing ground squirrels playing tag, and the chattering camp robber impatiently waiting for the party to get up so he can steal their breakfast, is an equally pleasant way to begin the day.

If intrigued by the latter prospect, a word of caution is in order. *Take care to avoid camping under trees with large dead branches (better known as widow-makers), or by snags or toppled trees.* (It's unlikely there will be any in the assigned camps, however keep this in mind if cross-country camping.) If during your travels you do see a truly dangerous tree in a camp or where it would endanger hikers, report it. The Park has a "Hazard Tree Plan" and wants to remove unsafe trees from the trail.

When selecting a place to sleep, keep in mind that *cold, like water, flows downward* and collects in basins and low spots. The temperature may be several degrees warmer up on the little rise, than in the pretty meadow. Water is a cold companion to sleep by, and is best avoided if at all possible.

There are three ways to lose body heat: Radiation is the emission of body heat from skin areas exposed to the elements. Conduction is the absorption of cold by the body. Examples are sitting on the ground, or handling cold objects such as a fuel bottle. Convection is the loss of body heat from wind blowing across unprotected body parts.

Radiation is the leading cause of body heat loss. An uncovered head may lose up to 50% of the body's total heat production at 40°F. A woolen facemask or baklava will make for a much warmer sleep. Also if the hiker's feet get cold, he should put on a hat.

Since overnight campsites must now be pre-selected, choosing a camp will not be a particular problem. Following these guidelines will save much time and inconvenience in setting up camp.

TO MAKE CAMP

1. Pick an established site with no vegetation. Avoid enlarging or damaging the site. Be especially careful not to damage any young saplings. Young trees in camping areas have a hard time surviving.

2. Carry a stove. **No fires are permitted in the backcountry.** Upon reaching camp, determine where the cooking and sleeping areas will be.

3. Locate the water supply. Fill the water pot and put it on to heat. Remember, the higher the altitude, the longer things take to cook. A stove exposed to cold and wind takes twice as long to cook. Make a circle around your stove and pot with

your closed cell foam pad, (fastened with a clothespin), or create a windbreak with food sacks or rocks. Also use lids (or aluminum foil) when cooking.

4. Take out the ingredients of the evening meal, and begin preparation, taking care to check whether foods are to be re-hydrated with hot or cold water.

5. Set up the tent or tarp and prepare the bed. Identify guy-lines with a white hankie or something light to show their location after dark.

6. If there isn't a toilet in the area, retire to the most obvious forest area reserved for those purposes, *taking care not to lose one's bearings and get lost after dark!*

7. If in bear country (and just about the entire trail is), hang food or string packs (15-feet high) between trees. Leave pack with all pockets unzipped or rodents will chew holes. (Rattling pans and flashing a light in his eyes will generally rout a marauding bear.)

8. Make one last check that camp is secure for the night against wind and weather, and that all tie-downs are tight. Shoes left out should be turned upside down tightly tied to a bush or tree. Rodents have been known to drag them away, and it's a long walk out without shoes!)

9. Place flashlight, hankie and anything else that may be needed during the night beside or inside the sleeping bag, then off to sleep.

BACKCOUNTRY ETIQUETTE

Yes, we know, you came out here to get away from civilization, but certain courtesies still apply. Step aside for the descending hiker. Give pack horses and stock the right of way. Don't roll or throw rocks down the trail or over drop-offs. If you accidentally dislodge a rock the may possibly hit someone below, yell "ROCK!"

Never cut switchbacks or corners. This destroys the trail, kills vegetation and causes soil erosion. Whenever possible, travel on rocks, roots or snow.

Walk softly. The wildlife will be less disturbed. Respect other hikers and campers. Some really did come out here to get away from people, while others will welcome your camaraderie. They're tired too, so don't expect them to do chores for you, and don't expect to "borrow" anything. You brought what? A **RADIO**! And you want to play loud rock music? Please, don't even think about it. Deafening decibels have no place anywhere, let alone in this land of solitude.

A WORD ABOUT HYGIENE

Some hikers cut down on pack weight by carrying fewer clothing changes. They wear the same clothes for the entire trip, washing them as time, weather, necessity and inclination permit. They usually carry several changes of clean underwear, and bathe either by sponge bath or jumping in a stream or river. REAL showers are available at the Henry M. Jackson Visitor Center at Paradise if you want a shower bad enough to add the uphill mileage to get one. There are no showers at Longmire unless you rent a room. There are slso showers at the Highlander Tavern in Ashford as you leave the park.

THE GOOD LIFE, BACKCOUNTRY STYLE

Every backpacker has their own favorite way of doing things. They scrounge an ounce here, a quarter-pound there, devise a short cut or easier way of doing this and that, and generally try to make life on the trail a little easier on themselves. As the years go by, this economizing evolves into a relatively comfortable backcountry lifestyle out of a very light pack. Beth lives like a queen out of a 35-pound pack for 10 days on the trail. There are dozens of other tips and hints, but these may serve as a starter:

COOKING, EATING AND DISHWASHING

. The most inexpensive thrift store Teflon pot will be a perfect backpack weight, will save hours of scouring, and can be discarded and recycled once back home with no regrets when ruined. To keep the inside of the pack clean, carry the cook pot in a large heavy-duty plastic bag.

. A dunk bag, stitched from nylon net will make an ideal dish and utensil storage bag, and eliminate dish drying.

. Individual packets of sugar or sweetener are neater and easier to carry than the bulk variety.

. "Natures own" is the very best brand of pot cleaner. Sand or river grit is dandy for scouring pots and beats any of the commercial abrasives for getting down to business. (Just remember to wash at least 100' from rivers, streams or lakes.)

. Popcorn packaged in its own lightweight aluminum foil pan (and with the hardened oil already in) makes a wonderful treat to include in the cache of second-half supplies.) Just be sure to carry out all trash including the pan and any unpopped kernels.

. Some kind of pot gripper will be needed. Pin the loop or ring to the inside top flap of the pack so its location is always known.

. Store all cooking and dishwashing supplies in individual plastic bags in the cook pot. Repackage soap into exact portions. Even biodegradable soaps pollute.

. Check all cooking instructions before leaving home to see what ingredients are called for but not included. Take individually wrapped portions.

. Several lengths of plastic mending tape or duct tape stuck to the water bottle and plastic containers help identify contents, plus providing pre-cut repair tape for fixing everything from torn clothing to ripped sleeping bags and packs.

BEST FOOT FORWARD

. The most expensive boots in the world can be excruciatingly painful if the hiker forgets to cut his toenails before leaving home. (A rather tricky operation when tried with a penknife on the trail.)

. A good foot powder liberally sprinkled in the socks *before packing them* will eliminate carrying a powder can and will render the socks ready for immediate wear. Roll each pair tightly, secure with a rubber band, and package in a plastic bag. Foot problems are probably the #1 culprit causing people to quit the trail. Taking good care of your tootsies should be one of your top priorities!

MORE TIME, WEIGHT AND EFFORT SAVERS

. Each evening, fold the map to expose the next day's travel. Carry it in a clear plastic holder and tuck it between the pack and frame, or for even greater convenience, tuck it between someone else's, and in turn carry theirs (then you can get to it with out taking your pack off). Maps can also be carried in a large pocket stitched on the front of the pant leg.

. Several plastic sandwich bags carried in a side pocket of the pack will find many uses. Keep them handy.

. Use a **monocular** instead of binoculars. For those who squint and look through only one eye anyway, monoculars save half the weight and half the cost, but still show the same sights!

. Organize the pack carefully. A place for everything, and everything in its place.

. Always fold dry sides of tarps or tents together or 'in' when packing them while wet or damp. Package them in plastic bags to keep the inside of the pack dry too.

. Deflating an air mattress is simple if, a moment before rising, the awakened sleeper opens the plug or valve, and lets his body weight push the bulk of the air out of the mattress. (It's a good way to roust reluctant risers too!)

. Hook the camera strap to the top and center of the pack frame, NOT around the neck where it will saw away with every step. The frame will carry the camera's weight, and have it immediately at hand when wanted.

. Unless you have a camera with an automatic ASA setting, use all one type and speed of film (such as ASA 200 or 400) to avoid forgetting to switch settings.

FIRST AID
and
EMERGENCY PROCEDURES

ACCIDENT AND RESCUE INFORMATION

1. Be calm. Do not move the patient until the extent of injury has been determined.

2. Treat in this order:

EXCESSIVE BLEEDING: Apply pressure directly to bleeding area. If this does not control bleeding, apply finger pressure to artery where it passes over a bony surface between the wound and the heart.

BREATHING: Give mouth to mouth resuscitation if patient stops breathing. If heart stops beating, give external cardiac massage and interrupt it ever 30 seconds to fill chest 2 or 3 times by mouth to mouth resuscitation if second person is not available. Use cardiac massage with extreme caution.

SHOCK: Elevate lower body, keep warm and dry. Avoid pain with analgesics and careful handling.

FRACTURE: Always check first for neck and back injuries before moving (see below). Splint with anything available including undamaged limbs. Pad well. Try to immobilize joint above and below fracture.

HEAD INJURIES

A. Control scalp hemorrhage by direct pressure.

B. Look for bleeding from ears, mouth, or nose, and unequal pupils or unconsciousness. These indicate urgent evacuation to hospital.

C. If above not present and patient is conscious.

MAY WALK OUT IF:

. Aware of time and place
. Minimal headache at spot of injury
. No nausea or vomiting
. No paralysis or weakness
. No neck stiffness

MAY NOT WALK OUT IF:

. Severe headache
. Unequal pupils

MAY NOT WALK OUT IF ... (continued)

. Pulse less than 45
. Nausea and vomiting
. Loss of orientation
. Defect in vision field

NECK INJURIES:

A. Suspect neck and back injury on a fall of any distance.

B. If neck sore, or weakness or loss of sensation anywhere below, fracture is possible.

C. Exert traction to head (pull away from body) and turn it to face forward if no resistance is felt. If fixed in odd position, splint it as is.

D. Avoid any forward or sideways bending of the head by placing a rigid splint vertically at the back of the head and neck and bandaging or taping it securely to forehead and chest.

BACK INJURIES:

A. Feel for tender spots and check for paralysis or sensory loss before moving.

B. Do not sit patient up or flex forward at any time.

C. Evacuate on rigid stretcher with clothing pad under small of back. Do not evacuate until rigid splinting is available.

D. Type of evacuation is more important than speed in neck and back injuries provided victim is protected from exposure while waiting.

ANKLE SPRAINS

A backcountry sprain can be inconvenient at least, debilitating at worst. Since the injury may in fact be a broken or chipped bone or torn ligament, think R-I-C-E until a final evaluation can be made.

R.I.C.E. *R = Rest.* Get off the ankle. *I = Ice* (or ice cold water) cool the ankle to contract the blood vessels and numb the site. Alternate cold on for 20 minutes, then off for 20 minutes until swelling goes down. *C = Compression.* Put stretch bandage on to restrict movement. *E = Elevation.* Elevate ankle to reduce swelling and pain.

THE FIRST AID KIT

Packaged in a small, compact waterproof container, the following items may be carried for years and never put to use, but in time of need, they're invaluable. The following items are recommended as the minimum contents of a basic first aid kit.

ITEM	HOW MUCH	USE
Gauze bandage	3" roll	wrapping
Adhesive tape	2" roll flattened	taping
Band-aids	10 - 1"	small lacerations
Butterfly band-aids	6	closing lacerations
Gauze pads	4 - 3x3"	larger wounds
Ace bandage w/clips	1	wrapping sprains
Merthiolate	1/2 oz. bottle	disinfectant
Burn ointment	1/2 oz. tube	burns
Needle	1	opening blisters
Razor blade	1 single edge	miscellaneous
Aspirin/Ibuprofen	2-4 dozen	pain relief
Salt tablets	24-36	cramps or heavy perspiring
Antiseptic	small plastic bottle	disinfecting wounds
Antacid tablets/Gavascon™	24-36	nausea/heartburn
Blue Benadryl	24	colds, sneezing, allergies
Moleskin	2 packages	blisters
Neosporin/Polysporin	small tube	open wounds
Anti-itch cream (Hydro-cortisone)	medium tube	bug bites
Triangular bandage	(if not carrying bandana or scarf)	sling
Dental Floss	end of roll	flossing/sewing
Safety pins	7-8	lots of uses
Tweezers		tick removal

SECOND AID

Mountaineering medicine is American Red Cross First Aid applied with the supplies at hand, knowing it may be 24-48 hours until further help is available.

The main factor to remember is to keep the victim warm, regardless of the nature of the accident or injury. In the mountains it doesn't take long to die from exposure if not kept warm. (*Remember that the victim will begin to lose body heat as soon as his activity ceases and he is laid on the ground.*) The sleeping bag may become the most vital of the first aid supplies.

Reassure the patient and keep him comfortable. Maintaining confidence and morale is also vitally important.

The trained first aider or most experienced person should direct first aid. While he makes a careful examination of the victim, an assistant should gather first aid kits, combine and inventory supplies.

After immediate treatment has been given:

A. Decide whether the patient may be evacuated under his own power (and if in doubt, assume he cannot.)

B. Determine whether the party has sufficient manpower and strength for an evacuation or whether outside assistance should be summoned.

If immediate evacuation is not possible, begin preparations for bivouacking. Allow rangers to evacuate the injured.

RESCUE INFORMATION

1. **THINK OVER THE WHOLE SITUATION.** Take time to get in command of all the facts. Then if outside help is required:

MAKE A LIST SHOWING:
1. Extent of injuries
2. Exact location of accident
3. Time of accident
4. Manpower, food and equipment at scene
5. Name, address and phone number of victim
6. Names and phone numbers of other party members

SEND FOR HELP, two people if possible, and send a copy of the above information with them. *Always* leave someone with the injured person.

MARK THE ROUTE on the way out if the accident occurred off the trail. If possible, travel on the trail. The exit will be swifter and safer than attempting to travel cross-country without a trail.

BE CAREFUL!

IN AN EMERGENCY

Once out, telephone **911, (360) 569-2211** or contact the nearest Park Ranger if the accident happened within the Park. Tell him:

1. Information listed above.
2. Your location according to the mileage point where you are in this book or the distance by road, trail and off the trail.
3. Type of terrain
4. Probable time to reach the accident
5. Equipment and manpower required
6. Where YOU will meet the rescue party
7. How you can be contacted by telephone until the arrival of the rescue team.

STAY ON THE PHONE until assured by rangers or responsible mountaineers that help is on the way.
Wait for the rescue party and guide them to the scene if at all possible.

THIRD AID: WHAT A POUND OF CURE IS WORTH

The real topic of this discussion is not cure, but prevention. Prevention of anything preventable: getting too cold, blisters, sunburn, bug bites, muscle cramps, snow blindness.

The hiker must decide early in the game whether to expend his energies in these matters before or after the fact. He can take pains to prevent blisters, and can prevent the blister's pain. He can take a minute to put on sunblock, or he can gamble on a dangerous ultraviolet burn. He can do battle with the bugs by perpetual motion swatting, or by permitting repellent to do much of the battling for him.

He can be defeated from within his own body by muscle cramps and the dismaying effects of heat exhaustion, or he can take salt tablets, Electrolyte drinks or Ibuprofen so the cramps and strange effects never occur in the first place.

It also consists of paying attention to your surroundings. Use caution in crossing slides and avalanche chutes. Loose rocks, branches and hazards of all kinds are all around. Be aware. Watch your footing.

Prevention doesn't have to be a big deal or a big ordeal. It's mainly a matter of common sense, like putting on sunglasses *before* crossing a snowfield or bright rocks, putting on bug repellent *before* the bugs get bad, and watching where you're going. Problem prevention is like defensive driving. Avoiding even one accident or injury makes it all worthwhile. Practicing prevention should become second nature when dealing with nature.

HYPOTHERMIA, The Silent Killer

Hypothermia is the silent companion which stalks everyone in the outdoors, quietly waiting to strike unexpectedly. It swiftly attacks the unprepared. Frequently the few warning signals it does give are ignored, both by the victim and his partners.

It is a condition where body temperature is lost due to getting cold or wet. The temperature continues to drop until death results. The whole process can take surprisingly little time. Speed and warmth are essential to reverse the condition.

As the person's temperature starts to drop, the brain and heart cease to function normally. Thinking and judgment is impaired, and general comprehension is dulled. Muscle coordination is affected. Incredibly, according to Mountain Rescue, most hypothermia cases develop in air temperatures between 30 and 50 degrees. Most people find it hard to believe such temperatures can be dangerous. The obituaries prove otherwise.

Lack of precaution leads to fatigue. Fatigue leads to exhaustion. Exhaustion leads to exposure and hypothermia. The first visible symptoms of **exhaustion** are poor reflex actions (recurring stumbling, poor control of arms and legs), need for frequent and prolonged rest stops, and a dazed careless attitude with a decreasing attention span.

Other visible symptoms of **hypothermia** are uncontrollable shivering, drowsiness, confusion, weakness, diminished mental capacity, irritability and problems breathing.

Once hypothermia is recognized, stop at once and get the victim into dry clothing and into a sleeping bag. If necessary have someone warm strip down and get in the bag with the victim. If conscious, administer warm liquids.

MOLESKIN IN TIME SAVES NINE (blisters, that is)

Several pre-cut pieces of moleskin or molefoam should be carried in the first aid kit for blisters or, better still, for blister prevention. Try both types out beforehand to see which you like better.

If irritated spots are caught and covered as soon as they are suspected, blisters will not develop. It is VERY important to eliminate the irritation at the first sign, or the hiker may find himself with well-developed blisters by the time he gets his boots off.

This may mean several extra stops while hikers go through the wearisome unlacing and lacing operations, but better to spend the time this way than to lose days and/or hikers because of needless foot problems.

Procedures

Shoulder blisters from a rubbing pack strap can also create a problem that can be relieved by a generous application of moleskin or a corner torn from the Ensolite™ mattress. It may also help to readjust the weight distribution of the pack so it rides higher or lower, or so the straps ride on a new spot.

WHAT TO DO IF LOST

IF IN POSSESSION OF THE PACK AND SURVIVAL GEAR

Stop and try to relax. Just as exposure is the greatest danger in accidents, *panic is the main hazard of those who are lost.* Things aren't as bad as they may appear at the moment. That pack contains everything needed to get along like it was the maid's night off, so don't panic. *Just don't part with the pack for any reason!*

First mentally retrace your steps. When did you leave the trail or campsite, or get separated from your party? Have you been climbing or descending? (If descending, then the trail must be above you.) Have you been bearing to the right or to the left? Have you come around a ridge or crossed any creeks or streams? Have you passed beneath any cliffs? Can you see a glacial river below you? Do you know which one it is? Can you see Mount Rainier? Is it on your right or left? Is the Wonderland Trail between you and the Mountain, or is it behind you? Is the ridge opposite you yesterday's ridge or tomorrows? Can you see a trail on it?

Get out your map and go over all these questions again, trying to relate the answers to the map. First mark your last definite known location. Can you determine a specific location on the next ridge or any landmark you can identify on the map, and where does that place your estimated elevation?

Do you have your compass with you? Do you know how to use it? Remember that the declination for this area is 22.5 degrees east.

If it is some time yet before dark, and the Wonderland Trail is between you and the Mountain, **KEEPING YOUR PACK ON,** begin to contour, (neither climbing nor descending, but remaining at roughly this same elevation), work your way toward the Mountain. If you were correct that the Wonderland Trail was between you, you're bound to cross the trail eventually. (And unless you've traveled for several hours off the trail before realizing you were lost, it shouldn't take too long before you come across it.)

Now is the time to use your whistle. The standard distress signal is three blasts. Then wait and listen. The distress answer call is two blasts. The sound will carry a *LONG* ways, so keep whistling every few minutes.

If darkness is closing in, and you feel you won't meet the trail before dark, begin to look for a place to make camp. Make some dinner. Use food sparingly. Bed down early, and as comfortably as possible so you'll be well rested tomorrow. Above all, don't panic. Just remember how lucky you are to have that wonderful pack full of survival gear.

The next day, resume your trek toward the Mountain until you cross the trail.

If the situation is reversed, and YOU are beyond (below) the trail, **DON'T** go too far, because you may be heading off into some of the real wilderness surrounding the park. If after an hour you haven't crossed the trail, prepare to set up housekeeping until you're found. Any further travel will make you harder to find.

IF *NOT* IN POSSESSION OF THE PACK AND SURVIVAL GEAR

Head toward any visible lake, stream or river. Such water might yield fishermen as well as fish.

Follow the same procedures as above in trying to get back to the Wonderland Trail. Remember that all ridges radiate from the Mountain, and all glacial rivers eventually lead to civilization. Outside the park, most logging roads eventually lead to a real road, but it could be a LONG way out.

Search parties will begin looking for you as soon as you are reported missing, so don't panic and don't give up hope. (You did remember to leave your schedule with a responsible person, didn't you?)

RESCUES ARE EXPENSIVE

In March 1993, the Park Service began considering a "pay for rescue" policy. They calculated that the rescue of four New Yorkers off the Mountain had cost $25,000, a fee which is pretty standard if a helicopter is required. They noted that rescues off Mount Rainier are some of the most expensive in the country because of the degree of difficulty entailed. While this pay policy is still only under consideration, it will eventually be implemented.

RULES, WRITTEN AND OTHERWISE

THE ELEVENTH ESSENTIAL: "I agree to comply..."

Wildfire has been the major destroyer of forests at Mount Rainier in the last 1,000 years. Fourteen major fires have been documented scientifically since 1230 A.D. Other major fires occurred in 1403 A.D., 1503 A.D. and 1628 A.D.

Forests that grew following that last fire include the 360-year old stands in the Carbon, Mowich, Puyallup and Nisqually drainages. The 300-year old stands in the Ohanapecosh and White River drainages began following a major fire in 1703. It is suspected that extensive fires in the mid to late 1800's were ignited by early

European settlers in the region. Huge sections of the Cowlitz drainage burned in 1856 and again in 1885. The White River suffered a major fire in 1858. Some of these areas are still sparsely forested.

One, the old "silver forest" burn (1894) still in evidence near Narada Falls, is attributed to James Longmire and a friend who were returning to Longmire from Paradise Valley. Their pack horses spooked when stung by yellow jackets, so after getting to Longmire, the men decided to go back up the trail and get rid of the yellow jackets. They got rid of a lot more than they expected. The ensuing fire got out of hand, and soon the whole ridge was ablaze. The silver snags soon became known as the silver forest, and twenty years later were the timbers used to build Paradise Inn.

North-facing slopes have burned less frequently, which accounts for why that's where most older stands are. The south-facing slopes: the White, Cowlitz, and Nisqually River drainages have burned most frequently. A 1982 study of the subject also showed that valley bottoms and ridge tops are the major natural firebreaks. In fact in spite of massive fires, every major river valley contains a streamside corridor of old-growth forest.

Park records show that since 1931, when written records on such things were begun, 57 (or over one-third of the 160 forest fires within the park, were caused by man.) The other two-thirds were caused by lightning. Between them, 1,421 acres of priceless virgin forest was destroyed.

Since 1973, campfires and cookfires are no longer allowed in the backcountry. **Not even smoking is permitted while on the Wonderland Trail.** It is permitted in camp, *but please consider carefully the incredible responsibility of striking a match or lighting a cigarette in the midst of a billion feet of flammable timber.*

RULES OF THE ROAD

In addition to rules mentioned previously, other park regulations pertaining to the Wonderland Trail are:

You **must** have a permit for either cross-country travel or camp use on the Wonderland Trail unless you are just doing a one-day trip.

Firearms are not permitted in the park.

Cutting of green plants, shrubs or trees is prohibited. Boughs should **never** be cut to make a bed or for firewood.

Regulations prohibit the use of nails in trees, they also prohibit defacing of buildings, signs or other park equipment.

Feeding, teasing, touching or molesting any form of park wildlife is against park rules (and very unwise!)

Dogs and cats are not permitted on trails nor are they to be taken cross-country.

CHALLENGING THE LAW OF AVERAGES

Even though in print here, these are the "unwritten rules" for wilderness travelers. There is no enforcement of them, and seldom anyone to know if they are broken. But each hiker must decide the validity of them for himself, and test the wisdom of his judgment with his life when he begins his practice of survival in the wilderness.

A foolhardy hiker may disregard one or all of these points and emerge unscathed; however a look at the annual alpine accident reports will show that a great many were not so lucky. In fact, a careful study of those same records will reveal that most mountaineering 'accidents' are not accidents at all, but are actually the results of various combinations of disregarded rules.

Nature is a worthy adversary. Those who respect nature will be rewarded with untold wonders and delights, but justice can be swift and terrible for those who violate or underestimate the might and dangers awaiting the unwary in the wilderness.

THE BACKPACKER'S CODE

. Carry at all times, the clothing, food and equipment necessary. '

. A party of three is the (Mountaineer recommended) minimum.

. *ALWAYS leave the trip schedule with a responsible person.*

. **NEVER** become separated from your ten essentials. (Page 59).

. Keep the party together and obey the leader or majority rule. (And decide in advance which it will be, leader or majority.)

. Never climb beyond your ability and/or knowledge.

. Judgment must not be swayed by desire when planning a route or turning back.

. Follow the precepts of sound mountaineering as set forth in textbooks of recognized merit.

THE LEGACY OF THE WONDERLAND

THE EYES OF TAXES ARE UPON YOU

Mount Rainier National Park belongs to all of the two hundred seventy-five million citizens of our great nation. To be counted among the few persons fortunate enough to actually get to trod this magnificent backcountry: walk its trails, sleep in its fragrant forests, drink its cool (boiled) waters, catch its fish and eat its berries, is a privilege accompanied by proportionate responsibilities.

Keeping the park in its native unspoiled state can only be accomplished by a deliberate effort on the part of all who partake of this national treasure. The dedicated National Park Service personnel have done wonders with both limited staff and funds to restore severely impacted meadows, stabilize eroded areas and replant native vegetation in overuse-damaged sites. The hard-working trail crews build the bridges, clear the blow-downs, rebuild damaged trails and do any other thankless task that needs to be done. But with a little help from "The Mount Rainier Fan Club", future generations will find the same wonderful experiences which we enjoy today.

Each person who ventures into this precious piece of real estate should do so with a personal pledge of minimum impact to the land. Take up the challenge to "leave no trace."

"No trace" travel first takes commitment. The rest is common sense and dedication to do no harm. The rest is common sense. It's as simple as traveling in small groups, staying on the trails, sitting on rocks instead of on flowers or other vegetation and staying out of fragile heather or flower fields.

Use the pit toilets provided at the trail camps, or if none are available, go at least 300' from any water sources. Bury human waste in a "cat hole" at least 6 inches deep in the organic layer of the soil. In the wild, human wastes should be disposed of by leaving them exposed on the surface, scattered to maximize decomposition.

Litter and trash must be carried out. This means everything: orange peels, cigarette butts, food scraps, bottles, cans, foil, Styrofoam, grease and paper. EVERY-THING. Remember, if you carry it in, carry it out. Carry extra Ziplock bags for this purpose. Put all bagged trash in the bottom of the pack until reaching the garbage can at the next trailhead. Better still, be a good guy and *take it all the way home with you.* Hauling trash out of the park costs the government a fortune, so do your part, and take it out yourself.

Good outdoor manners are contagious. Seeing one hiker pick up trash and litter will encourage others to do the same. Leave the camp and trail in the same condition you would like to find it. And as the old (but true) cliche says, other than edibles, take nothing but memories and pictures, leave nothing but footprints, and kill only time.

Part Two

THE TRAIL LOG

LONGMIRE TO DEVILS DREAM CAMP

Of all the places to begin the Wonderland, more people choose Longmire than any other jump-off point. It is home to Wilderness Information Center, campsite reservations, and up to the minute information on trail conditions.

The well-conditioned hiker should encounter no difficulty by beginning here, however the unexercised neophyte will begin kicking himself for not getting in shape long before making it to the top of Rampart Ridge.

But the fact remains that, in spite of all the words to the wise and good advice, the average hiker still generally starts off "cold" and gets conditioned on the trail as he goes. In truth, this method of getting in shape works perfectly well *IF* applied in moderation and taking shorter bites for the first two or three days.

It was old incorrect signs on this segment which inspired this book forty years ago. This section is best done by ignoring the mileage signs in the very beginning, and instead just working from point to point. First to the top of Rampart Ridge, then to Kautz Creek, Pyramid Creek, Fisher's Hornpipe Creek, Devils Dream Creek and then to camp. If each segment is enjoyed for what it is, the total trip is completely enjoyable and rewarding.

TRAIL CONDITION: For the most part this is an excellent broad wooded trail, best done (psychologically) a "chunk" at a time. There are few distant views on this section, for the major part of the trail will be in dense forest, punctuated only by the few creeks.

The hike consists of a steep climb, a short descent, then another very long climb. From Longmire, little time is wasted in going up and over Rampart Ridge. The following descent to Kautz Creek is fairly short and loses very little altitude, which is fortunate, because the trail climbs just about the entire rest of the way.

ELEVATION GAIN/LOSS: Climb: 2400 ft.   Descent: 200 ft.

MILEAGE: According to the sign at the trailhead by the Hiker Center.

```
            Cougar Rock   1.6
      Rampart Ridge 1.6   (actual 2.0-)
            Paradise   5.7
      Indian Henrys 6.2   (actual 7.1+)
```

Longmire to Devils Dream

TRAIL BEGINS: At Longmire by the above sign. The trail heads east and parallel to the right of the Nisqually Highway.

LONGMIRE TO DEVILS DREAM CAMP

THE TRAIL

0.1+   Trail junction with Wonderland Trail to the north and east. Sign reads:

WONDERLAND TRAIL

← Longmire 0.1   (actual 0.1+)
Cougar Rock > 1.5   (actual 1.3+)
Paradise River Camp 3.5>   (3.7+)
Paradise 5.6   (actual 7.0+)

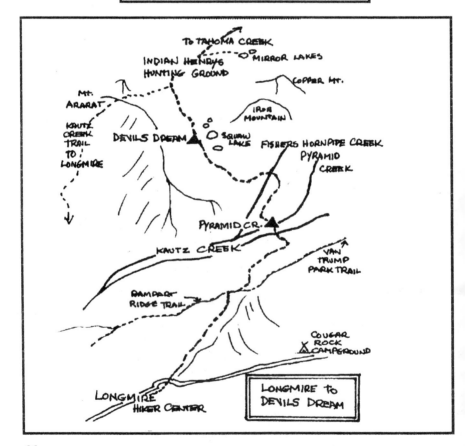

Second sign reads:

```
┌─────────────────────────────────────────────┐
│              WONDERLAND TRAIL                 │
│                                               │
│     ← Rampart Ridge 1.5   (actual 1.9-)       │
│     ← Pyramid Creek 3.1   (actual 3.7+)       │
│     ← Devils Dream 5.1    (actual 5.8+)       │
│     ← Indian Henrys 6.1   (actual 7.0+)       │
└─────────────────────────────────────────────┘
```

0.3+ **NISQUALLY HIGHWAY.** Trail emerges by the parking area to the right, then crosses the road and continues north. (Use caution when crossing the highway, especially on weekends). Enter forest and begin to climb immediately.

Sign on north side of highway reads:

```
┌─────────────────────────────────────────────┐
│              WONDERLAND TRAIL                 │
│                                               │
│     ← Rampart Ridge 1.4   (actual 1.6+)       │
│     ← Pyramid Creek 3.0   (actual 3.5+)       │
│     ← Devils Dream 5.0    (actual 5.6-)       │
│     ← Indian Henrys 6.0   (actual 6.8-)       │
└─────────────────────────────────────────────┘
```

0.7+ 253' of erosion control steps, followed by 14' **WATER** bridge (First water since Longmire.)

1.0- Overgrown talus slope visible to the left through the trees. Lots of vine maple, huckleberries and wild blueberries.

1.8- **TRAIL JUNCTION WITH VAN TRUMP PARK TRAIL** to the rightfollows. The top of the rise is visible.
Three signs:

```
┌─────────────────────────────────────────────┐
│              Comet Falls 3.9 →                │
│              To Paradise Road 5.8 →           │
└─────────────────────────────────────────────┘
```

```
┌─────────────────────────────────────────────┐
│             VAN TRUMP PARK TRAIL              │
│                                               │
│               Mildred Point 3.1               │
│               Van Trump Park 3.3              │
└─────────────────────────────────────────────┘
```

Three signs:

```
┌─────────────────────────────────────────┐
│           WONDERLAND TRAIL               │
│                                          │
│   Rampart Ridge Trail 0.2 →   (actual 0.2+) │
│      Pyramid Creek 1.8   (actual 2.0+)   │
│    Devils Dream Creek 3.8   (actual. 4.1-) │
│        Longmire 1.5   (actual 1.7+)      │
└─────────────────────────────────────────┘
```

The Wonderland Trail continues to climb and then curves to the right becoming a gentle rolling trail.

2.0-   **TOP OF RAMPART RIDGE.** (elevation 3,800') Wide junction with trail to left. (No horses are allowed on the Wonderland beyond this point.)

Signs:

```
┌─────────────────────────────────────────┐
│           WONDERLAND TRAIL               │
│                                          │
│    ← 1.6 Pyramid Creek Camp   (1.8+)     │
│    ← 3.6 Devils Dream Creek    (3.9+)    │
│      ← Indian Henrys 4.6   (5.1+)        │
│        Longmire 1.7 →   (2.0-)           │
└─────────────────────────────────────────┘
```

```
┌─────────────────────────────────────────┐
│          RAMPART RIDGE TRAIL             │
│                                          │
│         ← View Point 1.2                 │
│   ← Longmire 3.0   (not verified via this route) │
└─────────────────────────────────────────┘
```

Trail is good and broad, descending gently. Sparse tree cover. Huckleberries.

2.4+   Kautz Creek audible. Begin to leave meadow area. Descent gradual. After a switchback to the left, the trail by the river is visible far below.

2.8+   Large piece of lava to the right of the trail. Rough trail, rock bordered in places. Note the many dead trees, both standing and fallen, skeletons of the Kautz Creek mudflow of 1947. The trail turns right and winds toward the river. The trail becomes steep and slippery from the small, round glacially polished rocks. A "roller-skating" descent.

3.1-   **KAUTZ CREEK BRIDGE.** (elevation 3,400'). The bridge is one long log with a fixed handwire.

Kautz Glacier, the snout of which is about 1-1/2 miles above this crossing. The glacier is about one-fourth mile wide and over three miles long. Originating at the summit, it drops over 9,000 feet in 3 miles. The Kautz is one of the mountain's more active glaciers, moving several inches a day. This accounts for the abundance of Glacial flour (powdered rock) which gives the river its milky color.

It is sobering to realize when standing in this gorge, that an estimated 50-**MILLION** cubic yards of material swept through here during the October 2, 1947 mudflow. (Or over four times as much concrete as was used in the construction of Grand Coulee Dam.)

On that October date, not far above here on the glacier, a cloudburst deposited nearly six inches of rain in a very short time. Kautz Creek was already nearly flooding due to previous heavy rains.

The excess of water soon carved a narrow gorge in the massive river of ice, channeling the water and harnessing its might. The power was so immense it sliced clear down to the rock debris beneath the glacier.

A vast depression was formed and filled with water, but the weight and force were too overwhelming, and the remaining ice at the foot of the glacier began to collapse. The vast wall of water surged into the box canyon in front of the glacier.

Ice and boulders jammed between the narrow canyon walls, creating a temporary dam and partially holding back the inevitable flood.

When the pressure grew too great, and it finally collapsed, the resulting surge swept down through the forest wiping out everything in its path. Observers said boulders 13-feet in diameter were carried along like corks.

The mass, then the consistency of wet concrete, moved 5-1/2 miles into the Nisqually Valley, covering the Nisqually Road to a depth of 50 feet. (The present road is now elevated to that height above the old road.)

Trees that did manage to remain standing still died of suffocation within a year when the cement-like layer hardened and cut off the air to their roots.

Trail markers in this vicinity are usually washed out and replaced yearly.

The high cliff of the west wall stands to the right.

Switchback up the west wall in a steep climb. Watch for rolling rock from above. At top of wall, trail turns right and parallels Kautz Creek.

3.3+   Trail still on cliff above river. Dropoff area about 50' in length, but trail is wide and not dangerous. Leaving here, the Wonderland resumes climbing and cuts north into the forest.

3.5+   Old moraine. Level area.

3.8+   Sign:

PYRAMID CREEK CAMP
Stoves Only

PYRAMID CREEK (elevation 3,750') is crossed via a bridge with a fixed-wire handrail. This white-water stream originates in Pyramid Glacier 3,500 feet above. **WATER**

Pyramid Creek draws its name from Pyramid Peak which was named by surveyors who used it as a triangulation station in 1897. There are only two campsites in this nice forested camp. This would be a good lunch stop too.

4.1+   Trail turns to the right and climbs steeply. Switchbacks follow.

4.7-   **FISHERS HORNPIPE CREEK** (elevation 4,300') another wonderful lunch stop, with fresh huckleberry dessert right at hand.

This peculiar name was picked by Ben Longmire while he was building the trail to Indian Henrys. He said "it sang a regular 'Fisher's Hornpipe' to us at our camp."

25-feet from the far side of the bridge, an abandoned trail cuts to the right. The area ahead has bridges and puncheons going every which way over usually muddy areas.

5.3-   The sheer face of Satulick Mountain is visible to the left about a half-mile away.

5.4+   **DEVILS DREAM CREEK** (creek elevation 4,850'). This name is another legacy of Ben Longmire's vivid imagination. "Because it is as crooked as a Devil's dream," observed Ben. It may come by that crookedness honestly. It lies on a fault, one of the clearest faults in the park. The Devils Dream Fault, roughly parallels Devils Dream Creek, then crosses Indian Henrys Hunting Ground. It runs diagonally from roughly northwest to southeast.

5.6+   Switchback by (deep) Devils Dream Canyon to the right. Very sheer drop-off. **EXERCISE EXTREME CAUTION.** Good forest, good huckleberries,

5.9+   **DEVILS DREAM CAMP** (elevation 5,000'). Sign:

> **DEVILS DREAM CAMP**
> Stoves Only

This camp has seven individual sites and two group sites. In drought years, water may be so low that only a murky wasp sink hole remains. In that case, Squaw Lake is a betterwater source, but is 1/2 mile uphill beyond Devils Dream.

There is also a real outhouse here.

DEVILS DREAM CAMP TO KLAPATCHE PARK

Rise and shine with the dawn, for this day will be a full one both in terms of things to see and distance to cover.

The first "packs-off" stop will probably come less than an hour out of camp when getting to Indian Henrys. Resist the temptation to linger too long though, because there are many miles to travel today, and many more wonderful sights to see. The second stop will probably be when the party pauses to look for evidence of old flood damage at Tahoma Creek. Here's a chance to get a good look at the devastation the old Mountain can unleash when she cuts loose.

Tahoma Creek will be crossed via the highest, longest and strongest bridge on the Wonderland. It is 250' long and 100' above the creek. The bridge has 475 deck planks, 3,500 feet of steel cable and 1,400 cable clamps. Originally built with log towers in 1976, it was upgraded to steel towers in the mid-80's. One of the trail crewmen who helped build the original high log-tower bridge, told us a lahar occurred during construction in 1976. "We returned to work one morning and were amazed to find mud on the towers and cables almost 100 feet above the creek!"

Emerald Ridge is best tackled before the heat of day, because the final mile is an open climb, and can get pretty uncomfortable when done in full sun. The respite at the top will provide the rare opportunity for a genuine "straight down" bird's eye view of a glacier. In fact, many a never-to-be-forgotten lunch has been eaten by hikers lying on the grass near the edge who, between courses, try to guess how many hundred feet it is to the glacier below.

At the base of the Emerald Ridge descent, the South Puyallup River is especially memorable for the magnificent display of high "cathedral organ" andesite columns located just 200' beyond the junction of the South Fork trail and South Puyallup Camp. It's worth every second of the five minutes or so it will take to hike the full length of them. They actually originate due south (directly left) of the trail junction but are not evident in their full glory until a little farther west. The stream that serves as water source for the camp is a good place to fill water bottles on the way to see the columns.

Enough time should also be allowed to do the afternoon hike up to St. Andrews and Klapatche Parks in as leisurely a pace as possible, for it is uphill just about all the way. This is a tough stretch for the novice or unconditioned.

This will be a "big" day. Two big climbs, two big descents, and some really spectacular scenery.

TRAIL CONDITION: From Indian Henrys, until the final mile to the top of Emerald Ridge, (except for the immediate vicinity of Tahoma Creek), the switchbacking trail will be either climbing or descending under good forest cover.

The climb to the top of Emerald Ridge, and for about a mile down the other side, is open and unshaded. Only a large boulder or lone tree near the trail provides the occasional spot of shade. But the view at the top is worth everything that it took to get up here. It's fabulous! This upper section of trail is very unstable in spots, due to the rumbly rocks underfoot which occasionally tend to create the sensation of roller-skating. Old timers called rocks like these "ball bearings to hell."

The South Puyallup River has a good suspension bridge, high above the water. Decades ago, when the author crossed an ancient river-level one-log model, the log appeared to end in mid-river. (Actually, the high water was just washing over the north end of it.) The day was saved when some husky hikers approaching from the opposite direction hauled another log down to bridge the gap. Hair-raising though the suspension bridge may be, it's safer than the old log and boulder hopping crossing.

The trail to St. Andrews Park is generally undistinguished and tends to seem longer than it is. After climbing above the open meadows overlooking the river, the trail re-enters the forest and the remainder of the trip is made in the shade and on a good soft trail.

Debris flow
in progress
at Tahoma Creek
July 26, 1988

Photo by G.G. Parker, Jr., USGS

DEVILS DREAM CAMP TO KLAPATCHE PARK

ELEVATION: Gain: 3,786'   Loss: 3,386'

TRAIL BEGINS: By the Devils Dream Camp sign.

0.00   Begin short uphill stretch through small meadows and tree cover. Soon a 40'-high rock cliff is visible 200 feet to the left. If doing this trip in autumn, look for 'chicken of the woods' in this area. It shows up here every year.

0.2   A pretty meadow visible 250 feet to the left through the trees. Trail encircles, then enters Murphy Meadow. Small rise ahead.

0.5-   **SQUAW LAKE** (elevation 5,100'). Top of small rise. Wonderful flower meadows! Climb to clump of trees, a meadow, then more trees. This three-acre lake was the favored hangout of one of Indian Henry's wives. (He had three.) She used to like to wait here for him while Henry was stalking out a little dinner in the nearby meadows. Many erosion control steps follow. (Logs with dirt fill). Also nice pink and green rock steps.

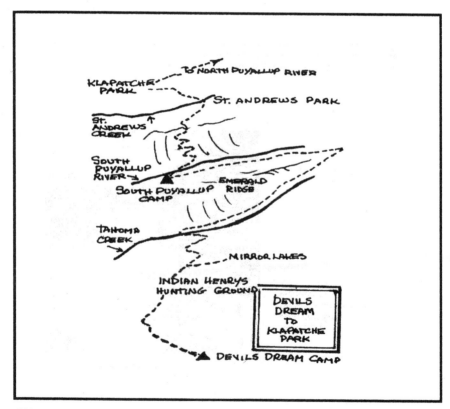

1.2- **INDIAN HENRYS** (elevation 5,500') Trail junction with Kautz Creek Trail after entering large meadow. Signs read:

> ### KAUTZ CREEK TRAIL
> Nisqually - Longmire Road 5.7-→

> ### WONDERLAND TRAIL
>
> ←-Mirror Lakes Trail 0.2   (0.3-)
> Devils Dream Camp 1.0 →   (1.2-)
> Pyramid Creek Camp 3.0   (3.3-)
> Longmire 6.3 →   (7.1+)

This lovely mountain meadow extends from the south slope of Pyramid Peak to Satulick Mountain and Mount Ararat. It was named by P. B. Van Trump for a Cowlitz Indian named Satulick (or Sotolick) whom the white men nicknamed "Indian Henry". Records show it was also a favorite resort of a small band of Klickitat Indians.

Nearby Mount Ararat was so named by Ben Longmire. He concluded it might have been the mooring place for Noah's Ark after he found pieces of petrified wood and a tree stump encircled by an iron ring on the 5,996' peak.

Among other tidbits of history concerning this remote and isolated spot, is that this was once the location of the "Wigwam Hotel," a tent-city establishment run by the former Sue Longmire and her husband early this century. A government bulletin from 1912, listed prices here of $.75 for a bed with a weekly rate of $15.00 for bed and board. Having your freight packed up from Longmire to Indian Henrys was 2 cents per pound. Where's that kid when you need him?

Then there's an old Indian legend which says there's a rock and ice likeness of Indian Henry graven on the slopes of Mount Rainier. Unfortunately, the Old Indians didn't say where to look. (Some think it was high on Success Cleaver.)

Continue north through more flower meadows, and drink in the "too beautiful for words" view of the Mountain.

Look over the picturesque patrol cabin. This is the oldest of the original ranger cabins still in use. This one was built in 1915.

WATER. Log footbridge over creek. Go upstream for water.

1.5-   **MIRROR LAKE INTERSECTION.**

Signs read:

WONDERLAND TRAIL

Indian Henrys 0.2 mi   (0.3-)
Kautz Creek Trail 0.2   (0.3-)
Devils Dream Camp 1.2   (1.5-)
Tahoma Creek 1.2   (1.3+)

MIRROR LAKES TRAIL
← 0.7 mi.

When conditions are right, these four small lakes (tarns) offer some of the most perfect reflections of the Mountain of any found in the park. Gone is the picturesque shelter cabin, which stood here for so many years. Gone too is the privilege of camping here. Camping must be either at Devils Dream Camp or Klapatche Park.

There is a crosscountry camping area beyond Mirror Lake in the Pyramid Peak area where two site permits are issued per night. There is no water beyond Mirror Lakes for those camping there. Also gone is a sign that stood

---

NOTICE OF CLOSURE

On December 10, 1946 a Marine transport plane
carrying 32 US Marines crashed on the upper slopes
of the S. Tahoma Glacier. There were no survivors
and their bodies remain entombed in the glacial ice
of Mt. Rainier. Out of respect for these young men and
their families all climbing routes on the
South Tahoma Glacier are closed.

National Park Service
Department of the Interior

(The climbing route has long since been reopened.) The Wonderland Trail begins a gradual descent.

1.7+   View rock to the left with two short trails a few feet apart leading to it. From it, the South Puyallup River (far below) is visible. Leaving here, the descent steepens. Stream to the right of the trail.

1.9-   Steep short switchbacks. River visible below. High rock cliff to the left. Seven puncheon bridges follow within the next 1,000 feet.

2.2+   Switchback to the right, then left. River gorge visible to the left.

2.4-   **WATER.** A 25-foot foot log over a good (fresh) stream. Water will be scarce from here to other side of Emerald Ridge. Leaving here, break into the clearing above the river. End of forest cover. Viewpoint shortly ahead, then descend a weaving trail over the moraine.

2.7-   **TAHOMA CREEK** (elevation 4,200'). This suspension bridge is a narrower version of the Carbon River bridge: high (100'), long (253') and swinging! (Not a bridge for the faint hearted. One pundit writing about this bridge likened crossing it to an Indiana Jones exploit.) The north shore, with its huge boulders and a deep layer of grit is the graveyard of many former bridges. Read the recent history of this little beauty and what passed under it on page 18. A side note for winter hikers, From October to May, the "decking" (slats) are lowered on one side to prevent the weight of snow build-up. Off-season hikers could still make the crossing by using a harness or "swami-belt", a short sling and carabiner or two clipped onto the cable. It would be necessary to unclip at each vertical connecting cable. This is not recommended! *Do it at your own risk!*

2.8-   **TAHOMA CREEK ACCESS TRAIL.** Two signs:

> **WEST SIDE HIGHWAY 2.2**   (actual 2.1+)
> (This trail is detailed on page 211)

At this writing, the West Side Highway is closed. Second sign reads:

> **WONDERLAND TRAIL**
>
> Indian Henrys 1.4   (actual 1.6-)
> Devils Dream Camp 2.4 →   (actual 2.8-)
> ←Emerald Ridge 2.0   (actual 1.4-)
> ←So. Puyallup River 3.8   (actual 3.8+)

Crossing Tahoma Creek   Ed Walsh Photo

3.3-   Switchback to the left above Tahoma Creek. The trail crosses higher above this stream. Wait to get water.

3.5+   **WATER.** Switchback to the right, then re-cross same stream on a 15-foot log-edged puncheon bridge. This is the last water for 2.5 miles, nearly to the South Puyallup River. Bridge is at the end of a short meadow. Note high cliffs above after leaving the east end of the bridge.

        Temporary tree cover. The end of the south fork of the Tahoma Glacier visible straight ahead.

3.6+   Short drop-off to the right of trail. One lone symmetrical tree to the right about 50 feet below. South Tahoma Glacier above.

3.7-   Cliffs to the left about 300 feet above the trail. Ahead begin crossing of long, fairly flat stretch of moraine.

3.8-   Switchback to the left. Watch for marmots in the rocks. They're especially friendly here, and either race you or follow you up the trail. (Don't feed them!) Switchback to the right by the shady corner. This is a good place

3.7-   Cliffs to the left about 300 feet above the trail. Ahead begin crossing of long, fairly flat stretch of moraine.

3.8-   Switchback to the left. Watch for marmots in the rocks. They're especially friendly here, and either race you or follow you up the trail. (Don't feed them!) Switchback to the right by the shady corner. This is a good place from which to look for steam puffs on the Mountain, (a little reminder of the thermal processes cooking away in Mama Rainier's kitchen down below). Look for them in the rock cliffs straight ahead. When seen, they come in short puffs like Indian smoke signals.

4.1+   Survey peg

4.2+   A short series of switchbacks with spectacular views for next .5 mile.

4.3+   **EMERALD RIDGE** "The Prow" (5,500') Exposure to the right where the bank has fallen away into the glacier. *Exercise extreme caution!* Not much farther to the top.

       The ridge is an open rolling meadow with many large boulders. Allow enough time to study all the activity and phenomenon on and around the glacier: (rockfall, the distant waterfall, the sun-cups higher up, etc). Look for goats on the moraine and on Glacier Island. The steam puffs will be in the area of the rock cliffs below Point Success.

       Glacier Island is a remnant of the previous Mount Rainier before it was reduced to its present size.

       Upon leaving, this ridgetop, the trail begins to descend. **Exercise caution next half mile. There are areas of extreme danger.** *Do not allow children to run.*

4.6+   **VERY exposed section.** The two-foot wide ridge top trail is very exposed on both sides. To the right it drops several hundred feet down to the glacier, to the left, a sudden drop to the base of the moraine.

4.7+   Switchback to the left above the glacier, then to the right above the cliff on the left. Be cautious here, the trail is rumbly rock, and the drop-off would be memorable (in your obituary).

4.8-   Another switchback to the left by a steep drop to the right. This is directly across the valley from the distant west end of the bedrock outcropping at the base of the glacier.

5.1-   A broad turn to the right (after having done seven steep switchbacks and turns above the river). Trail now wider and not quite so rocky. The wobbly knees and "sewing machine leg" will soon subside. Forest cover here is grown over a moraine base.

5.4-   Switchback to the left above the river shortly before coming to a point high above the joining of the two forks of the river, now about a half mile west of the previously mentioned bedrock at the base of the glacier.

5.6+   Switchback to the left in a stand of alder and fir. Still traveling high above the river. An open switchback to the right follows.

5.9-   **WATER.** Tiny streamlet crosses trail from the left. (This is the first water since shortly after leaving Tahoma Creek.) The trail takes a sweeping horseshoe bend left, then right to a young forest grown over old moraine. Another streamlet ahead followed by the beginning of heavy tree cover.

6.3-   100-foot open stretch followed by moderately steep and very rocky winding trail. Ahead is an 18-foot puncheon bridge over a fresh stream that tumbles over moss-covered rocks. St. Andrews ridge to the right.

6.6+   **SOUTH PUYALLUP TRAIL JUNCTION.** Dry stream crossing preceding junction. Sign reads:

WONDERLAND TRAIL	
Emerald Ridge 1.7 →	(actual 2.4+)
Indian Henrys 5.1 →	(actual 5.4+)
←Klapatche Park 3.7	(actual 3.7+)
No Puyallup Camp 6.6	(actual 6.4-)

Take ten minutes before leaving this junction to follow the South Fork Trail to the west for about 500 feet and discover the magnificent display of andesite columns on the left. This is one of the most spectacular sights in the park. They're truly one of the wonders of the Wonderland Trail! They're also a therapeutic little reward after that challenging descent from Emerald Ridge.) These columns are known as "The Devil's Pipe Organ.")

SOUTH PUYALLUP CAMP. One of the nicest forested backcountry camps. On the south side of the river, it is protected from the wind, and the sites are scattered at generous distances from each other. A stream flows through the camp.

A second sign at this intersection reads:

SOUTH PUYALLUP TRAIL	
←Westside Road 1.6	(actual 1.6)
←So. Puyallup Camp 0.1	(actual 0.1-)

The Devil's Pipe Organ by South Puyallup Junction

Beth Rossow Photo

6.6+   **SOUTH PUYALLUP RIVER BRIDGE.** (elevation 4,000'). A nice sturdy 50' bridge with pole railings.

This turbulent little river boils furiously down the mountainside with its churning chocolate-milk colored water echoing the ominous reverberating BONG-G-G of boulders crashing together under water.

6.9+   15-foot bridge before entering forest cover.

7.4+   9-foot bridge by a small clearing.

7.9+   Back under good forest cover. Trail climbing steadily.

8.4-   Stream crosses trail by a talus slope.

8.7-   **ST. ANDREWS PARK** (elevation 5,800'). A lovely little alpine park. The lake is the headwaters of St. Andrews Creek (and empties via a natural culvert by the trail). This park and lake are apt to be snowbound until August if winter snows were heavy.

The only sign in St. Andrews Park is the following trail sign:

> ← WONDERLAND TRAIL →

9.0-   Scenic view of Sunset Amphitheater (12,522') at the head of the Puyallup Glacier. The prominent rock is 7,675 foot high Tokaloo Rock.

10.2   **KLAPATCHE PARK INTERSECTION.** (elevation 5,400'). Junctions of the Wonderland Trail and the St. Andrews Creek access trail.

Sign reads:

```
St. Andrews Trail 0.8    (actual -0.8)
← West Side Road         (actual 2.2+)
```

Klapatche Park is a lovely high alpine park with four good campsites. Fresh water comes from a spring 250 yards across the lake. Aurora Lake has been described recently as a "scum puddle" that even filtering and boiling wouldn't help.

Klapatche is likely to be well "populated" if and when the West Side Road ever opens again. The easy access and the popularity of its flower fields and beautiful scenery make this park a favorite of Mount Rainier devotees.

There have been several successful revegetation projects around the lake to repair the meadows and way trails.

From Klapatche campsite at sunset, the distant Golden Lakes look to some like city lights. Others describe them as looking like shining golden coins, a distant beaconing treasure. All agree, the experience of seeing the Golden Lakes sunset phenomenon is one of their most memorable sights.

One final sign reads:

```
"STOVES ONLY."
```

The Wonderland Trail to Golden Lakes continues on North from Klapatche Camp.

KLAPATCHE PARK TO SUNSET PARK
(Golden Lakes)

The sights encountered this day will come first as a surprise, then as a shock. Memories of this section will be those of the ravages of both nature and of man. First seen will be the power of ice and water (the site of the destruction of the mammoth North Puyallup River bridge which was damaged extensively by avalanches in 1947, 1948 and 1952), and later in the day by the far greater destruction by fire on the slopes of Colonnade Ridge and the hills beyond.

70+ years later, the tragedy of a major burn continues to be seen firsthand as the trail passes through the still charred remains of a once majestic and dense old-growth forest. Miles of silver snags amidst the younger forest are grim reminders of what one small spark can do. But we do have a view!

THE TRAIL

KLAPATCHE PARK TO SUNSET PARK

TRAIL CONDITION: Varied conditions exist on this section of trail, beginning with a fairly steep descent to the North Puyallup River. However this swift drop is under forest cover and on nice trail nearly all the way. Hiking time will be an hour or less from Klapatche. The photo on the back cover was taken shortly after leaving camp.

After crossing the river, the trail seems to be considerably flatter than indicated on the USGS map. It never really gets down to business in gaining any real elevation until about 1-1/2 miles beyond the river crossing. (And by then, Golden Lakes are only about 3-1/2 miles away.)

The main old fire area will be seen from afar before actually coming to it. (From the huckleberry heaven area, it is visible across the gorge by looking to the next hump of the ridge. The trail can be seen slicing upward through the young forest.

ELEVATION: Gain: 1,800'   Loss: 2,150'

MILEAGE: Our mileages, since there is no longer a sign at Klapatche Park intersection.

```
        N. Puyallup River    2.8-
        Golden Lakes    7.6+
        Indian Henrys    9.0
```

Klapatche Park to Golden Lakes

TRAIL BEGINS: Kalpatche Park intersection. The trail circles Aurora Lake and drops over the north side of the ridge.

Sign:
KLAPATCHE PARK TO SUNSET PARK

```
┌─────────────────────────────────────┐
│                                       │
│        ← St. Andrews Park Trail       │
│        ← Wonderland Trail →           │
│                                       │
└─────────────────────────────────────┘
```

0.3- First switchback. Begin quite steep descent.

0.7- After 7th switchback, enter heavily treed area. Ahead, the (slightly better) trail travels through a slide area.

1.1- **WATER.** Cliffs above. Ahead, the trail opens up and switchbacks, following the contour of a gully coming off the peak above.

1.4+ Short climb. Ahead the trail turns and crosses slide area Trail improves once under cliffs. Travel over the next mile will be swift.

2.2- 15th switchback followed by a 15-foot puncheon bridge over run-off.

2.8- **"THE ROAD."** (The end of the West Side Highway.) The road has been closed for the past several years due to mudflow damage at Tahoma Creek. If and when it ever reopens, it will probably only be open to Klapatche Point.

Horse travelers might be able to make it all the way up the West Side Road at present, however since it is not patrolled, doing so could be risky. There is a horse camp at the North Puyallup. Signs read:

```
┌─────────────────────────────────────┐
│                                       │
│         NORTH PUYALLUP TRAIL          │
│                                       │
│    Westside Road 2.7   (actual 2.7-)  │
│                                       │
└─────────────────────────────────────┘
```

A second sign by a very nice rock wall reads:

```
┌─────────────────────────────────────┐
│                                       │
│          WONDERLAND TRAIL             │
│                                       │
│    North Puyallup Camp    0.1         │
│    Golden Lakes Camp 5.0   (actual 4.9-) │
│    Klapatche Park Camp 2.8  (actual 2.8-) │
│    So. Puyallup Camp 6.6   (actual 6.4-) │
│                                       │
└─────────────────────────────────────┘
```

A third reads "No Horses". Duplicate signs are across the road.

Other mileages from this point are:

> North Mowich River   11.4-
> Mowich Lake   15.1
> Indian Henrys   12.3-
> Longmire   19.6-

2.8-   **NORTH PUYALLUP RIVER BRIDGE.** (elevation 3707'). This sturdy wooden bridge is high above the rushing waters of the gorge. After crossing the river, the road forks. The right fork goes to the camp. The left fork paralleling the river is the Wonderland Trail.

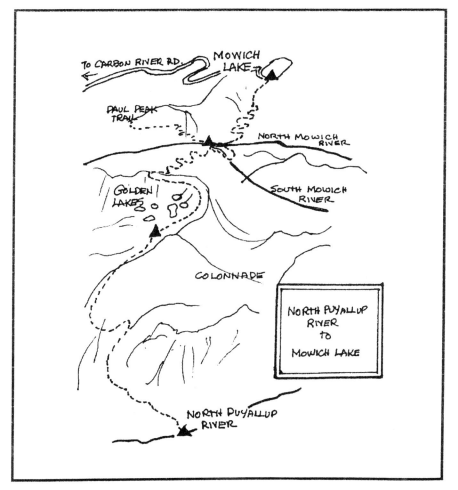

NORTH PUYALLUP RIVER to MOWICH LAKE

North Puyallup Camp is located on the north side of the bridge. There are only three sites, (in a row) , so if you don't want anyone walking through your camp, take site #3. About the only thing that makes this a good place to camp is its location. Klapatche or Golden Lakes are nicer, but sometimes the schedule makes this a handier choice. (Also, this is a warmer and more protected camp than Klapatche.)

3.0-   **WATER.** Very nice new bridge followed by rocky trail. More water ahead.

3.3+   Slide gully.

3.6-   Slide gully. Trail "rolling". Rock slopes beside trail. Heavy fern undergrowth. Begin gentle ascent. Archway log over trail ahead.

3.8+   **WATER.** 8-foot bridge over stream. Trail through heavy forest. Good mushroom area. No switchbacks. Slowly gaining elevation.

4.2-   Tree cover thinning out. Much bear grass, red huckleberries and salal. Now climbing steadily. Silver snags from old burn visible above. Still traveling beneath it.

4.6-   Back under forest cover. Climbing steadily. Listen for audible water ahead.

4.8+   **WATER.** Two notable bridges in a row. Log railings and plank surfaces. Very nice spot.

4.9+   Trail comes around ridge. Still climbing, with consistent elevation gain across old burn area just ahead.

5.1+   Round a bend, then back under forest cover. Abundant blue huckleberries ahead, then tree cover thins out.

5.6+   Long puncheon trail. Blue huckleberries in all directions as far as the eye can see. WOW! **WATCH FOR BEARS! (with blue lips!)**

5.7+   Entering old burn area again. Interesting rock formations high above the trail. Ahead desolate area. No trees. Large rock slide. Trail climbing and exposed in places. It climbs along the side of a ridge that burned.

6.4   **TOP OF THE RIDGE.** (elevation 5,200').

6.5+   Ancient faint wooden pole reading "M/W -1" in grassy meadow. (This pole has been here at least since 1940.)

6.9+   End of forest cover. Small footbridge. Trail begins to descend. Ahead it runs over gentle rolling ridges and crosses several (dry) bridges.

7.2-   Large pond visible to the left.

7.3-   **WATER.** Look for small deep lake to the left. Another faint weathered wooden pole reading "M/W 2."

7.6+   30-foot puncheon bridge. Large lake visible below.

7.8-   **GOLDEN LAKES PATROL CABIN.** (elevation 4950'). Large lake behind it. There are actually fifteen or more small lakes here, most of which comprise the headwaters of Laughingwater Creek. The area is so named because of the golden sunsets reflected in the lakes.

Signs read:

GOLDEN LAKES CAMP
Stoves Only
Camp at designated site only

DON'T BE A MEADOW STOMPER

The patrol cabin has a broad-roofed front porch (no camping on porches allowed.) 5 good campsites. Use water from lakes (and remember to treat it.) A composting toilet is nearby.

Fishing used to be outstanding here, particularly at the outer lakes, and is still about as good as you'll find anywhere in the park. The largest of the lakes, about 1,500' below the camp is reportedly good for 8 to 12 inch trout. (See fishing specifics on page 74). Creel census forms are in a box by the Patrol cabin.

GOLDEN LAKES TO MOWICH LAKE

While perhaps not as spectacular in scenery as the opposite eastern leg of the Wonderland, the west side of the Mountain has a distinct sublime "wilderness" feel that is not as evident for as long a time anywhere else on the trail. This is for good reason: to the west is the Glacier View Wilderness area.

This is due as much to the psychological distance between contact points with civilization as it is to the remoteness of the area. The hiker knows that should there be an emergency, he may have a long hike out.

To the north, a similar condition exists. If it's tourist season, Mowich Lake, or the Paul Peak Trail to the Mowich Lake road, would be the first sure contact with people. However if hiking "out of season," then the exiting hiker may have an even longer hike toward Carbonado, or a climb over still another ridge to the Ranger Station at Carbon River. This is highly unlikely because the roads to both the north and south terminus of this section are checked frequently by the rangers, and are traveled by curious sightseers right up to the time the snow flies.

Indeed, thoughts of what MIGHT be crosses the minds of most hikers at least once during their travels on the West Side. It's just not like the other sections where help is more readily available

Added to this is the possibility that the Wonderland hikers will have the entire section to themselves (especially if the West Side Road is closed.) Unlike all other segments of the trail, people generally just don't come into the West Side for the heck of it. About the only ones using it are those doing the Wonderland Trail, a few fishermen and an occasional trail crew. If you like solitude, you'll love the West Side.

Thus, it's also a wonderful place to bring a fishing pole, a good book, a sketchpad, or maybe even a Bible, and spend an extra day replenishing the needs of the soul as well as those of the body.

The Old Sunset Park Patrol Cabin

Beth Rossow Photo

GOLDEN LAKES TO MOWICH LAKE INTERSECTION

TRAIL CONDITION: After leaving Golden Lakes, the trail climbs a short distance nearly to the top of the gradually descending Colonnade Ridge. Then, for over a mile, it traverses along the southwest side of the ridge, again frequently in or overlooking more of the old 1928 burn.

About 2 miles out of camp, the trail crosses over the top of the ridge, and drops over the edge before entering the heavily forested north slopes of the ridge overlooking the South Mowich River.

The 2 1/2 mile descent from "the pass" will be made in just an hour or so, and the hiker will probably find himself at the North Mowich shelter in plenty of time for a leisurely lunch.

If that is his destination for the day, it will have been a short easy day. Even if continuing on, he will still have ample time to be at Mowich Lake before dinner.

The trail climbs continually after crossing the North Mowich River, gaining over 2,300 feet in the 3-1/2 miles to Mowich Lake. It's pleasant climbing, however, on an excellent trail, through thick woods with several pleasant respites provided by cool tumbling streams and an occasional glimpse of the Mountain.

ELEVATION: Gain: 70'   Loss: 2,420'

MILEAGE: According to sign by Golden Lakes Patrol Cabin:

WONDERLAND TRAIL

N. Puyallup River 4.8   (actual 4.8+)
Klapatche Park 7.5   (actual 7.8-)
N. Mowich River Shelter 7.4   (actual 6.3+)
Mowich Lake 11.2   (actual 10.0)

TRAIL BEGINS: At the Wonderland Trail sign in Sunset Park. Pass the lake on the left, then trail and campsite on the left.

0.7-   30-foot bridge. Immediate area heavily forested with thick underbrush.

1.2-   Trail climbing slightly and out in the open again. The ridge was burned over in 1928.

1.5+   **WATER.** Small pond visible to the left. Round the ridge where the Sunset Fire Lookout tower used to be.

1.8+   Trail visible in the distance, climbing to the top of a small ridge. Very good trail with some forest cover.

1.9+   **THE "PASS"** at about the end of the Colonnade Ridge. A "side trail" leads up to a small knoll. (The side trail was actually an old fire trail built by bulldozer brought in from the outside. It is now part of an X-country ski trail). The Wonderland descends from here into the forest. (32 switchbacks to the South Mowich River.)

2.5+   End of slide area run-out following switchback #5.

3.2-   Switchback #11 by rocks and devastated area. Many old downed trees, all else green.

3.5+   Switchback #14. Trail in this area is generally level but winding. Looks like an Olympic mountain trail. Mushrooms galore!

4.7+   Three switchbacks (#26-28) within 200 feet. Trail very steep. Lush undergrowth.

5.3-   **WATER.** Switchback followed by one 80' and one 50' bridge over first (fresh) water since Golden Lakes, then three more small bridges. Trail now flatter, rolling and winding.

5.5-   River audible. Flat (sometimes muddy) trail approaches river.

5.7+   **SOUTH MOWICH RIVER,** (elevation 2700'). This is one rugged river, and there may or may not be a log crossing. When Beth measured the trail, one year there was a deep waterfall cascading over the Log Bridge in the afternoon. Early the next morning the water had dropped a foot and a half. A lot depends on when you cross.

         This river is hard on bridges. The carcasses of several previous bridges with handwires still attached can be seen lying on the shores. Trail crews keep a supply of logs seasoning nearby because of the continual need for bridge replacement. Ask rangers or others on the trail what to expect here.

         The signs are on the north shore, before the trail enters the forest.

WONDERLAND TRAIL
South Mowich Shelter

Sunset Park 6.0	(actual 5.7+)
No. Mowich 0.5	(actual 0.3+)
Mowich Lake 4.3	(actual 3.7-)
Spray Park 6.5	(actual 7.2-)

HORSE CAMP
Use Fireplace - Build No Other Fires

6.0- **SOUTH MOWICH SHELTER.** (elevation 2,600'). A beautiful shelter in a densely wooded, picturesque setting. Several clean comfortable campsites surround the shelter. One john serves all.

Water is from the stream 250 feet away.

A word of explanation about the shelters here is in order. There are actually **three** shelters in this area, all nice log cabin style with open fronts. The first, **the South Mowich Shelter**, is on the north side of the South Mowich River.

The second shelter is **the original one**, unmarked by a sign. It is on the south side of the North Mowich River.

Number 3, **the North Mowich Shelter**, is on the north side of the North Mowich River. Mowich River is the horse camp.

6.3+ **NORTH MOWICH SHELTER**

Ed Walsh Photo

The South Mowich Crossing

NORTH MOWICH SHELTER TO MOWICH LAKE

ELEVATION GUIDE: Gain: 2,329'   Loss: 100'

MILEAGE: According to sign at North Mowich Shelter (The #3).

WONDERLAND TRAIL
North Mowich Shelter

Spray Park 6.0   (actual 6.6-)
Mowich Lake 3.8   (actual 3.7-)
So. Mowich 0.5   (actual 0.3+)
Sunset Park 6.5   (actual 6.3+)

HORSE CAMP
Use Fireplace
Build No Other Fires

TRAIL BEGINS: From the South Mowich Shelter, take the wooded trail north to the North Mowich River. Cross river to North Mowich Shelter sign (above).

0.1-   Switchback. Trail climbs above river on a carpet of thick moss as it travels through a beautiful section of forest.

0.5+   **PAUL PEAK TRAIL JUNCTION.** (elevation 2,600'). Signs:

WONDERLAND TRAIL

← Mowich Lake 3.6   (actual 3.7-)
← Spray Park 5.7   (actual 5.8)
So. Mowich River Shelter   (0.8-)
Golden Lakes 6.3 →   (actual 6.8-)

PAUL PEAK TRAIL

Mowich Road 3.5

(There also used to be a sign here indicating that from this point Mountain Meadows is 5.0 miles, and the Grind- stone Trail is 3.0.)

Note: Upon leaving here, the trail to Mowich Lake is *PERSISTENT!* It climbs with little relief for nearly 3 miles.

0.8-   Switchback followed by a long climb to the east with no switchback.

1.1+   Dry stream bed containing much devastation. Ground cover is Oregon grape and salal. Ahead is a switchback by a giant old Douglas fir and beneath a very steep hillside.

1.3-   Cross (dry) rocky streambed. Rock "seat" by the trail.

1.5-   Stop and listen to the stress noises of these trees as they creak and groan. This is a particularly audible forest! Following this, the trail switchbacks by a very long old nurse log.

2.0-   10-foot bridge over (dry) stream followed by 8-foot bridge over a tumbling stream with beautiful moss covered rocks. A 20-foot bridge over a trickle follows.

2.3-   Two switchbacks followed by a very steep pitch and another switchback. When the Mountain is visible, stop and look for a deer head in the rock formations on the upper reaches. It was the Indians who first saw the resemblance, and since "Mowich" is Chinook Jargon for "deer," legend has it the sight of this head led to naming the river and lake "Mowich." For more information, see pages 126 and 134.

Carl Fabiani Photo

123

2.8-   **CRATER CREEK** (elevation 4, 500') with beautiful falls above. The grade then steepens and trail leaves the stream area.

3.2-   8-foot puncheon over trickle culvert. One 22' wood bridge, more culverts, rock built-up trail and puncheons in the area.

3.5-   **SPRAY PARK TRAIL JUNCTION.** (elevation 4,850'). Signs read:

```
┌─────────────────────────────────────────┐
│          WONDERLAND TRAIL                │
│                                          │
│   ← Mowich Lake 0.4    (actual 0.2+)     │
│   N. Mowich River 3.5 →  (actual 3.5-)   │
│   10.9 Golden Lakes →   (actual 9.8-)    │
└─────────────────────────────────────────┘
```

```
┌─────────────────────────────────────────┐
│          SPRAY PARK TRAIL                │
│                                          │
│   Eagle Roost Camp 1.5   (actual 1.7-)   │
│   Spray Park 2.6    (actual 2.8+)        │
└─────────────────────────────────────────┘
```

From this junction, the Wonderland Trail goes to the left, and the Spray Park Trail to the right.

3.7-   **JUNCTION WITH SOUTH SIDE OF MOWICH LAKE** camping area and parking lot. (elevation 4,929'). The old parking lot is now the designated campground. Campers should be aware that they are expected to pitch their tents on a hard-packed gravel surface. Maybe you can borrow a tire iron from a drive-in tourist to pound in your tent stakes. The new parking lot (indistinguishable from the camping area) is on the other side of the barricade, beyond the bathrooms. No need to bear bag food here. There's a food cache at the Ranger Station (south side of lake) where you can stash stuff overnight. Did you bring a bathing suit? Swimming is allowed in Mowich Lake. Brrrr...

Signs:

```
┌─────────────────────────────────────────┐
│          WONDERLAND TRAIL                │
│                                          │
│    Ipsut Camp 5.5   (actual 5.7+)        │
│    N. Mowich River 3.9   (actual 3.7-)   │
└─────────────────────────────────────────┘
```

```
┌─────────────────────────────────────────┐
│          SPRAY PARK TRAIL                │
│                                          │
│   Eagle Roost Camp 1.9   (actual 1.9-)   │
│   Spray Park 3.0   (actual 3.0+)         │
└─────────────────────────────────────────┘
```

MOWICH LAKE TO CARBON RIVER

Some interesting sidelights on this area are in its history. This exceptionally clear, 200'-deep, 122-acre lake was first discovered by geologist Bailey Willis while exploring for resources for the Northern Pacific Railroad. Willis first thought it to be a crater lake, (and it was so named on early maps), Although this was soon disproved, (it's a glacial cirque), the creek which flows from it still bears the name Crater Creek. The white discoverers were Johnny-come-lately's, however, because the Indians had known all about this area for centuries, and had already named the lake and the pass. In Chinook language, Mowich means "deer" and Ipsut (originally 'Ipsoot') means 'hidden place."

At the same time Willis was exploring the North side of the Mountain, and the railroad was contemplating plans for the area, James Longmire, on the other side of the Mountain, had discovered the mineral springs. Had the word not gotten out about the therapeutic benefits of "Longmire's Medical Springs", the thundering herds might today be thronging to Mowich Lake instead of to the South side. Viewed in that perspective, the name is appropriate. It indeed is still pretty much a hidden place. Incidentally, for early season hikers, the road to Mowich is seldom open before the 4th of July. It's usually barricaded at the Paul Peak trailhead.

In any event, here the hiker must make a choice. Should he take the (actual) Wonderland Trail with its shorter faster trip over Ipsut Pass, or go the higher and longer (but far more scenic) alternate route through Spray Park?

The following factors should be considered before making the decision.

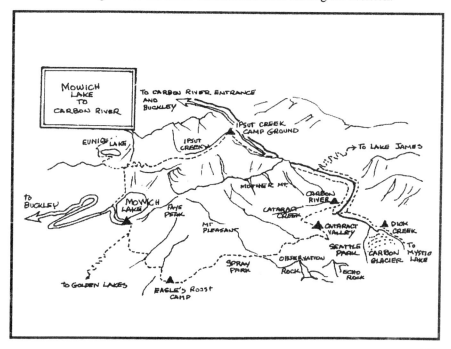

MOWICH LAKE TO CARBON RIVER VIA IPSUT PASS

For those whose objectives are speed and minimum distance, then this is the route to take. Less than an hour out of Mowich Lake (4,929'), and after having gained less than 100 feet in elevation, the trail crosses over Ipsut Pass, then descends the entire remainder of the way to the Carbon River.

The time saved may put hikers taking this route a full day or two ahead of their fellow hikers traveling to the same destination via Spray and Seattle Parks. This is also the preferable choice early in the season when most of Spray and Seattle Parks are still under snow.

There will be few distracting views once over Ipsut pass, for the hiker is separated from Mount Rainier, first by 6,116-foot Castle Peak (immediately southeast of Ipsut Pass) and later by multi-summited Mother Mountain as he descends her northern flanks. The valley down which he travels provides his only scenery. With the exception of the first views from the top of Ipsut Pass, this route is generally undistinguished.

It is, however, the route those desiring to do the "true" Wonderland Trail must take, because the following trail is not a part of the Wonderland Trail, but is an alternate to it.

ALTERNATE ROUTE

MOWICH LAKE TO CARBON RIVER VIA SPRAY PARK

This is one of the oldest sections of trail in the Park. It was built by Bailey Willis in 1883-84, originating in Wilkeson and ending at Spray Park.

To many Mount Rainier fans, Spray Park is their favorite. For beauty, views, countless great photo sites, in fact, an abundance of everything trails are hiked for, Spray Park has it! Few persons have the will power to pass through without at least a rest stop and, of those who do, their desire to return is compelling.

The trip from Spray Park on, however, is not without difficulties. Even in summer the hiker can count on crossing snowfields in the vicinity of the 6,400-foot divide between Spray and Seattle Parks. (We crossed 12 in mid-August one year.)

The descent into Seattle Park is steep and persistent and especially harrowing after a rain, when the pitched trail turns to mud. (The Ipsut Creek Trail, however, is mostly rock-based, and even when the trail is very wet, it is rarely slick and muddy.) There is also the matter of where to stay. Since there is no camping allowed in either Spray or Seattle Parks, the first place to camp is Cataract Valley, or continue through to the Carbon River Camp or two more miles to Ipsut Campground. Hardy hikers can make the entire trip from Mowich Lake to Carbon River via this route in one day, but their legs will rebel toward the end. There's a lot of climbing and even more descending on this stretch.

This route was once considered a segment of the Wonderland Trail. However about thirty years ago, official Wonderland status was switched to the Ipsut Pass Trail, with Spray Park becoming the alternate route. Although perhaps not the "official" trail, this should be the choice of those who are hiking to see the beauties and glories of the mountain, for Spray Park's grandeur is breathtaking, and the panoramic view of Mount Rainier from the Park is one of the finest you will see.

The Spray Park Trail Log begins on page 132.

THE WONDERLAND TRAIL

MOWICH LAKE TO CARBON RIVER VIA IPSUT PASS

TRAIL CONDITION: A good trail offering one spectacular view at the Pass, then a rapid descent to the Carbon River for the traveler wanting to do the actual Wonderland Trail or loop the Mountain in the minimum time and distance.

After skirting the west side of Mowich Lake, the trail gains a scant hundred feet in elevation before dropping over Ipsut Pass. (A side trip to Eunice Lake and/or Tolmie Peak would certainly be an option to consider for those taking this route.) The first few hundred feet beyond the pass, the trail drops rapidly down the east wall with a series of fairly steep switchbacks. Though this first half mile is memorably steep and rocky, once the trail enters the forest, the hiker's knees quit complaining.

Although most of the actual switchbacks are under forest cover, the straightaways run back and forth across the high open meadow. This is no problem for the eastbound traveler who won't take long getting down the slope, but to the counter-clockwise hiker making the climb in the late afternoon, there will be little relief from the sun except that which is provided by high weeds and tall flowers. This is also an area where the hiker would do well to keep a wary eye for rockfall from the cliffs and sheer north walls bordering the pass.

This is a unique forest area. Forest fires are rare in this valley, thus there are trees along the trail that are more than 1,200 years old. The most famous among them is one which is now the largest known Alaska cedar in the world, (A larger one was found on the Olympic Peninsula, but it recently toppled.) Once down the steep stretch, the trail is a brisk hike through a pretty forested valley.

NOTE: There is no water after leaving Mowich Lake until coming to a stream at the base of the switchbacks at 2.5-miles.

MOWICH LAKE TO CARBON RIVER VIA IPSUT PASS

ELEVATION: Gain: 171'   Loss: 2,880'

MILEAGE: Park Service Mileage: Carbon River Road 5.4 (actual 5.3-). This mileage measurement was begun at the signpost and trail junction at the south end of Mowich Lake, since this is where round-the-Mountain travelers would emerge.)

TRAILBEGINS: South or west of Mowich Lake. A network of interlaced trails eventually all merge at the northwest margin of the lake.

0.0   South end of Mowich Lake across the picnic & camping area. Travel north across the camping area and follow the road to the sign.

0.2-   Sign at access trail junction reads:

> ### LAKESHORE WALK
> Ranger Station   0.1

A few feet further, another sign reads:

> ### WONDERLAND TRAIL
>
> Eunice Lake 2.4   (not measured)
> Tolmie Peak 2.8   (not measured)
> Ipsut Campground 5.5   (actual 5.3-)

Trail heads north along edge of lake. Easy trail skirts lake via several small puncheon bridges.

0.5-   Junction with access trail coming in from Mowich Lake road on the left. Signs read:

> Ipsut Pass 1.0   (actual -1.0)
> Mowich Lake Camp 0.5   (correct)

> ### NO CAMPING AND NO CAMPFIRES
> ### AT EUNICE LAKE

Trail begins slow climb up and away from lake.

0.9+   Pass base of cliff and talus area. Excellent trail with gradual climb. Nearly flat in spots.

1.4+   **TOLMIE PEAK TRAIL JUNCTION.** Sign reads:

```
┌─────────────────────────────────────────┐
│                                          │
│           TOLMIE PEAK TRAIL              │
│                                          │
│     Eunice Lake    (actual 0.9)          │
│     Tolmie Peak    (actual 1.8)          │
│                                          │
└─────────────────────────────────────────┘
```

Another reads:

```
┌─────────────────────────────────────────┐
│                                          │
│           WONDERLAND TRAIL               │
│              IPSUT PASS                  │
│                                          │
│   Ipsut Campground   (actual 4.3-)       │
│   Mowich Lake        (actual 1.4+)       │
│                                          │
└─────────────────────────────────────────┘
```

The Wonderland Trail runs northwest, while the Tolmie Peak Trail cuts off to the west.

This 5,939-ft. peak was named for a young Scot, Dr.William F. Tolmie, Hudson Bay Company's surgeon at Fort Nisqually. Dr. Tolmie was the first white man known to explore what is now Mount Rainier National Park. In August 1833, he employed five Indians as guides on a botanical expedition into the area in search of medicinal herbs. It is thought he and the Indians climbed what we now know as Tolmie Peak. Prof. Bailey Willis chose the name "Tolmie Peak" in 1883.

1.5-   **IPSUT PASS.** (5,100'). Sign reading

```
┌─────────────────────────────────────────┐
│                                          │
│              IPSUT PASS                  │
│             Elevation 5100               │
│                                          │
└─────────────────────────────────────────┘
```

Look for the first of six switchbacks within 200 feet. Trail rocky, increasing briefly to a 30-40 degree grade. Nineteen switchbacks eat up the next 9/10 mile.

1.8-   Trail at base of sheer rock cliffs.

1.9- Large Alaska cedars beside trail preceding a switchback. Seven more switchbacks follow.

2.3 Temporary tree cover.

2.5+ WATER. No bridge. *First water since Mowich Lake.* Two more streamlets follow shortly. Tree cover. Trail heads north temporarily, steepness diminishing.

2.7- Looking back, the trail over the pass is visible from here. (If traveling from the east, this is the first time it is visible.)

2.8+ Trail running a small ridge. Water on both sides.

3.3+ 25' bridge. **WATER**. Heavily forested.

3.4+ 95-foot combination built-up trail and puncheon bridge. To the left is a good view of Gove Peak ridge. Ipsut Pass is where this ridge converges with the low point of Castle Peak ridge.

Just uphill of the bridge, on the left when descending, is the large Alaska cedar. The biggest one being the current record holder as the largest 'Chamaecyparis nootkatensis' in the U.S. Alaska cedars are distinguished by their "wilted" appearance, light bark, sparse branching and yellow-green foliage. Also, the wood is yellow instead of brown like that of western red cedar.

These particular trees are over 1,200 years old, and they are the oldest trees in the park. Their longevity is attributed to two factors, abundance of water and lack of disturbance by fire. They generally grow at elevations of 3,000 to 4,850 feet, and like moist North-facing slopes where cold air sweeps down a valley. That description fits perfectly the Ipsut Creek valley which coincidentally has not experienced a forest fire for over 1,200 years.

A PLEA: These ancient trees are not only some of the wonders of the Wonderland, they are some of the treasures of our nation. It's hard to believe that these giants are still alive after 1,200 Mount Rainier winters. Please do not betray the trust of being given this knowledge of their age and where- abouts to harm or damage the great trees. Unless you're a Spotted Owl, don't even touch them, please.

3.6- Trail dropping fast. Two switchbacks. Trail paralleling Doe Creek. Ahead, a 30-foot bridge crosses a rushing stream which cascades over a glass-smooth rock bed. A very scenic spot.

3.9- Switchback preceding footlog and horse ford over Doe Creek. This beautiful little creek begins in a permanent snowfield high on Mother Mountain.

Dinni Fabiani Photo

Find these roots, and you've found the tree.

4.1-   "Bear tree." An ideal fun photo spot as long as neither Smokey nor Yogi are home. Bridges follow, then rocky trail parallels Ipsut Creek. WATER and footlog beside an immense moss-covered boulder.

4.3   Ipsut Creek and trail converge, followed by two 15-foot bridges over (sometime) good streams. Heavy undergrowth. Much devil's club, heavy fern and thimbleberry. Trail rocky.

4.7+   Switchback. Begin final descent before trail junction.

5.1-   **JUNCTION WITH IPSUT CREEK CAMPGROUND TRAIL** (to the left). Ahead, and a short distance to the left, a short side trail leads to Ipsut Creek below the falls. From this same point, the Wonderland Trail continuing east (to the Carbon River Loop and beyond) goes to the right.

        Note the moss-draped trees in this area. This is a classic example of temperate rain forest.

5.4+   **IPSUT CREEK CAMPGROUND TRAILHEAD** (elevation 2,320') and parking lot.

ALTERNATE TO THE WONDERLAND TRAIL

MOWICH LAKE TO CARBON RIVER
via
SPRAY PARK

TRAIL CONDITION: A good trail which begins by traversing lower Fay Peak to the vicinity of Lee Creek, then climbs steeply from Spray Falls Trail junction to the lower Spray Park Meadows, but resumes a gradual climb from there to the park proper. For the most part it is broad and in excellent condition. With the exception of those places noted in the trail log where caution must be exercised, it is a good trail on which to introduce the whole family to the wonders of the Wonderland.

ELEVATION: Gain: 2,020'   Loss: 4,250'

MILEAGE: Park Service mileages (according to the sign at the Mowich Lake Trail terminus):

TRAIL BEGINS: Due south of the lake. It is well marked.

WONDERLAND TRAIL

Ipsut Campground 5.5   (actual 5.7+)
N. Mowich River 3.9   (actual 3.7-)

SPRAY PARK TRAIL

Eagle Roost Camp 1.9   (actual 1.6+)
Spray Park 3.0   (actual 3.0+)

THE TRAIL

0.2   Junction with Wonderland Trail coming up from Mowich River. Signs:

SPRAY PARK TRAIL

3.0- Eagles Roost Camp 1.5   (actual 1.6+)
Spray Park 2.6   (actual 2.8+)

```
┌─────────────────────────────────────────────┐
│                                               │
│              WONDERLAND TRAIL                 │
│                                               │
│         Mowich Lake 0.4     (actual 0.2+)     │
│         North Mowich River 3.5   (actual 3.2+)│
│                                               │
└─────────────────────────────────────────────┘
```

In 1890, Fay Peak (6,500') the south side of which you're now traversing was named in honor of Miss Fay Fuller of Tacoma. That year she became the first woman to reach the summit of Mount Rainier.

0.8- **LEE CREEK**, bridged with side-by-side footlogs. A second fork of this creek is 120' farther along.

Lee Creek drainage separates Fay Peak and Hessong Rock (6,385'). The latter was named for an early photographer who took many popular pictures of the area.

1.2+ Talus.

1.5+ **EAGLE CLIFF.** (elevation 4,800'). 85 feet south via a short side trip. CAUTION: If doing this as a family trip, be extremely careful that children do not run ahead down the short trail to the cliff. The cliff fencing is not visible until the last few feet of trail.

In 1898, early geologist and climber I. C. Russell stood on this same spot and declared it "One of the most sublime pictures of noble scenery to be had anywhere in North America." The North Mowich Glacier was much larger when Mr. Russell made that statement. By age dating the lichen, scientists have determined that the glacier has retreated more than 1.4 miles from its location in the late 1800's.

At the base of Eagle Cliff, a half mile away and 1,000 feet straight down by the North Mowich River, was the site of the third largest mining effort in the Park. The ambitious operation had a sawmill, blacksmith shop, flume, power plant, small railroad and numerous prospector cabins.

The remains of the last half dozen buildings, two tunnels, small ore cars narrow gauge railroad track plus tons of tools and equipment are no longer discernable as nature has erased all evidence of man's intrusion nearly a century ago.

Not a hint of the interesting history of the spot is told by the sign which reads simply:

```
┌─────────────────────────────────────────────┐
│                                               │
│                 EAGLE CLIFF                   │
│                                               │
└─────────────────────────────────────────────┘
```

Don't attempt to go down to do any exploring from here. There is nothing left to see, and the route in was not from up here, but came in up the valley, near the Paul Peak Trail.

Incidentally, while here, do you see the Deer's Head on the Mowich Face of Mount Rainier?

It's the resemblance of a deer's head, neck and antlers in a large prominent collection of rock bands and snowfields on the upper left portion of the Mowich or West Face of the Mountain. According to John H. Williams, author of 'The Mountain that was God' (published 1911), the Mowich Rivers were so named by the Indians from their belief that, in the great rocks on the northwest side of the peak, just below the summit, they saw the sight of the Mowich, or deer. Photo on page 123.

1.9-   **EAGLE'S ROOST CAMP.** A side trail leads to the small camp. It has 7 numbered sites, and an "air- conditioned" outhouse (no roof).

EAGLES ROOST CAMP
0.1 km   (actual 0.1-)

2.0   **JUNCTION WITH SPRAY FALLS TRAIL.**

SIDE TRIP TO SPRAY FALLS
(.2+ round trip)

These spectacular falls cascade almost 400 feet over an old andesite flow.

Cross log bridge over Grant Creek, traverse musical rocks and follow trail to edge of creek. For a better view of the falls, cross stream from rocks on near side to base of falls.

Be careful; everything is wet and slippery!

Signs read:

SPRAY PARK TRAIL

Spray Parl .08   (actual 0.08+)
Mowich Lake 2.0   (actual 2.0)
North Mowich Shelter 5.2   (actual 5.3+)

> **SPRAY FALLS TRAIL**
> Spray Falls 0.3   (actual 0.1+)

About 3/4 of a mile below, Spray Creek merges with the North Mowich River.

2.2   Sixth switchback by mossy streamlet with nice sitting log. There are six more switchbacks to go.

2.6+   **BEGINNING OF SPRAY PARK PROPER.** (elevation 5,400'). Spray Park starts at the log bridge that crosses Grant Creek. The spectacular view of Mount Rainier straight ahead lets you know you have arrived.

No sign, but some mileages from this point are:

> Seattle Park 2.1
> Cataract campsite 3.8+
> Ipsut Campground 9.3-

No camping is allowed at Spray Park. Many side trails intersect the main trail. To explore the park, stay on a defined path to avoid trampling the flowers and fragile groundcover. These way (social) trails lead to tree islands, small lakes or scenic picnic spots. Down the main trail and to the right (over a knoll) is a picturesque lake, perfect for a picnic and some spectacular photo opportunities.

Take time to get a good look at Mount Rainier's rugged northwest face, split down the middle by Ptarmigan Ridge. To the left is the legendary Willis Wall, the most formidable climbing route on the Mountain, because of the continual rockfall and avalanches, and to the right is the Mowich Face. All of these routes are very difficult climbs which have claimed a number of victims. What appears to be the summit of Mount Rainier (about 8,500 feet above you) is actually Liberty Cap (14,112'). Behind it, out of sight, is the true summit of the Mountain (recently remeasured at 14,411.1') Columbia Crest, the high point of the mile-wide crater which still vents steam.

Between you and the Mountain are some smaller peaks. To the left is Echo Rock (7,870') an old lava vent, then to its right, Observation Rock (8,364'). In the foreground is the tiny and almost touchable Flett Glacier, and to its right, on Ptarmigan Ridge, is Tillicum Point (6,654').

The beauty of this view from the north inspires eloquence, but of all the writing we've seen, Bailey Willis captured it best in 1883when he wrote:

"Southward, 9,000 feet above you, so near you must throw your head back to see its summit, is grand Mount Tacoma; its graceful northern peak piercing the sky, it soars single and alone. Whether touched by the glow of early morning or gleaming in bright noonday, whether rosy with sunset light or glimmering, ghost-like, in the full moon, whether standing out clear and cloudless or veiled among the mists it weaves from the warm south winds, it is always majestic and inspiring, always attractive and lovely. It is a symbol of an awful power clad in beauty."

Better hang packs if going off exploring Spray Park. (This is a popular park with the bears too.) They can sometimes be spotted on the slopes of Hessong Rock and Mt. Pleasant. (Hessong Rock was another of the sites explored by early prospectors. One report we read said that when the Alaska Gold Rush hit, the prospectors here were so anxious to go to the greener pastures, they even left their tools up on Hessong Rock).

3.5+ EAST SIDE OF SPRAY PARK. Here the trail approaches timberline and continues to climb towards a ridge. It passes through a large alpine meadow which may be dotted with snowfields.

3.8+ Beth calls this climb toward the ridge, "the stairway to heaven." Looking northward, it is now easy to identify the Carbon River valley and spot several familiar peaks.

High points on the prominent ridge to the north (from left to right) are: Hessong Rock (6,385'), Mount Pleasant (6,454'), and Mother Mountain (6,389'). In the distance, (90 miles to the NNE), you may be able to see the snowy slopes of another volcano, Glacier Peak (10,541'). Also visible are a number of Cascade Peaks, including Chimney Rock (on the eastern edge of the Snoqualmie Pass area), and Mount Stuart (on the Southern edge of the Enchanted Lakes Wilderness Area) about 50 miles distant as the crow flies.

From here the trail continues to climb, crossing volcanic rock, lava and pumice slopes. (Dwight Crandall in his book "The Geologic Story of Mount Rainier" notes that this pumice in Spray Park came from eruptions of Mount Rainier between 2,000 and 2,500 years ago).

4.1 **"THE TOP OF THE RIDGE."** (elevation 6,400'). This is the infamous permanent snowfield you have to cross. The trail is identified by painted rocks and cairns. Starting in late June, trail crews mark the best route across the snow with brightly flagged wands.

Descend diagonally (dropping about 250 feet in elevation) across the large snowfield. Head toward a large rock formation which is marked with several cairns and arrows painted on the rock.

Note to those going from east to west: *The large rock cairn marking the trail at the top of the ridge may not be clearly identifiable from the bottom* *of this snowfield. If for any reason (fog or other inclement weather) you are not able to follow wands or previous hiker's footprints, you will need to get out your compass and make your ascent to the ridge on a bearing of about 230 degrees (SW). Once on the ridge, if you did not come out at the right place, the trail into Spray Park should be easily spotted. During your climb to the ridge, you should not encounter any cliffs (which are too far down the ridge), or steep prolonged snowfields (which would mean you are heading too far up the ridge toward Flett Glacier).*

4.2+   At the rock formation, change direction, turning somewhat leftward (toward the North) and proceed across additional snowfields toward the trees. The trail may be visible at this point and if it isn't under snow, there may be melt-water running across it. In either case you should be able to see the trail in the distance. Ahead the trail is on small flat rocks.

4.6+   **WATER.** Cross streamlet. First water since Spray Park. Plenty of water from here on.

4.7   Short (20 foot) cliff-like wall. Do not descend it, stay on the trail. Follow trail 200 feet across talus to point at the base of cliff.

4.8+   Trail crosses 50 foot wide stratified bedrock slab.

4.9+   A few steps to the right, far below and to the east, is an excellent view of Seattle Park. This stretch of trail also affords a good view of the Carbon River gorge at the base of Mother Mountain.

5.1+   **SEATTLE PARK** outer edge, (elevation 5,500'). You'll know Seattle Park by the flowers, streams and erosion control trail steps.) These steps are wonderful, but in a hard rain, going down them is like walking down a fish ladder. Beware too of these brown sands when wet, they're as slippery as ice. (This "sand" is actually pumice from the same eruption of Mount Rainier mentioned earlier.) From here there's a good view of Seattle Park (proper) and the valley. Trail markers are either wands or bright paint on the rocks.

5.5-   A faint 50' side trail leads to a pretty little waterfall.

5.6-   **TRAIL CROSSES MARMOT CREEK** via double log bridge. There was a sign here until 1966 (when it disappeared), which read:

CAMP 12 - AUGUST 7, 1912

MOUNTAINEERS CAMP

6.1+   After re-entering forest cover, the next half mile contains fifteen switc backs and turns. Occasional steep pitches. Trail follows creek.

6.4+   20-foot bridge. Passing beneath cliffs. Trail continues into deep woods and tall timber. Broad trail with 20-30 degree grade.

6.7+   CATARACT VALLEY CAMP (4,700') Sign reads:

CATARACT VALLEY CAMP
NO WOOD FIRES

A short spur trail to the right goes to the camp. This lovely camp in deep forest, has 7 individual sites and 1 group site and a clean, roofed latrine. Two small streams pass through the camp area. (For those who can't decide whether to stop at Eagle's Roost or here, this is the more highly recommended camp.)

7.4+   Nice big sitting log preceding the first of 12 switchbacks. A tornado-like wind-throw ripped through here during the winter of 1983-84 wreaking terrible havoc in this once beautiful old forest. Shortly before this storm took place, the authors of "The Forest Communities of Mount Rainier National Park" noted that the lower Cataract Valley had no evidence of catastrophic disturbance for well over 1,000 years. But a few short minutes changed all that as you are about to see.

7.7-   Switchback #8. Many beautiful ferns line the trail. The cliffs across the valley on lower Mother Mountain become visible for the first time.

8.0   Large blowndown log is partially suspended over The trail. The sheer lower cliffs of Mother Mountain are now visible across the valley directly in front of you. The final switchback on this leg is just ahead.

8.2-   The destruction of the forest in this area is almost total. Trees were uprooted, sheared off and flung in all directions. Those few left standing show the tell-tale sign of a tornado in their tops, which are not snapped, but twisted off.

Pass completely under another large downed tree. Several small switchbacks as you reenter undamaged forest.

8.4-   Signs at Wonderland Trail junction with Carbon River Loop, Corner D. For continuation to Mystic Lake see page 149. The trail to Carbon River Camp or Ipsut Creek Campground continues on page 145.

Here's a later old Mountaineer Camp sign:

CARBON RIVER LOOP

One of the major trail intersections in the Park occurs along the banks of the Carbon River. It is here that four major park trails intersect to follow both sides of the river, and to cross it at two places. We refer to this area as the "Carbon River Loop" (not to be confused with the adjacent "Northern Loop"). It is comprised of four distinct trails, (north, south, east and west). Each "corner" of the loop connects to a segment of the Wonderland Trail or an alternate to it. (See map next page.)

The most common entry point to the Carbon River Loop will be from the Ipsut Creek Campground near the Wonderland Trail. Therefore, the description of the Loop will begin in this northwest "corner" and will proceed clockwise with a description of each of the four segments. However, we have also provided "reverse" mileages for those hiking these trail segments counter-clockwise. In this case, simply read each trail segment description "from the bottom up."

For those wishing to cross the river from west to east, we recommend the northern (lower) river crossing, because it connects to the east segment of the Loop which is one of the nicest miles of hiking found in Mount Rainier National Park. This eastern segment of the Loop is rarely traveled because signage leads most hikers to believe that it only leads to Lake James. It is true that the north and east segments of the Loop are longer (by .5+ mile) than the far more commonly used west and south segments. But the east side of the Loop travels through lush forest, whereas the western Loop mostly traverses the steep west bank of the Carbon River in the open, without the benefit of shade.

If crossing the river from east to west, we recommend the suspension bridge route. The northern (lower) crossing's log bridges and trail might give a westbound hiker some route finding problems, especially if visibility is restricted.

THE CARBON RIVER

The Carbon River has a beauty all its' own. It's hard to believe when you look into the swirling brown waters that fish could survive, but they do: char have been caught just downstream from the Ipsut Creek Campground! Far downstream from the Park boundaries, the silt-laden waters of the Carbon merge into he Puyallup River, below the town of Orting. Known thereafter as the Puyallup, the now-merged waters of the North and South Mowich, Carbon and Puyallup Rivers eventually find their way into Tacoma's Commencement Bay. Because of the Carbon's close proximity to the Ipsut Creek Campground and several miles of trail, it is easily accessible and offers an invitation to explore the riverbed itself.

But Beware! Behind the beauty lurks danger. Because it is so laden with rock flour, the river's water is unfit for drinking, and the water's opaqueness makes it impossible to tell how deep it is at any given point. Also be aware that this river's water is extremely cold, runs very fast, and is full of tumbling boulders and other debris. The river (and its many braided channels) change course frequently and leave the landscape looking different every year. Also, the grey rocks and their similarity in appearance up and down the river bed may make it difficult to find distinguishing landmarks (particularly when mist rises off the river in warm weather, during periods of inclement weather, or early morning or late evening.)

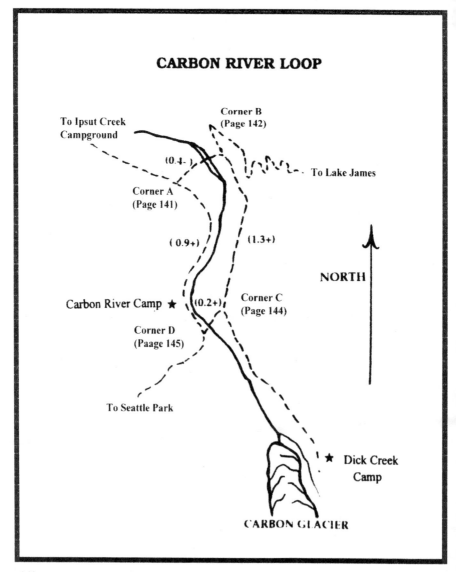

CARBON RIVER LOOP - NORTH

Corner "A"
(Lower River Crossing via Log Bridges)

Mileage begins at sign (below) located at the junction of the Wonderland Trail and the trail (described here) to the Northern Loop. It should be noted that the signage on both ends of this trail segment inaccurately refer to it as the Northern Loop Trail, when in fact, it is only a connector between the Wonderland Trail and the Northern Loop Trail. This trail begins by descending a talus slope, and turning to the east.

From W to E	From E to W	
0.0	0.4-	Sign reads:

```
┌─────────────────────────────────────────────┐
│              NORTHERN LOOP                    │
│                                               │
│   4.6 Windy Gap (7.6km)     (actual 4.6+)    │
│   6.5 Lake James (10.8km)   (actual 6.7+)    │
│                                               │
│            WONDERLAND TRAIL                   │
│                                               │
│   1.5 Carbon Glacier    (actual 1.7-)        │
│   5.6 Mystic Lake    (actual 5.7-)           │
│   Isput Campground 2.0    (actual 2.2-)      │
└─────────────────────────────────────────────┘
```

0.1-	0.3+	First log bridge (with wire rail) across side channel of Carbon River. From the bridge the trail enters a forested "island".
0.2-	0.2+	Abandoned trail on right. Main trail veers left.
0.2+	0.2-	Second log bridge (with wire rail) crosses another side channel of the river. Looking east from this bridge, you can usually see the third and fourth bridges across the river and the trail switchbacking up the far slope. From this vantage, all three bridges are in a line, (though this may change in future years as frequent bridge washouts require rerouting this trail segment).
0.3-	0.1+	Third log bridge (with wire rail) crosses the largest side channel. There are no cairns marking the trail across the riverbed to the next bridge and it is possible that water maybe running along the trail.

<u>Note to hikers traveling from east to west</u>: routefinding may be difficult, especially between the first bridge you cross and the second. If you get lost, proceed no further. DO NOT CROSS THIS RIVER WITHOUT A BRIDGE. It should not be attempted under any circumstances. If you are unable to find any of the four lower crossing bridges, go back the way you came, hike south on the West Loop Trail to Corner C and cross the river via the suspension bridge.

0.3+   0.1-   Fourth log bridge with wire rail crosses the Carbon River. Trail climbs quickly up the river bank in three switchbacks to trail junction.

0.4-   0.0   Intersection with Northern Loop (Lake James) Trail (page 160 and 176) and Carbon River Loop - East, (Corner B) below.

CARBON RIVER LOOP - EAST

Corner "B"
Northern Loop Trail between Log Bridges crossing
and Suspension Bridge

Mileage begins at sign (below) located at junction of the Carbon River Loop - North (lower river crossing via log bridges), and the Northern Loop Trail. The trail begins by traversing the eastern slope of the Carbon River bed, heading south through old growth forest.

From   **From**
(N to S)   **(S to N)**

0.0   1.3+   Sign reads:

```
┌─────────────────────────────────────┐
│                                      │
│       NORTHERN LOOP TRAIL            │
│                                      │
│   1.5 Carbon Glacier   (actual 1.6+) │
│      Windy Gap 4.3    (actual 4.3+)  │
│      Lake James 6.2   (actual 6.4+)  │
│                                      │
└─────────────────────────────────────┘
```

```
┌─────────────────────────────────────────┐
│                                          │
│          NORTHERN LOOP TRAIL             │
│                                          │
│      Wonderland Trail 0.2   (actual 0.4-)│
│      Ipsut Campground 2.2   (actual 2.6+)│
│                                          │
└─────────────────────────────────────────┘
```

0.1-   1.2+   Cross streamlet. Look up to see the lower moss-covered reaches of Alice Falls.

0.2-   1.0-   Cross first of three log bridges (with rails) across branches of Spukwash Creek. Steep liffs visible above. This Klickitat Indian name (also formerly spelled Spunkwash and Spuckwash) means "many small streams."

0.4+   0.9-   Cross streambed (could be dry) via two 20' log bridges. Wide trail climbs gently through the trees.

0.5+   0.08   "The green cathedral". The forest here is beautiful with moss-covered boulders and a gradual ascending soft, needle-covered trail through thick forest. Lust ferns line the "cushioned" trail. Crescent Mountain momentarily visible to the southeast. This is one of the nicest sections of forest on the entire trail.

1.0+   0.3-   Finally! Padded rocks! Numerous moss-covered rocks provide cushioned seats. You halfway expect to see a forest gnome pop out from behind a stump and sit beside you! If there were little people in the forest, this is where they would live. This wonderful section of forest looks like it was designed by Walt Disney.

1.1-   0.2-   Lush undergrowth makes this trail the quintessential stretch of Mount Rainier forest hiking. Thick moss adorns everything.

1.3+   0.0   Intersection with Wonderland Trail (to Mystic Lake), and Carbon River Loop - South.

CARBON RIVER LOOP - SOUTH

Corner "C"
(Upper River Crossing via Suspension Bridge)

Mileage begins at sign (below), located at the junction of the Wonderland Trail and the Carbon River Loop - East (Northern Loop trail to Lake James). The trail begins by heading west (as the Wonderland Trail) toward the river.

From   **From**
E to W   **W to E**

0.0   0.2+   Sign reads:

> **Wonderland Trail**
>
> Carbon Glacier 0.4   (actual 0.3-)
> Mystic Lake 4.5   (actual 4.5+)

> **NORTHERN LOOP TRAIL**
>
> Windy Gap 5.4   (actual 5.5-)
> Lake James 7.3   (actual 7.5-)

> **WONDERLAND TRAIL**
>
> Carbon River Camp 0.3   (actual 0.3-)
> Ipsut Campground 3.1   (actual 3.3-)

0.1-   0.2-   Cross the Carbon River on a spectacular metal suspension bridge with wood decking. According to MRNP Trail Supervisor Carl Fabiani, who oversaw the bridge's construction, the deck is now noticeably higher above the river than when it was built. (Apparently because the river has eroded away the riverbed beneath it). In 1984, the bridge was built (from a prefabricated "kit" brought in by helicopter). It is suspended from four 24' towers, and spans 205' from bank to bank.

The bridge deck sways easily, especially if more than one person at a time is aboard. Walk slowly and steadily down the center of the wood planking to minimize swaying if you're prone to seasickness! Also, keep a close eye on small children (the sway might surprise them).

Once across, the trail descends the west bank of the river a short distance to the next trail sign.

0.2+   0.0   Intersection with Spray Park Trail and Carbon River Loop - West. Corner D, (below)

CARBON RIVER LOOP - WEST

Corner "D"
(Wonderland Trail Between Suspension Bridge
And Log Bridges Crossing)

Mileage begins at signs (below) located at junction of Spray Park Trail and Wonderland Trail from Ipsut Pass (and Ipsut Campground). Trail begins headed north across a forested slope.

From   **From**
(S to N) **(N to S)**

0.0   0.9+   Sign reads:

```
┌─────────────────────────────────────────────┐
│             WONDERLAND TRAIL                  │
│                                               │
│       Carbon Glacier 0.6   (actual 0.5-)      │
│       Mystic Lake 4.7   (actual 4.8+)         │
│       Carbon River Camp 0.1   (actual 0.1-)   │
│       Ipsut Campground 2.9   (actual 3.1+)    │
│                                               │
└─────────────────────────────────────────────┘

┌─────────────────────────────────────────────┐
│             SPRAY PARK TRAIL                  │
│                                               │
│       Cataract Valley 1.6   (actual 1.6+)     │
│       Seattle Park 3.2   (actual 3.5+)        │
│       Spray Park 5.3   (actual 5.3+)          │
│                                               │
└─────────────────────────────────────────────┘
```

| 0.1- | 0.9- | 62' log bridge (with wire rail) over Cataract Creek. Nice resting spot on north side of creek. Spectacular view of this cascading stream. |

| 0.1 | 0.8+ | **CARBON RIVER CAMP.** (3,100') The first campsite is 65' from the main trail, nestled among the scattered logs of a blowdown. Camp has four individual sites, one above another, also one uncovered toilet. Site 4 is the nicest. It even has a small table fashioned out of an old wire spool. (A memento of the suspension bridge construction, we'll bet.) The trail leading to the Ipsut Creek campground used to change annually with the river, however in 1990 it was moved off the valley floor and should now be safe from damage. At one time the Carbon River Road came up this far! |

Ahead the trail passes under overhanging cliffs. Carbon Glacier and Willis Wall visible to the south.

| 0.2- | 0.7- | Trail crosses two large metal culverts in a thicket of devils club. Trail now descends to the river bank and leaves the forest. |

| 0.6+ | 0.3- | Large 35' sitting log (on river side of trail). Trail is now only a few feet away from the river. |

The trail now enters the forest. Descent is gradual, and the trail is rocky, sometime crossing talus. Note for hikers headed north to south: Carbon Glacier and the left skyline of Mount Rainier (Curtis Ridge) soon become visible.

| 0.9+ | 0.0 | Intersection with Carbon River Loop - North, Corner A, (lower river crossing via log bridges). Described on page 141. |

The Carbon River Suspension Bridge   Ed Walsh Photo

CARBON RIVER TO SUNRISE
VIA MYSTIC LAKE

This segment will appeal to glacier fans, for it has not just one glacier, but two of them, — and both at very close range. In fact, much of this segment will be spent within sight of these glaciers, both beside them and above them. But the trip will begin with little hint of the grandeur and proportion of things to come.

There are two approaches: from the Wonderland Trail via Ipsut Pass, and from the Ipsut Creek Campground (connected by a .3+ spur). Regardless of the starting point, this stretch of the Wonderland connects with Corner C of what we refer to as the "Carbon River Loop". This loop offers hikers a choice of two routes toward the continuation to Mystic Lake.

The choice of route through the Carbon River Loop will depend on how a hiker wishes to cross the Carbon River. For eastbound hikers, we recommend the northern (lower) river crossing, via log bridges, and for westbound hikers, the southern (upper) river crossing, via the suspension bridge. The four trail segments of the Carbon River Loop are described on pages 131, 141 and 146.

Once past the southern river crossing, the scenery changes abruptly as the trail begins a steady climb up the steep east side of the glacier. The climb will be long, hot, and at moments uncomfortable. Nevertheless few tarry for long after looking at the rugged Northern Crags towering overhead and the massive gaping Carbon Glacier below them.

Where there are glaciers, there's danger, a fact deserving of some serious consideration during the two or so days spent doing this portion. The greatest danger comes not from the glaciers themselves, but from rock. Rock in the form of cliffs, rock-fall, rockslides, exposed rocky trails and rock falling off the glacier. (The latter poses no problem unless the hiker leaves the trail and makes side trips to or beneath the glaciers.)

Once safely on the lower slopes of Pacific Point, beyond Dick Creek, it takes nothing but determination and strong legs to finish the climb to Moraine Park and on to Mystic Lake.

Moraine Park is a spacious and open rolling meadow with a straight-on view of Willis Wall. The Mountain looks close enough to touch, but don't try from here. A little further ahead is a short side trail leading to a spectacular view.

Get a good night's rest when camping at Mystic Lake because the following day will be a long one if you're going on in to Sunrise. Try to get an early start tomorrow too, for it will be a "fun" day, and the hiker will want a little extra time for exploration and sightseeing. The descent to Winthrop Glacier won't take too long, but the climb up to Skyscraper Pass on Packtrain Ridge will be slow. The grade is persistent and constant, but a good consistent rest step will soon eat up the miles and leave the hiker little worse for wear.

An hour or so from the top, the forest cover will begin to thin, then disappear completely, and there will be Skyscraper, with an open invitation to "bag this peak." It's an easy gentle climb and, if time permits (it takes about an hour round trip), accept the invitation. Once seeing the peak in retrospect on the distant skyline, hikers invariably regret it if they didn't make the climb when the opportunity was there.

Hikers "smell the oats in the barn" once they get to the gap, but the distance is deceiving. There are still almost two hours of hiking ahead before reaching Sunrise and the campgrounds.

The descent from the west side of the pass won't be difficult but take time to stop and study Berkeley Park and the more distant Grand Park as they come into view. The relatively short distance and easy access to Sunrise make both areas good ones to bring the whole family back into some day. (The Berkeley Park shelter is 0.7 mile farther down the valley, and is not visible from the Wonderland Trail.)

Soon the small sign posts on the top of the divide by Frozen Lake will be silhouetted against the skyline (looking momentarily like crosses at Calvary), and a little more plodding will find the party peering over the fence at Frozen Lake. (Fenced because it's the water supply for Sunrise.)

From the lake on, the "high road" goes into the area of the Visitor Center, while the "low road" will deliver the group to the Lower Campground, still over a mile from the "civilized" area of Sunrise. Access trails from both areas lead to the next segment of the Wonderland Trail which drops down over the steep hill to the White River Campground.

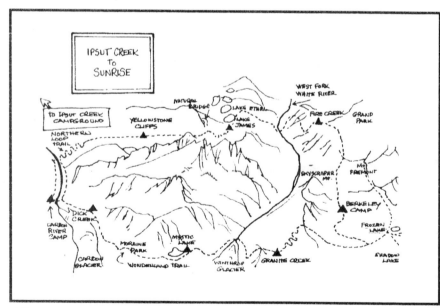

IPSUT CREEK TO SUNRISE
VIA MYSTIC LAKE

TRAIL CONDITION: The initial two-mile stretch of this trail was once a road which facilitated access to the glacier, It went nearly to Cataract Creek. (It has been rerouted countless times by the river, and more recently (in 1989 and 90) by the Park Service. To those who do much hiking in the backcountry out of Ipsut Creek, adding those extra 2+ miles to the beginning and end of every trip becomes a nemesis.

The Wonderland Trail beyond, climbing up beside the Carbon Glacier is "hairy" as our young hikers put it, but fabulously interesting! Beyond, the trail is in excellent condition all the way through to Sunrise.

IPSUT CREEK CAMPGROUND TO CARBON RIVER LOOP

TRAIL BEGINS: This measurement begins at the Ipsut Creek Trailhead, south of the campground. (The sign at the campground says "Wonderland Trail". It is, in fact, a 0.3- spur trail leading to the Wonderland Trail.)

Sign reads:

```
┌──────────────────────────────────────────┐
│                                            │
│           WONDERLAND TRAIL                 │
│                                            │
│    Northern Loop Trail 2.0    (act 2.2-) → │
│    Carbon Glacier 3.5    (actual 3.7-) →   │
│    Mowich Lake 5.3    (actual 5.3-) →      │
│                                            │
└──────────────────────────────────────────┘
```

0.2-   Sign at side trail heading to the right reads:

```
┌──────────────────────────────────────────┐
│              IPSUT FALLS →                 │
└──────────────────────────────────────────┘
```

0.3-   **WONDERLAND TRAIL JUNCTION.** The right fork climbs uphill to Ipsut Pass, the left fork, (straight ahead) leads to the Carbon River Loop at Corner A, and from each corner of the Loop (clockwise) (B) to Lake James, (C) Mystic Lake, and (D) to Seattle & Spray Parks.

IPSUT CAMPGROUND TRAIL JUNCTION TO SUNRISE
VIA MYSTIC LAKE

WONDERLAND TRAIL

← Northern Loop 1.7   (actual 1.7-)
← Carbon Glacier 3.2   (actual 3.4-)
(our measure above is to the Carbon Glacier sign)
← Mystic Lake 7.0   (actual 7.2-)

WONDERLAND TRAIL

Mowich Lake 5.0   (actual 5.1-) →
Ipsut Pass 3.5   (actual 3.6-) →

Another sign (a few feet down the Carbon River segment of the trail) reads "No horses". This applies to those going south to Seattle and Spray Parks and east to Lake James and Mystic Lake. Horses or (other pack animals) are allowed on the Ipsut Pass trail only.

0.6+   Abandoned trail intersection on left.

1.0   Old 2' high stump on left. A shortly ahead is a 48' barrier log on the left.

1.3   Trail enters a devils club and salmonberry thicket alongside a channel of the Carbon River.

1.5-   Begin crossing an old rockslide at a 15 degree angle. There used to be a sign on the trail which said that this slide occurred in 1905. (This was a BIG event and a major slide!)

1.7+   End of slide crossing.

2.0-   Cross a vine maple draw. It is exactly two miles to the Ipsut Trailhead from here.

2.2-   Carbon Loop trails North and West. (Page 141). Proceed from here over river crossing of your choice. As described in the Carbon River Loop Chapter, we recommend the northern (lower) river crossing from this point. Trail continues (below) following Corner C.

Resuming from Corner C

CARBON RIVER LOOP JUNCTION TO MYSTIC LAKE

TRAIL RESUMES: This measurement resumes at the Southeast corner of the Carbon River Loop, (Corner C), where the Northern Loop Trail intersects the Wonderland Trail, just east of the suspension bridge. (page 144). From here to Dick Creek Camp is tick territory, so check yourself during your next rest stop. Trail heads southeast, climbing across a forested slope.

3.3+   Large resting rock juts into trail from the uphill side. The trail now climbs steadily across boulder-strewn slopes just beneath a sheer rock wall. The snout of the Carbon Glacier looms directly ahead.

3.7-

CARBON GLACIER
DANGER
Falling rock, swift water, cave-ins.
Stay away from Glacier and river.

Heed the sign! Resist the urge to explore it closer. This is an active glacier. There is always danger from rockfall, icefall and boulders melting out of the ice.

CARBON GLACIER. (elevation 3,400'). An unobstructed view of the glacier snout that is now less than 500' away. The Carbon Glacier terminus is the lowest of any glacier in the lower 48 states. Does the thick layer of rock surprise you? This glacier is not pretty and white as one would expect, but instead is dark gray. Much of the rock you now see on the glacier is from a major rockfall which occurred on the face of Willis Wall in 1911! It constitutes most of the glacier's surface rock today. Some experts believe this rock serves to "insulate" the glacier and is one of the reasons the Carbon's terminus is so low.

As the rocky trail continues to climb across the steep east bank of the glacier, you will be serenaded with a constant crescendo of pops, bangs, and occasionally, startlingly loud rockslides, all courtesy of the glacier.

Take a moment to cast a wary eye on the sheer lower cliffs of the Northern Crags, located above you.

3.7+   A streamlet emerges from beneath a large rock on the uphill side of the trail.
        The edge of the glacier is now about 150' away! Loose rocks and gravel
        make for slippery footing, especially if wet and you are descending.) The
        trail now climbs more sharply up the slope.

3.8+   Sign:

> **DANGER**
> TRAIL CLOSED
> STEEP WASHOUT
> ← NEW TRAIL

This is the first of two switchbacks. Shade is hard to find, but the
magnificent panorama of Mount Rainier and the Carbon Glacier more than
compensates for it.

The upper reaches of Willis Wall are visible. This rock face contributes
of some of the glacier's incredible rock topping, as do the crumbly rock
walls of lower Curtis Ridge. This huge ice conveyor groans down the
mountain with its' load of rock, dumping it into the swift waters of the
Carbon River. The erosive powers of water, fluid or frozen, are a marvel to
behold!

Dinni Fabiani Photo

Mountaineers of old seemed to wax poetic at sights like this, and Edmund Meany was no exception. Here are some excerpts of his inspiration from this point:

"CARBON CLACIER"

Thy open lips of ice doth pour
A gushing stream in noisy flood
A stream .released in joyful roar;
Behold! A glacier's milk-white blood.

    Grind, grind, grind
        to crumbling dust these stones!
    Grind, grind, grind
        The Mountain's shatteredbones!

How weak the pen, how vain the brush
    to catch the hues of this deep gash!
How here revealed thy power to crush,
    How awful is thy breathing's crash!

    Grind, grind, grind
        The rocks however hurled!
    Grind, grind, grind
        Thou mill-stone of aworld!

New life from death, eternal whirl,
    How brief each puny span of life!
How long the atoms, grinding swirl,
    Ere seized anew for a season's strife!

    Grind, grind, grind
        to powder every stone!
    Grind, grind, grind
        New life will deathatone!

I mount thy shoulders' utmost height,
Where threat"'ning ice-cliffs poise andnod,
    Where avalanches roar in flight,
    Like flying demons cursed of God

    Grind, grind, grind
        and grind exceeding fine!
    Grind, grind, grind
        My Father's will and thine!

Edmund S. Meany
- August5, 1909

3.9- Trail reenters forest. Less than 100' ahead is a duplicate of the "trail closed" sign above, on the uphill end of the abandoned stretch of trail.

4.0 Log bridge (with wire rail) crosses Dick Creek.

4.1- **DICK CREEK CAMP.** (elevation 4320'). A nice spot offering three good tent sites as well as hammock trees. The **WATER** source is nearby Dick Creek by the footbridge (Dick Creek drains the Elysian Fields 1,700 feet above and flows west into Moraine Creek, a tributary of the Carbon River. It was named for Dick Williams, a former Park employee.) Just west a cliff drops away to the glacier.

Sign reads:

```
┌─────────────────────────────────────────────┐
│                                               │
│              DICK CREEK CAMP                  │
│              NO WOOD FIRES                    │
│                                               │
└─────────────────────────────────────────────┘
```

The Wonderland Trail from this point is rocky, steep, and increasingly rugged. The climb (via 15-20 good switchbacks under good forest cover) begins almost immediately after leaving the camp.

4.8- Boulder cliff above trail.

5.1+ **WATER.** A swift fresh stream (and falls above) which cascades down from subalpine areas just south of Pacific Point. Stepping stones across water. This is a good place for a rest stop, to have a drink of the cool (treat it) water and bask on the comfy rocks.

5.2+ 71-foot wide slide area. Trail rocky and unstable.

5.3- Begin long, gentle half-mile traverse.

5.8+ End of traverse, begin switchbacks.

6.3+ **MORAINE PARK.** (elevation 5100'). Beginning of this beautiful alpine park aptly named because it is built on the moraine of an earlier edge of Carbon Glacier. Enjoy the excellent view of the Mountain from this glorious open flower meadow and the antics of some of the large colonies of Moraine Park whistling marmots.

Beyond this point the trail passes through a small grove of trees into a large open rolling meadow. If going on to Mystic Lake (1.1+ miles farther), continue through the meadow before climbing the rise to the east of the park.

Ahead is a way trail at the small pond (at the top of the divide), which leads to a viewpoint overlooking the Carbon Glacier and a head-on look at the Mountain. Avalanches are frequently seen falling from precipitous 3,600-foot high Willis Wall with its 300 foot thick ice cap. Covering a diameter of a mile and a half, the base is the beginning of the Carbon Glacier.

This tiny pond is called Reflection Pond by some and Frog Pond by others because late in Summer it's black with pollywogs.

6.6+   Beginning of steep climb and final ascent.

6.8+   Climb still steep. Trail rocky over (dry) creek bed. Many large comfortable boulders for great rest spots. Musical selections will be presented by one of the famous Mount Rainier whistling marmot choirs.

6.9-   Final switchback. Open hillside, sparsely treed. At top of rise, is a nice grove of trees. A pretty little lake lies south of the trail (not visible from trail). Sign reads:

```
MYSTIC LAKE 0.8
```

Leaving here, the Wonderland descends to the valley in 5 switchbacks.

7.2-   A pleasant little storybook valley, complete with bubbling brook and footlog crossing. Note the large rectangular cave high up on old Desolate (to the left). That's a natural (not man-made) cave, and though it looks impressive, it doesn't go very far back into the Mountain..

Note the view of Skyscraper Mountain far to the east. That gap to the right of Skyscraper will be crossed tomorrow if continuing east. Begin the final short haul to Mystic from this point, taking care not to shortcut and make footsteps erosion can follow.

7.4+ **MYSTIC LAKE.** (Elevation 5700 feet). Sign reads:

```
MYSTIC LAKE
NO FIRES
Camp only at Campground
Beyond far end of Lake Trail
```

Visiting professors J. B. Flett (after whom Flett Glacier was named), and H. H. Garretson named this lake after seeing what they thought was a mysterious whirlpool near the lake's outlet.

For the next 0.4- miles, the trail skirts the south side of Mystic Lake through the meadow. It is a good quick trail with a bridge and several boardwalks over typically muddy areas.

7.8+   Signs:

```
┌─────────────────────────────────────────────┐
│                                             │
│              MYSTIC CAMP 0.2 →              │
│                                             │
└─────────────────────────────────────────────┘
```

```
┌─────────────────────────────────────────────┐
│                                             │
│              WONDERLAND TRAIL               │
│                                             │
│   Mystic Camp 0.2 (0.3 km)   (actual 0.3-)  │
│   Ipsut Creek 7.6 (13.1 km)  (actual 7.8+)  │
│                                             │
└─────────────────────────────────────────────┘
```

```
┌─────────────────────────────────────────────┐
│                                             │
│                 MYSTIC LAKE                 │
│                     ←                       │
│          Ranger Station 0.2 mi. 0.3 km.     │
│                                             │
└─────────────────────────────────────────────┘
```

8.1+   Camp only at the designated camping area. There are 7 individual sites here and 2 group sites. Pick a nice hillside site with views of Old Desolate and Mineral Mountain.

The general area is very marshy, and early in the season, the mosquitoes are nearly intolerable. They defy **any** repellent! Be sure to hang packs. (Cables are already strung). There was once a penned sign here which read "No mice — just bears." The old-time bears must have been pretty fertile bruins. Lots of their descendents still live around Mystic Lske. A mother Bear with three (no kidding, THREE) cubs greeted virtually everybody coming through in 2001.

Mystic continues to be a good fishing lake, even though no longer stocked. It's a favorite among fly fishermen, but even non-anglers will enjoy watching the fish rise and feed in the evening when the surface of the lake seems to come alive.

There's no sign of the old Mineral Mountain Mine on the North side of Mineral Mountain anymore. It's another vestige of history now reverted to nature. Those old miners were a hardy bunch. The only access from here was by foot or horse. All ore had to be taken out in saddlebags on mules to Wilkeson, Carbanado or Fairfax. Whew!

Edmund Meany was inspired here too. He called Mystic Lake, "Just a laughing little mirror, just a shining little gem."

MYSTIC LAKE TO SUNRISE

ELEVATION: Gain: 2,570'   Loss: 1,990'

MEASUREMENT BEGINS: At signs where trail leaves the lake. Climb a short rise to the top of the hill overlooking lake. Descent begins through small open meadow, then switchbacks down the steep gully.

0.2-   Signs are:

> **MYSTIC CAMP**
> No Wood Fires

> Mystic Lake 0.2   (actual 0.2-)
> Ranger Station 0.4   (actual 0.4-)

0.3-   Sign reads:

> Mystic Camp 0.1   (actual 0.1+)

The Wonderland Trail in this vicinity is a nice trail. It soon descends steeply to the now audible creeks.

1.0-   Stream crossing via two one-log bridges (the second with a wire handhold). This swift stream originates in a snowfield high on Mineral Mountain.

1.2+   Old riverbed crossing. Rock cairn marks the trail.

1.2+   **WEST FORK OF THE WHITE RIVER CROSSING.** Look for cairns visible on far side. Bridges are probably out because river keeps re-routing in this area. It's difficult to gauge depth because the water looks more like chocolate milk. (Also note that cairns do not always mark the best river crossings. Hikers need to scout around and judge for themselves where to cross.)

If you have to ford this, don't do it alone. Wait for other people and do it as a group. It would help to pass packs across. If wearing pack across, undo your waist strap, get a stick and plant it downstream so each step is supported. Cross at angle to flow.

This swift turbulent river originates at about the 4,700-foot terminus of the Winthrop Glacier. You're crossing part of the headwaters of the White

River, which once flowed north to Puget Sound through the Kent-Auburn Valley. During flooding in 1906, it jumped to a new channel to flow into the Puyallup River. Engineers have now made the change permanent. Today this water will ultimately turn the turbines which will generate 63,400 kilowatts of electricity, and is enough to supply the power for two or three small cities. (And here you are jumping across it!)

When the power is not needed locally, it is "put into the grid" and may be diverted to as far away as California. By the time the White River gets to the generating plant, two miles north of Sumner, it will be draining 425 square miles of rugged country on the western slope of the Cascades.

On August 16, 1989, in the biggest rock avalanche since the Little Tahoma event, (page 13) debris fell from the cliffs of Curtis Ridge (at about the 11,800' level) in the north side of the Mountain onto the Winthrop Glacier, finally stopping at about the 6,400 foot level. Fortunately there were no climbers on the glacier when the house-sized boulders came roaring down. But in Seattle, at the University of Washington Geophysics labs, 75 miles away, seismic instruments registered the activity. It was the first time such a rockslide had ever been detected and located remotely.

(For information on the east fork of the White River, see page 179).

1.5- Small stream crosses trail Avalanche area. (Note all tree tops are broken off at the same height). MANY downed trees! After leaving here, begin paralleling river. (In 1991 there was a little rerouting begun here to put the trail on higher ground.)

1.8- Rolling trail through beautiful forest grown on old moraine. West Fork still to the left. Blue huckleberries.

2.0+ Leave tree cover. Begin final descent to the river. Trail still on moraine. Great view here!

2.2+ View of falls across glacier.

2.3- Top of a rise. Big boulder seat to the right of the rocky trail. Area of large moraine ahead, then trail enters woods.

2.5- **WINTHROP CREEK.** (elevation 4900'). This creek originates from the second largest glacier on the Mountain. (3.5 square miles in size, 5.0 miles in length). The glacier was named for popular nineteenth-century author, Theodore Winthrop, who saw it in 1853 and described it in a book called *The Canoe and the Saddle.*

Footlog crosses this chocolate milk creek. This creek is one the many tributaries of the White River and will merge with the West Fork about a mile downstream.

On far side of bridge, begin persistent 2-mile climb to Granite Creek.

2.6-   **GARDA FALLS.** A former trail camp beside Granite Creek. (Camping prohibited here now.) This falls was named in honor of Miss Garda Fogg of Tacoma by a popular turn-of-the-century park photographer. 25' log bridge crosses the creek.

2.9-   **WATER.** Streamlet crosses trail. Last of the tree cover for a while. Trail ahead is open, and very rocky. Several switchbacks follow.

3.1+   Last switchback directly above the glacier. Bad dropoff. Trail rocky and open. Begin steep climb with many switchbacks. Ahead trail enters woods. *Steep!*

3.3-   Several bridges over marsh and streamlets. Trail very steep in places.

3.5-   Right turn followed by switchback. This marks the top of the very steep stretch. (However the trail continues to have occasional short steep pitches.)

4.3-   Two 2-log bridges (side by side logs).

4.5+   **GRANITE CREEK CAMP.** (elevation 5,730'). A 17-foot split-log crossing over swift water. A good camp (2 sites) on the east side of creek. **Water** to the left of trail. Leaving here, the trail climbs gradually through spruce forest, crossing several small bridges.

> **← GRANITE CREEK CAMP →**
> Stoves Only

4.7+   9-foot bridge at base of gully. (no water) Trail climbs more gradually.

5.0+   **A historical spot.** This was the site of an early prospector cabin. It contained signatures dating from 1935. The remains stood until the mid-1970's. **WATER** available from stream.

5.3-   Trail enters the sparsely-treed subalpine meadows.

5.6+   End of sparse forest cover. Skyscraper Mountain in full view. Gradual climb through open meadow to the saddle.

5.9+   **TOP OF SKYSCRAPER RIDGE.** Great views in all directions. Glacier Peak and the Stuart Range to the north, Echo and Observation Rocks on the western horizon, and an unobstructed view of Mount Rainier and Little Tahoma. Trail narrow and rocky. From here Skyscraper is a 20-30 minute climb and well worth every minute of it.

6.0+   From the saddle, begin to descend through the rock slide area above and below the trail.

6.3+   Begin series of little bridges. A good view of Little Tahoma straight ahead. The foot-wide pumice trail descends steadily.

6.6-   Stone bridge over running water (culvert pipe.) Shortly ahead is a bridge over swift tumbling (fresh) **WATER.** Glacier Peak visible to the north. Trail begins to cross open rolling meadow. Fresh springs 20 feet to the left of trail (**ice cold water**).

6.7-   Traverse rock area. Berkeley Park visible below.

6.8-   Footbridge over run-off ditch. Cross open meadow with good view to the north of Grand Park and Mount Baker 100 miles farther to the north.

7.0+   Top of rise. Cross short open meadow with a few alpine firs, then a short descent to Porcupine Flat.

7.2-   **NORTHERN LOOP TRAIL JUNCTION** (elevation 6,400') coming in from the left from Berkeley Park. Signs ahead (at 7.2+) read:

> **WONDERLAND TRAIL**
> Sunrise 2.3   (actual 2.3)

> **WONDERLAND TRAIL**
> ← Mystic Lake   (actual 7.2-)
> Northern Loop Trail →
> Berkeley Campsite 1.5 →

The trail junction is on open mountainside. Depending on the time of year, upon leaving here, you will either pass through much pretty pink lava and volcanic rock, or cross snow patches.

7.4+   Pretty rock borders on a very "Wonderlandish" trail.

7.7+   Little melt lake and permanent snow patch to right of trail. (This is a reminder that you are at high elevation. This trail is well-traveled by tourists who don't respect it for the high-country it really is and are frequently not prepared for the sudden changes of weather which can occur just an hour from their cars.)

7.9+   **FROZEN LAKE INTERSECTION. (elevation** 6,730'). This is one of the windiest, coldest spots on the whole trail (and when it was a campsite, it had to have been **the** coldest!) Keep in mind the wind chill factor if lingering here. The many signs are as follows:

WONDERLAND TRAIL
←Mystic Lake   (actual 7.9+)
Northern Loop Trail 0.8   (actual 0.7+)
Berkeley Campsite 1.5→   (actual 2.2+)

WONDERLAND TRAIL
Sunrise 2.3   (actual 1.6+)

MOUNT FREMONT TRAIL
Fremont Lookout 1.3

BURROUGHS MOUNTAIN TRAIL
Second Burroughs Mountain 1.5
Sunrise Camp   2.0

WONDERLAND TRAIL
Sunrise Camp 1.0
North Loop Trail 0.8   (actual 0.7+)
Mystic 7.0   (actual 7.9+)

SOURDOUGH RIDGE TRAIL
Sunrise 1.5 mi.

Sign along fence:

DOMESTIC WATER SUPPLY
KEEP OUT

Here the hiker must decide whether to go into the main Visitor Center area of Sunrise, the Sunrise campground or keep going to the White River Campground. From Frozen Lake, after a very short rise, the trail descends the entire way to the campground which is 1.3 miles behind the Visitor Center.

The "high road" is the more interesting of the two trails, (particularly if you're not going to the Sunrise Campground) for shortly after leaving Frozen Lake, a spectacular view of Sunrise comes into sight.

FROZEN LAKE TO SUNRISE VIA HIGH ROUTE

From Mystic Lake	From Lake James	
7.9+	10.5-	Frozen Lake Intersection
8.1-	10.6+	(Sign) "Water Supply - Stay Out"
8.2-	10.7+	(Sign) "Sourdough Trail"
8.2+	10.8+	(Sign) "Wonderland Trail"
		Junction with another trail to. Frozen Lake. 100-foot slide area has man-made retaining wall to left. campground visible below.
8.8-	11.3+	**Huckleberry Creek Trail Junction**
		"Forest Lake 1.9"
9.1-	11.7-	**Wonderland Trail Junction Sign:**
		Huckleberry Trail 0.5 (actual .3+) Mystic Lake 8.3 (actual 9.0-)|
9.5+	12.0+	**Sunrise Visitor Center Flag Pole**

VIA LOW ROUTE

FROZEN LAKE TO LOWER CAMPGROUND VAI LOW ROUTE

From Mystic Lake	From Lake James	The Lower Campground Trail cuts off to the right at Frozen Lake Intersection
7.9+	10.5-	Frozen Lake intersection at top of rise. Very rocky. Pink lavaabove and below trail
8.3-	10.8	Junction with service road. Bear right on road to camp 0.4+ Left via road to Sunrise 0.9
8.4-	11.0-	Sunrise Camp Sign:

> **SUNRISE RIM TRAIL**
>
> Wonderland Trail 0.8
> Sunrise 1.3

9.4+   Sign at Sunrise:

> **WONDERLAND TRAIL**
>
> Burroughs Mountain 1.1
> Berkeley Park 3.8   (actual)
> Lake James 11.2   (actual 12.0+)

At 6,400 feet, this "top of the world" park sits astride a three mile long plateau with an eagle's eye view of Mount Rainier, Little Tahoma, the Emmons and Winthrop Glaciers. To the south the Goat Rocks Wilderness Area and the second highest peak in the Pacific Northwest, Mount Adams, the can be seen. Mount Adams is also a volcano, and Goat Rocks are the remains of an old stratovolcano.

Because of the easterly site of Sunrise, it sits in the "rain shadow" of the mountain and is sheltered from storms coming in from the Pacific Ocean. The Mountain diverts the flow of moisture-laden air and causes it to lose the bulk of its precipitation over the southern and western slopes. That's also why it seems warmer and dryer at Sunrise than at Paradise, and why the subalpine flower meadows are slightly different from those found elsewhere around the Mountain.

This place was a favorite spot of the Yakima Indians and their leader, Chief Owhi, who loved to come here for hunting, horse racing and berry picking. Thus it was originally called Yakima Park (from 'Me-yah-ah-pah' meaning "place of the chief").

Much to the chagrin of the good people of Yakima, the name was changed to the more poetic "Sunrise." This was because of the predictable beauty of the sun rising over the Cascades, painting Sunrise, and the eastern flank of The Mountain, with it's warming rays and pastel colors long before lighting up the lower valleys.

National Park Service Photo

Can this be Sunrise? It can, and it is. Earlier this century (in 1931) the Rainier National Park Company built this "resort."

ALTERNATE ROUTE
NORTHERN LOOP TRAIL

This segment of trail has earned the worst reputation of any stretch in the park. Most experienced wilderness hikers agree it came by this reputation honestly.

No matter which direction it is traveled, the hiker will be impressed by the punishment it inflicts. Traveling clockwise, and coming in from the west, the relentless climb to Windy Gap will gain 3,000 feet in 4 miles from the northeast corner of the Carbon River Loop (or 3,500 feet in 6 miles if coming all the way in from Ipsut Creek Campground). From the Gap, it's still another 2.1+ miles (all down hill) to Lake James.

The second day, if anything, is worse. After losing 1,100 feet before breakfast is even digested, there's another unforgiving climb of 2,500 feet as a prelude to lunch. The afternoon will be spent on a 4.5 mile long climb gaining 1,700 feet before reaching Frozen Lake, still 1-1/2 miles out of Sunrise. Those going all the way into Sunrise will log a 12-mile day and will have climbed a total of nearly 5,000 feet.

If doing the loop from the east, making it into a two and a half-day trip and going on in as far as Berkeley Park that first half day or afternoon can make the trip a little easier. (Thus making the first full day shorter by 3.7+ miles.)

The next morning, a pleasant short climb to Grand Park will precede the 2,500-foot loss and get the westbound hiker to the West Fork of the White River before lunch. Then after a 1,100-foot climb he will be at Lake James in time for a little fishing before dinner.

Lake James is one of a series of five backcountry alpine lakes once known for their fine fishing. (And if the fish aren't biting at Lake James, maybe they are next door at Lakes Ethel, Marjorie, Oliver or Adelaide.) One young man we met at Lake James in 1969 swore he had caught a 32" Rainbow trout at Lake Adelaide. A word to the wise, however. Don't run on over to see if not wise in the ways of cross-country travel. It's rugged country, and there's only a faint unmaintained "way" trail to the more distant lakes.

If continuing on to Carbon River, the 4-mile descent from Windy Gap may make one wonder if the old knees are going to hold out.

In any event, take time to visit the natural bridge 0.8+ miles to the north, for the sight of it will well outlast the wobbly knees and the fish tales. It's about 200 feet high and spans a gulf of about 150 feet.

Don't be deterred by these derogatory comments from doing this trip some day, because in spite of everything, it is one of the most interesting and rewarding trips in the park. True, it's hard, but **very** worthwhile. (The secret of taking the effort out of this section is to do several other trips elsewhere first, then do this one **after** getting in good shape. Don't do it as a conditioner.)

In this section, the natural bridge isn't the only "wonder" to discover. There's Windy Gap — a spectacular piece of landscape which gets the author's vote as the most beautiful saddle on the Northern Loop trail. Flanked on the south by the jagged peaks of Sluiskin Mountain, the open meadows of the gap roll on leisurely for nearly half a mile.

If traveling east, the different and exquisite beauty of Grand Park will come as a memorable bonus too. The three square mile park is the only really large *flat* area within the park boundaries. Nearly everyone wants to return here on a separate trip some day to do some exploring and to follow that intriguing trail disappearing off toward Lake Eleanor. (Or come into Grand Park on the Lake Eleanor Trail from outside the park. It's a super shortcut to this beautiful spot.).

ALTERNATE TO THE WONDERLAND TRAIL
CARBON RIVER TO SUNRISE
via THE NORTHERN LOOP (Lake James) TRAIL

TRAIL CONDITION: The trail between the Carbon River and Windy Gap is an exceptionally good one. The segment from Lake James to the West Fork of the White River is also in excellent condition, easily navigated and makes for a pleasant trip.

From the West Fork up to Grand Park, the densely wooded trail is another good one, with the only problem (aside from the fact it's a long climb) being the absence of water. The hiker will have to listen carefully for the springs at mid-point, or there will be a 5.8-mile haul with no certain water source. Between Grand Park and Sunrise the trail is well traveled, well "populated," and with adequate water.

ELEVATION: Gain: 3,340' Loss: 1,550

TRAIL BEGINS: at northeast corner of the Carbon River Loop (Corner B) where the Northern Carbon River crossing (via log bridges) connector trail meets the Northern Loop Trail. Signs see (page 142). The trail heads north across an old forest slope. Mileage is from Ipsut Creek. Note: The first .9 mile after Corner B goes down river.

2.6-   Corner B signs. Lower crossing (Northern Loop) junction on east side of river. The trail to Mystic Lake goes to the right, to Lake James goes left. Trail doesn't begin real climb until first switchback.

2.8+   White rectangular sitting rock to left of trail.

3.5+   Switchback to the right by a ravine with many felled trees.

3.8+   Slab rock cliff to left of trail.

4.6-   Trail starts flat traverse through woods and continues in forest all the way to Bee Flat.

4.7+   Trail starts climbing again.

4.9-   Flat traverse with great views.

5.1-   **YELLOWSTONE CLIFFS** come into view. (base elevation 5,100', Cliff height: 600 feet). Water audible.

5.2+   Sign:

> ### YELLOWSTONE CLIFFS CAMP →
> ### Stoves Only

This camp, located a short way off the trail has two sites. **WATER** is from the nice babbling creek that crosses the trail leading into camp. Look for mountain goats here, both on Yellowstone Cliffs above the trail, and across on Crescent Mountain.

Check yourself for ticks when you're around Yellowstone Cliffs. The ones found here are the large wood ticks, not the smaller deer ticks that carry Lyme Disease.

Leaving camp, the meadowed switchbacks cross under an exposed area beneath Yellowstone Cliffs. Excellent views and a wild profusion of flowers.

5.5+   Enter the woods.

5.6+   Switchback to the left of an open slope.

5.8+   End of the cliffs. Bear grass covers the steep hillside to the base of cliffs. Boulders and stones line the trail.

5.9-   **WATER.** Stepping stone crossing over good (fresh) stream, but even better, wait for the next spot just around the bend (50-60 feet). It's an idyllic rest stop.

to call these tarns November, December and January Lakes. Now just a gentle climb to the top.

6.4-   **WINDY GAP.** (elevation 5,800'). Cross flat meadow.

6.4+   **NATURAL BRIDGE TRAIL JUNCTION.** Sign reads:

INDEPENDENCE RIDGE TRAIL

Natural Birdge 0.09   (actual 0.8+)

Richard Filley Photo

The Natural Bridge

SIDE TRIP TO THE NATURAL BRIDGE

The 200' stone arch is the eroded remnant of one of the Mountain's earliest andesite lava flows.

This worthwhile side trip will add an additional 1.6+ miles to this already difficult day, but it's easy mileage with the only real effort required in the last .02+ miles. There the trail descends, losing about 200 feet in elevation via 10 switchbacks.

The round trip, including a few minutes for picture taking, will take about an hour. The Park Service strongly recommends against going beyond the

NATURAL BRIDGE SIDE TRIP MEASUREMENT

BEGINS: At the above trail junction.

0.2+ Another talus slope to the left. View now to the north-northeast.

0.5- Round another small point. Trail fairly flat. Excellent view of West Fork of the White River and the 1965 Pigeon Peak Burn. Lake James and Lake Ethel visible below.

0.6+ Switchback to left, to the right by white boulders, then to the left again.

0.7+ Cross two (dry) runoff streams, then switchback to the right.

0.8+ **Viewpoint at the top of bridge.**

BACK ON THE NORTHERN LOOP TRAIL

Back at junction of Independence Ridge Trail by signpost. (The Independence Ridge Trail is no longer maintained beyond this junction.) Begin descent through beautiful open meadow and flower fields. Switchbacks ahead.

6.6- **WATER.** (Fresh) stream crossed via 18' footlog.

6.7- **WINDY KNOLL**, a good rest area in a lovely 'Wonderlandish' spot with sitting rocks and breathtaking scenery. This is about the "bottom" or eastern base of the Knoll. Leaving here, the trail ascends a few feet, then traverses an interesting rock area.

6.9+   WATER. A tiny streamlet trickles down the moss-covered boulders and crosses the trail. Ahead the jagged spires of Redstone Peak are visible to the east.

7.0-   Switchback to the left by an automobile-size moss-covered boulder on the right; switchback right, immediately before coming to a large boulder to the left of trail.

7.2-   Top of small rise. Good wooded trail. Begin final descent.

7.3+   Switchback to the right. An interesting gap and valley to left. (Look, but don't go.) Trail continues wooded switchbacking descent.

8.0-   PATROL CABIN TRAIL JUNCTION. Sign reads:

```
┌─────────────────────────────────────────┐
│                                          │
│          NORTHERN LOOP TRAIL             │
│                                          │
│        Lake James 0.3   (actual 0.4+)    │
│        8.8 Ipsut Creek   (actual 8.0)    │
│        Lake James Ranger Station .3       │
│                                          │
└─────────────────────────────────────────┘
```

Trail to Ranger Station goes to the right. Northern Loop Trail continues straight ahead.

8.1   WATER. 26-foot long foot log over swift (fresh) Van Horn Creek.

8.2-   LAKE JAMES CAMP TRAIL JUNCTION. (elevation 4,250'). The Lake James Camp was closed in 1989 and has been replaced by Redstone Camp. Lake James was named for James O'Farrell, one of the first rangers in Mount Rainier National Park. (Note: The hungriest and most brazen chipmunks on the Wonderland live at this trail camp!)

To fish Lake James and the other lakes beyond it without coming in via the Northern Loop Trail, you can access the area from the outside by coming up to the Park Boundary on Forest Service roads. (See Green Trails Greenwater Map No. 238). Road 74 comes in off of Highway 410 about 5 miles beyond Greenwater. Follow it, staying on the east side of the West Fork - White River Road. (Road 7550). Then hike the trail (about 2 miles) up the east side of the river until it intersects the Northern Loop Trail. From there it's 2.2+ miles (uphill all the way) to Lake James, and further still to the four other lakes.

Sign reads:

```
┌─────────────────────────────────────────┐
│                                          │
│          NORTHERN LOOP TRAIL             │
│           Lake James Cabin .6            │
│      Fire Creek Camp 5.1  (actual 5.0-)  │
│                                          │
└─────────────────────────────────────────┘
```

LAKE JAMES TO SUNRISE

ELEVATION: Gain: 3,985'   Loss: 1,965'

0.0   **WATER.** 20-foot log across (fresh) stream.

0.1-   Top of short rise. Begin descent.

0.5+   Right turn by talus. (This talus has a remarkably large colony of marmots. A whistle will bring out at least a half dozen.)

0.6   **WATER.** A small stream to right of trail.

0.7+   A moss-covered house-size boulder 30 feet to the right, followed shortly by another house-sized rock with trees growing on top, and a lily-pond to the left.

0.8+   Switchback right, a moss-covered sheer rock wall to the right. Switchback left, followed by an "S" turn, right then left. Dry streambed crossings ahead.

1.1+   Switchback right, then left. Trail steep, and root-bound, with many rock and root steps.

1.4+   Switchback left. Trail needle-covered under good thick forest.

1.6+   Switchback left, descend a steep pitch, then switchback right and left again on slope with huckleberry ground cover.

1.8-   Switchback left down another fairly steep pitch. **WATER.** Watch for a (not obvious) junction with a side trail to left, leading to gorgeous **Van Horn Falls** and (fresh) water. (Go look at the falls.)

> **BE SURE TO FILL WATER BOTTLES**
> This is the last reliable water
> until well beyond Grand Park at the
> northern edge of Berkeley Park

The trail continues east toward the West fork of the White River. The river is inaudible because of the falls, but it is very near.

1.9+   The Mount Fremont lookout is visible on the skyline, up valley on the left.

Immediately ahead is the river crossing. Follow trail to the footlog bridges (if in place) or scout for best ford.

2.0-   **WEST FORK OF WHITE RIVER.** (elevation 3,000'). (Hopefully) nice safe log bridges with log railings. As with all river crossings, the size and type of bridge may change from year to year, thus hikers may not find the bridge described here. This is especially probable with this river, and in all likelihood these bridges will be replaced by others by the time you get there. At this writing, there are two forks of the river to be crossed. (See more White River notes on pages 157 and 179.)

Look downstream for signs of the old burn on distant Pigeon Peak, a 275-acre fire that occurred in 1965.

2.2+   Trail junction. Sign:

```
Grand Park 3.7    (actual 3.7+)
Lake James 2.1    (actual 2.2+)
```

The West Fork Road is about 2 miles down this well-used trail heading north parallel to the river. See notes on this trail at the Lake James Camp Trail Junction, page 170.)

Continuing on the Northern Loop Trail from here, expect good soft wooded trail for next 1.8- miles.

2.5-   Moss-covered moraine. Huckleberries, many boulders and tall timber.

2.7+   Switchback left, followed by a steep climb and more switchbacks.

2.9-   Switchback left, then right by a rocky point. Ahead on the left are three large symmetrical boulders. This area is full of interesting boulders.

3.1-   Following end of main boulder area, switchback right by an area of sparse ground cover and tall trees.

3.3-   Level traverse on nice soft woods trail.

3.5+   Start climbing again. Switchbacks ahead.

3.7+   Switchback left above a point (200 feet to the right) high over the river.

4.0-   **WATER.** *LISTEN CAREFULLY* for a spring in the little green gully to the left. Hearing it will be the only clue to its location. It's 200 feet beyond the last switchback. Use only if desperate, and treat first.

West Fork River sound fading away here. Switchback left. This is the last time the river is audible.

4.2-   First sight of Mount Rainier since the Carbon River and the few views prior to Windy Gap.

4.4+   Look for signs of old forest fire: ash layer in the hillside, occasional burned snags. (Although the forest is lush and green). Climb gets *steeper!*

5.0-   **FIRE CREEK CAMP** (elevation 4,600'). Side trail leads to camp. This camp has 3 individual sites and 1 group site. When the ranger is in this area, he stays in a tent.

> **NORTHERN LOOP TRAIL**
>
> Fire Creek Camp   0.4
> Grand Park Ranger Station 0.4
> Lake James 4.7   (actual 5.0-)
> Grand Park 1.7   (actual 1.3+)

Sign reads:
5.1-   Switchback left in a fairly open area of huckleberries, then switchback right, still in the berries.

5.4+   Switchback left with a good view of Pigeon Peak across the river.

5.5-   Huckleberries so thick they nearly cover the trail. Switchback to the right under temporary forest cover. The top is visible from here.

5.6-   **PANORAMA VIEWPOINT** (elevation 5,696') of far distant Wonderland Trail east of Skyscraper Mountain, Mount Fremont Lookout, Lake James and Redstone Peak to the west, and White River below. A magnificent view, but a decidedly exposed rocky point. **EXERCISE CAUTION.**

5.9-   **TOP OF CLIMB.** Descend to Grand Park from here.

6.3-   **GRAND PARK** (elevation 5,600') trail junction. Sign:

> **GRAND PARK**
>
> Lake Eleanor 3.3   (not measured)
> West Fork (Fire Creek) Camp 1.6   (actual 1.3+)
> Lake James 5.9   (actual 6.3-)
> Berkeley Park 3.0   (actual 2.2+)

Grand Park is astonishingly beautiful to the eye, especially after the long climb to reach it. Bears are common here. The grassy plateau with a few islands of noble fir is unlike anyplace else at Mount Rainier. After looking out across the park, look over your shoulder to see the "reach out and touch it" view of Columbia Crest. Spectacular!

The 3.3 mile trail to Lake Eleanor is well defined. Lake Eleanor can also be reached via a short hike from a Forest Service road outside the park boundaries. About 5 miles beyond Greenwater, turn off Highway 410 onto Forest Service Road 73. After several miles cross Huckleberry Creek and go through the gate and around the ridge to the Park Boundary. There is only enough parking for 4 cars. Although there is no sign at the Boundary trailhead, the trail is pretty obvious. This "back way" in is shown on Green Trails Greenwater Map No. 238.

If going up to fish at Lake Eleanor, the camp there has 3 individual sites and 1 group site. A cross-country permit is required.

There is no camping here and no water in Grand Park.

6.4+   Beginning of sparse tree cover. Some shade along trail.

6.7+   Approximate end of Grand Park. Begin long descent.

6.9+   Switchback to the left, then right above a charming, long, flat valley far below (known as "Cold Basin.")

7.2-   A large rock on the left touches the trail.

7.3-   An excellent view to the west of the Carbon Glacier, Observation Rock, the top of Skyscraper Mountain and the distant Wonderland Trail east of Skyscraper. Trail open, but there are shady spots along the way.

Richard Filley Photo
Where the Wonderland Trail and Northern Loop meet

7.4+   South end of steep descent. Sparse tree cover, then begin another fairly steep descent.

8.0-   **WATER**. First definite reliable water source since west of the White River. A large (fresh) stream. Look for a variety of animal prints at this water. (They're thirsty too after that trip.) Leaving here, pass through a small stand of trees before breaking into a meadow.

8.1+   Prominent rock (75 feet long, 30 feet high) to left of trail. Alpine fir growing on shelf near top.

8.2+   **WATER**. Fresh stream crossing. Underwater moss on rocks. Beginning of sparse tree cover. End of open meadow. Steep climb ahead. There's a better water source just ahead, and *a real phenomenon: 2 streams flowing in opposite directions!*

8.5+   **BERKELEY CAMP** (Elevation 5,600'). Across the trail is the outhouse. **WATER** is from a stream to the right. There are several good designated campsites, three where the shelter clearing is still evident, one across the trail.)

         The trail winds around a tree island and breaks out to a good view of Skyscraper Gap. (Some call it Skyscraper Pass or Skyscraper Saddle.)

8.7-   **WATER**. Fresh stream. A forked talus area high above to the left is on the west slope of Mount Fremont.

8.8+   Large talus slope to the left. Room-size boulders a few feet off the trail. Climb now more gradual. No solid tree cover, but tree islands here and there.

         Ahead is another talus slope to the left and a Volkswagen-size boulder to the right. The peak of Skyscraper dominates the western skyline.

9.0-   Tiny streamlet crosses trail. Note the natural dam and pretty little waterfall on the stream to the right.

9.1-   First of two branches of stream crossing. Second fork crosses trail by large table rock above stream to the left. Climb is now very gentle.

9.2-   Wonderland Trail is visible high above and far in the distance to the south.

         This is the fo-rmer site of a charming little pump house that pumped water to Frozen Lake for the Sunrise water supply. The only remains of it are the pipe with running water coming out of the hill.

         Cross another fresh stream after leaving the old pumping station site.

9.3- Sign (pointing back to Berkeley Camp) reads:

> Berkeley Camp 0.5 → (actual 0.7+)

9.5+ **WATER.** Wide spot and stream access. Talus to right. The trail takes a gentle turn and gradually climbs above Berkeley Park. Check out the views of Mount Baker to the north, and the terrain you have just traversed. From the top of the rise, climbing out of Berkeley, you can see the Wonderland junction coming in from Skyscraper Gap.

10.1- **WONDERLAND TRAIL JUNCTION.** (elevation 6,400').

Signs:

> **NORTHERN LOOP TRAIL**
> Berkeley Campsite 1.5   (actual 1.5+)

> **WONDERLAND TRAIL**
> Sunrise 2.3   (actual 2.2+)

> **WONDERLAND TRAIL**
> Mystic Lake   (actual 7.1+)

10.1+ Top of small rise. Watch for marmots in rocks to right. Sandy pumice trail.

Ahead, the signs are visible on the ridge at Frozen Lake. Gradual climb on pumice trail.

10.8- **FROZEN LAKE INTERSECTION.** (elevation 6,730'). See description of trails into Sunrise on page 162.

SUNRISE TO WHITE RIVER CAMPGROUND

This stretch will be remembered as one of the quickest and easiest 3.1+ miles on the trail. It is basically a tourist trail all the way, as are all campground approach trails. It took Beth, (who is a very strong hiker in spite of having bum knees) approximately 40 minutes from top to bottom!

This is one reason why many hikers often choose to go right through to either White River Campground, or on to Summerland instead of other camps such as Sunrise or Berkeley. Another reason is that the Sunrise Campground is disappointing. The gravel service road through the center of the Sunrise Camp destroys the spell of the Wonderland.

The Swift 2,100-foot descent isn't quite steep enough to leave the hiker wobbly kneed, for the elevation loss is spread out over 3.1+ miles.

If continuing on to Summerland, the 1.5 mile trot down the White River Campground Road will provide one of the longest fairly flat stretches of hiking encountered on the trail for some, and be looked upon as another unwelcome brush with civilization by others.

ELEVATION: Gain: 0   Loss: 2,168'

ALTERNATE TRAIL

LOWER CAMPGROUND
TO WONDERLAND TRAIL JUNCTION

TRAIL BEGINS: Lower campground, across road from Frozen Lake Junction.

0.3-   Lower road. Picnic tables and garbage cans. A few feet farther, trail junction with Shadow Lake Trail. Sign reads

> **PICNIC AREA LIMIT**

0.4+   Begin slight climb followed by trail junction with (right) Burroughs Mountain Trail.

0.5+   Good view of the White River winding far below. Pumice trail now gradually descending.

1.1-   Trail Junction with Wonderland Trail.

SUNRISE TO WHITE RIVER CAMPGROUND

TRAIL BEGINS: (elevation 6,400'). Cross the parking lot, heading due south from the front of the Visitor Center to the hiker sign where the service road (left of building) begins.

ELEVATION: Gain: 0   Loss: 2,168'

0.0   Signs read:

```
┌─────────────────────────────────────┐
│                                      │
│         SUNRISE RIM TRAIL →          │
│                                      │
│      Wonderland Trail Junction 0.5   │
│           Walk-in Camp 1.3           │
│            White River 3.1           │
│                                      │
└─────────────────────────────────────┘
```

```
┌─────────────────────────────────────┐
│                                      │
│      EMMONS VISTA NATURE TRAIL)      │
│                                      │
└─────────────────────────────────────┘
```

```
┌─────────────────────────────────────┐
│                                      │
│          WONDERLAND TRAIL            │
│           Sunrise Rim Trail →        │
│        ← Emmons Vista Viewpoint      │
│                                      │
└─────────────────────────────────────┘
```

Take time for a good look at the mighty Emmons Glacier, whose ice mass (4.3 square miles) is not only the largest on the mountain, it is also the largest glacier in the U.S. outside of Alaska.

0.5+   Sign at trail junction with alternate Lower Campground Trail (above).
Upon leaving intersection, begin steep descent. Good view of Little Tahoma.

```
┌─────────────────────────────────────┐
│                                      │
│          WONDERLAND TRAIL            │
│                                      │
│          Sunrise Rim Trail           │
│        Northbound Follow Road        │
│            Sunrise Camp              │
│            Sunrise 0.5               │
│                                      │
└─────────────────────────────────────┘
```

1.5+   2-log bridge. Soft cushioned trail with a 90-degree bend. Trail now quite gentle. A very pleasant hike.

1.7+   First little Bridge. Second follows at 1.9+

2.4+   2-log bridge. Another follows at 2.6-

2.6+   Ten more little bridges (plus several longer board bridges) in next .04 miles.

3.1+   **WHITE RIVER CAMPGROUND and the road.** The trail emerges by space C-21, "Loop D" near the quaint and historic old ranger cabin.

Remember a day or two ago on the north side of the Mountain when you crossed the West Fork of the White River? Well here, 10+ miles away on the east side. is the other (main) fork. From here it flows east, southeast, then northeast, next a long run north, then at last west to Puget Sound. The Indians called this "S'kamish", an appropriate name meaning "mixed water". A look at the map will show that dozens of creeks, streams, lakes and valleys drain into the White River as it runs toward the sea. (See pages 157 & 172 for info on its companion branch).

Unlike every other camp along the Wonderland, this "civilian" campground has almost all known creature comforts: telephone, safe tap water, fires allowed, flush toilets, hospitality with "drive-in" neighbors, good shelter, garbage cans, possible food drop and even informative Campfire programs put on (Friday, Saturday and Sunday evenings) by a Park Naturalist. In spite of the fact fees are normally charged for camping, *fees are traditionally waived here for Wonderland hikers.* There is also a small Hiker Center in the White River Ranger Station.

If you're interested in the 3-1/2 mile (one-way) side trip up Glacier Basin to view the site of the old Starbo Mine (pages 32 and 33), follow the Glacier Basin sign at the west end of the campground. Viewing the debris left from the rock avalanche from Little Tahoma (page 13), isn't easy since the trail cuts inland from the river and bypasses it.

To continue southeast on the Wonderland Trail from here, follow either the road or the new segment of trail across the river 1.4- miles to the junction of the White River Campground Road and the Sunrise Road.

WHITE RIVER CAMPGROUND TO THE SUNRISE ROAD
(White River Campground elevation 4,232')
(continuing from above)

Follow the road to the right to the Loop D sign. At sign, turn left and follow the main road (or look for the new river crossing).

3.3+   Entrance and Ranger Station.

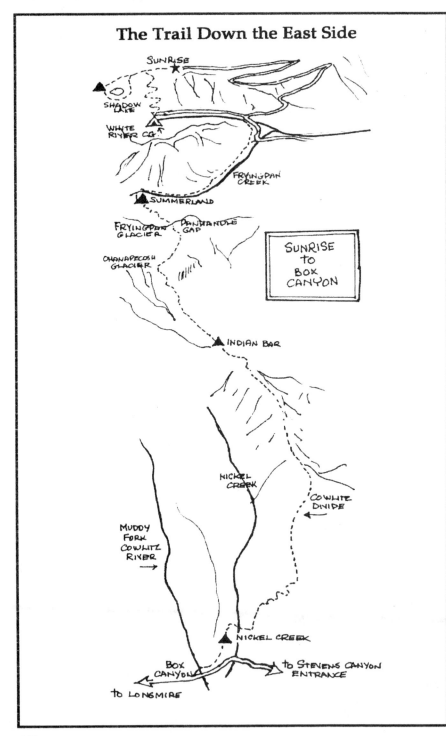

The Trail Down the East Side

SUNRISE

SHADOW LAKE

WHITE RIVER CG.

FRYINGPAN CREEK

SUMMERLAND

FRYINGPAN GLACIER

PANHANDLE GAP

OHANAPECOSH GLACIER

SUNRISE
to
BOX
CANYON

INDIAN BAR

NICKEL CREEK

COWLITZ DIVIDE

MUDDY FORK COWLITZ RIVER

NICKEL CREEK

BOX CANYON

to STEVENS CANYON ENTRANCE

to LONGMIRE

WHITE RIVER ROAD TO SUMMERLAND

The first mile of the trail from the White River Road to Summerland heads south paralleling the Sunrise Highway just a few feet off the road.

Only after the junction with the Fryingpan Creek Access Trail coming in from the then .1+ distant highway, does the Wonderland Trail again head into the backcountry and on to Summerland. Even then it's easy travel, for until reaching the horseshoe bend above Fryingpan Creek, the trail is fairly level and has little elevation gain.

Then the climb finally begins. The ridge, with Summerland high atop it, will frequently be visible, helping the traveler check his progress as he works toward the high camp.

Soon Mount Rainier will also come into view, then Little Tahoma, and the Wonderland Trailer will begin to experience some of the breathtaking scenery of the East Side. Not only will his camera and lenses seem inadequate, he'll find himself wishing for wide-angle eyes to help drink in all the expanses of wrap-around beauty.

The last half mile is a long one, but the three switchbacks, one right after another, signal that the reward of Summerland is only minutes away. From camp, the whole north face of the Mountain forms a white wall across the sky. No other alpine meadow on the trail is as close to glacier snows.

ELEVATION: Gain: 1,900'   Loss: 275'

WHITE RIVER ROAD TO SUMMERLAND

Regarding the two sets of figures, the top figure (the higher number) is the continuing count from Sunrise. The lower figure is the mileage starting at the road junction. You decide which count you like best.)

4.4+
0.0   Junction of White River road and Sunrise road. (Elevation at river 3965 feet.)

          Turn right and cross stone highway bridge over White River. Follow highway 1,000 feet to point where the Wonderland Trail cuts west into the forest.

4.6+
0.2   Wonderland Trail leaves road and enters the woods. The broad trail parallels the highway for nearly a mile, (above and frequently within sight of it), and then meets the Fryingpan Creek access trail.

Sign:

WONDERLAND TRAIL

5.1 Summerland   (actual 5.3+)
Northbound Use Road

White River Camp 1.5   (actual 1.5+)
Sunrise 4.6   (actual 4.4+)

5.6-
1.1+ **Frying Pan Creek Access Trail** junction.
Signs:

WONDERLAND TRAIL

Summerland 4.1 (actual 4.2-)
White River Road 1.0 (actual 1.1+)
White River Campground 2.3 (actual 2.6+)

Highway 0.1 →
Fryingpan Bridge

5.9-
1.5+ **WATER.** 34-foot bridge over a beautiful clear stream. The picturesque trail continues to climb gradually. To the south, look for the end of the first ridge to come into view.

6.0+
1.7- Entering primeval forest. Winding trail.

6.2+
2.0+ Trail climbs to short open meadow. Thimbleberries. *Watch for bears here.*

6.4+
2.2+ **WATER.** 25' bridge over a clear **stream** followed by five more little bridges.

6.8+
2.6+ (4,450' elevation). Horseshoe bend and switchback 50 feet above Fryingpan Creek. (Imagine how many centuries it took for the creek to carve this deep gorge). The rugged peaks of the Cowlitz Chimneys and Sarvent Glaciers visible to the south.

7.0+
2.8+   Switchback above Fryingpan Creek again. The ridge is visible high up above the creek.

7.1-
3.0-   Waterfall. Above large avalanche gully. Switchback, then climb hrough avalanche area. Note the grotesquely bent twisted trees and crushed and matted ground cover.

7.4+
3.3+   Semi-clearing with many broken trees. Summerland visible again high above.

7.5
3.5-   Mount Rainier summit visible for the first time. Enter open meadow, then Little Tahoma comes into view too.

8.4+
3.9-   Board bridge with handrails followed by 1-log bridge over stream. Another devastated area follows shortly, thousands of small downed trees.

8.8-
4.3-   Good new 44' bridge, boards and railings. In the remaining mile to the top, the trail switchbacks several times, crossing and re-crossing a (usually dry) streamlet.

8.9+
4.8+   Flower meadow with carved sign:

DON'T CUT WITCHBACKS
HELP PREVENT EROSION

With all the heavy traffic Summerland gets, this is vitally important!

9.3-
5.1+   Three switchbacks very close together mean the top is just minutes away. They are followed shortly by the junction with the short trail to the Summerland shelter cabin.

9.8-
5.3+   **SUMMERLAND**. (elevation 5,900'). This high rugged park was named for its beautiful flower displays by Major E. S. Ingraham (who in turn had the glacier named after him). Sign:

SUMMERLAND CAMP
Stoves Only

The Summerland shelter is one of the prettiest on the trail. It is a sturdy, three-sided stone building capable of holding 12 people (in a pinch) or about 8 people (and many rodents) comfortably. It sits atop a small ridge looking back down the valley of the Fryingpan. Most sites have spectacular views of the Summit, Little Tahoma, Emmons Glacier and Goat Island Mountain. Don't lean packs or hang equipment on the trees by the shelter. The trees are full of pitch.

But packs *must* be hung somewhere here, (daytime as well as at night). The chipmunks, ground squirrels and mice are voracious eaters and will empty an unattended pack in minutes. Even the marmots are aggressive here. In 1991 a marmot snatched a spoon of peanut butter right out of a camper's hand. It was his only spoon, and it took a 20-minute chase to get it back. Even hung packs aren't immune to critters, but the precaution will add to the sport of the chase.

Nights are interesting here too. With all the critters being so chummy, you never know what's going to snuggle up beside you. More than one party has been startled awake by a herd of elk snorting around in their camp. (These are the same creatures park literature describes as weighing 500-600 lbs, being the size of a horse, and are so strong they walk through barbed wire as if it wasn't there.) As Bart Simpson would say, "Yes Sir, Mr. Elk, Sir. You can have my space, Sir."

Bears abound here too. Five were in camp one night Beth camped while measuring. Other resident Summerland beggars include marmots, camp robbers and weasels. But it's the Ground squirrels that usually win in the competition for goodies. Their large cheek pouches can hold an amazing amount of pilfered booty. They've been seen waddling off with so much larder, they look as if they had a bad case of mumps.

Aside from the shelter (which is the designated group site) there are five individual sites. There will probably be a ranger tent too.

One site you won't see, but which is the most historic one on the trail, is an ancient Indian shelter, technically known as the Fryingpan Rockshelter, which is beneath an overhanging rock which was excavated near here in 1965. At 5,300 feet, it is the highest archaeological site in Washington State. Based on carbon-14 dating of charcoal and bone bits from the long-ago fires, and by the style of the stone knives and implements found buried near the site, it is estimated the shelter had been used for at least 300 years, and possibly for as long as one thousand years. Summerland has been a popular destination for a long time!

It's too bad there are no longer registers kept in the shelters, for those, plus the historic graffiti on the cabin walls made for some interesting reading.

Perusing the comments and adventures of those who came before revealed many fascinating stories.

Among the "weather comments" about the snow season at Summerland, one entry from July 15 (20+ years ago) noted that there was "LOTS of snow!" Another from October 16, was written during the first major snow of the year. (It's a short summer season up here.) We found one entry from November 11, 1966 when there was enough snow for the Ira Spring family to come in ski touring.

Also significant were the "goat comments" A man from Graham, Washington, noted that he saw 62 goats at Panhandle Gap on a July day. It isn't uncommon to see 50 or more.

One final note regarding snow. The author was surprised to find crevasses not far above the stream at Summerland. The area of the stream (in the little gully south of the main park) was a large snowfield which remained through late August the year this book was originally written, and heavily crevassed about 70 feet west of the trail. Several crevasses were 20 feet deep or more, and presented a true hazard to the several small children who scampered unattended among them.

Summerland also boasts outdoor plumbing with indoor conveniences (seat, burlap drape for a door, and air conditioning). A solar dehydration toilet was installed in 1990, but didn't work because it never got hot enough to kill the pathogens. Plans now call for installation of a composting toilet with a structure around it.

SUMMERLAND TO INDIAN BAR

After "overly populated" Summerland, the hiker usually feels he's at the opposite end of the population spectrum once he leaves for Panhandle Gap. Regardless of how many people are in his party, or near the Gap while he's there, it isn't uncommon to experience a distinct sensation of remoteness and solitude at this windy divide.

Though just a few hours' travel from the road, this location is a very lonely and solitary place.

The lovely rugged peaks, the steep snow slopes, the abundance of rock, and the lack of trees, all combine to create a sight that few but climbers ever see.

Take time at the Gap to study the map and get oriented in relation to the surrounding peaks and crags. A few minutes' patient survey of the Cowlitz Chimneys to the east may reward the observer with a look at the herd of goats known to inhabit the area.

Following Panhandle Gap, the high trail rolls on, descending and then climbing again for another 1.3+ miles before it begins the 1-1/2 mile long descent into Indian Bar, a real and unique fairyland. Indian Bar is a gravel deposit on the Ohanapecosh River above Wauhaukaupauken Falls and below the rocky headwall of the Ohanapecosh Cirque.

The final approach is unique, for unlike most "final hauls" where the hiker has no idea how close he is, here he first sees the shelter from almost a mile away. From then on, it's a simple matter to measure progress by just watching to see how much closer the shelter appears as he descends toward it.

SUMMERLAND TO INDIAN BAR

TRAIL CONDITION: This is a trail the hiker will still be talking about and showing slides of for winters to come: the reason being its adventuresome quality. The "trail" is defined by cairns and painted rocks at its high points.

There may be some route finding, a snow bridge or two, and at least one traverse across a steep snowfield before reaching the Gap.

From Panhandle Gap on, there will be more snowfields — and one that will stand out among the rest. It comes well after the hiker thinks he's beyond snow, and between the steepness and length of it, he'll begin to wonder if he didn't accidentally wander onto the Mountain. (This thought got more than a little consideration when the author's party crossed a crevasse at the top of this snowfield one year.) The descent to Indian Bar is rapid, for the chute-like trail wastes no time in losing 1,500 feet elevation as it drops parallel to the "Oh-my-gosh" Ohanapecosh Glacier.

The decision of whether to stay at Indian Bar (a really tempting choice) or keep going to Nickel Creek will be a tough one. The time schedule and the heart will have to be the judge, and unless you are really in a hurry, stay. It's possible to be at Indian Bar by lunchtime, if breaking camp at Summerland by 8:30. Continuing on will make a long day of it, for Nickel Creek is 6.6+ miles beyond Indian Bar.

If staying, there's plenty to do to keep busy: watching the bears play across the creek, picking huckleberries for dessert, or the most challenging chore, making a gourmet feast out of the grubbings left in the pack.

There's a tongue-in-cheek chuckle over the outhouses high up behind the shelter too. The trail up to them is reportedly so steep, it's advisable to rope up to make the trip. It's pretty well agreed, though, that they have the best view of any outhouse in the state

ELEVATION: Gain: 1,075'   Loss: 1,640'

MILEAGE: Begins at the sign near the shelter. Cross stream. (water source for Summerland) and begin climb.

0.2-   Sign:

> ## SUMMERLAND
> Fragile Meadow

Trail following is marked by dozens of rock cairns with orange or yellow paint slashes. If trail is snowy or foggy, work from cairn to cairn.

0.5-   Cross fork of Fryingpan Creek coming from snowfield and glacier above. Some route finding may be necessary from here on in early summer due to extensive snow at 6,000' to 7,000' elevation. This bridge is installed in early June and removed in late September. The trail switchbacks while climbing gradually. Summerland is now visible to the rear, looking very small and distant.

0.6-   Another 30' wide Fryingpan Creek fork. Ford it if the bridge is gone.

0.8-   West end of a (usually frozen) lake to the right. Cairns and red-painted rocks appear every 50-100 feet. Many snowfields follow.

1.2+   The climb of the final snowfield before the Gap begins in this vicinity.

1.4-   Nearly to the top. The area is recognizable by a large natural rock amphitheater. A short climb to the left into the basin provides a dandy look over the top and into the valley beyond. The trail here is back on rock momentarily.

Rodney Harwood Photo

Panhandle Gap

1.5-   **PANHANDLE GAP** (elevation 6,750'). This narrow gateway is the divide between the north and south sides of the Park. It's either the bleakest spot on the trail or covered with flowers in wild profusion. (Isn't it interesting that they grow here so high above the snow line?) Generally windy and misty. Pumice ground cover and a pipe trail marker. (If it isn't too windy, the peak to the left of the Gap can be climbed in a few minutes. It's a very pleasant little climb.)

On a clear day, the view is absolutely breathtaking! The entire Cascade Range is spread before you. On the distant northern horizon, the Canadian Cascades beckon from beyond Mount Baker and Glacier Peak. The upper Sarvent Glacier, just below the Cowlitz Chimneys, looks close enough to touch, while Oregon's Mount Hood stands pristine and symmetrical to the south, and massive Mount Adams stands guard to the southeast. Above you stands Little Tahoma, looking not so little from here. The massive Emmons Glacier sweeps from the summit into the depths of the White River Canyon to complete the panorama.

Watch for goats on the slopes to the east.

188   Trail markers beyond the Gap are primarily cairns, with a few painted rocks.

Between here and Indian Bar, keep an eye open for slabs of glacially smoothed and polished bedrock, souvenirs of the glaciers which helped sculpt this landscape between 25,000 to 10,000 years ago. The carved "scratches" are called "striations." They're caused by the file-like action of rocks carried downward by the glaciers.

As for how this pass got its name, well Frying pans have handles, don't they? And this gap lies at the end of the Fryingpan Glacier.

1.9+ Three fresh streamlets. Red rock cairns, and probably snow fields in this area. Watch for pipe trail markers too.

2.3+ A very blue lake (may be snow covered) and more snow fields.

2.7- Cross stream. Climb toward steep snowfield visible on the left. A rock scramble before entering the snowfield. This is an approximate 600-foot long climb. (And it was at the top of this pitch the author's party once crossed a small crevasse.) Soon after crossing over and beginning descent, pass "Tombstone marker" (looks like one) with no markings or paint.

3.2- Switchback by good viewpoint of the Ohanapecosh Glacier. Ohanapecosh in Indian jargon, means "look down on something beautiful". This must have been the spot where that name was picked.

3.5+ End of trees to the right of the trail. Shelter visible in the distance. Trail chute-like and sandy. (This "sand" is actually pumice). From the point where the trail enters sparse woods, start watching out for bears. These woods are full of them!

4.0+ Fresh stream to the left of the trail soon followed by open meadow across river from shelter cabin.

4.5- **INDIAN BAR SHELTER** (elevation 5,200') on south side of the Ohanapecosh River (which looks more like a creek at this point.)

There is a bridge over the river and a stone stairway to the shelter.

Sign on north side of river reads:

> **INDIAN CAMP**
> Toilet
> ← Wonderland Trail →

This shelter might well be referred to as the Wonderland Hilton, for it has all the comforts of home and a few like home never had. It has 10 REAL bunk beds (just the bed frames, no mattresses), a big fireplace full of rocks. (We told you the rangers had a sense of humor) and a large table/shelf. It even has a nearby natural rock bathtub complete with fresh running ice water a short distance below camp.

Indian Bar Camp has 3 individual sites and one group site. (The group site is the shelter).

The privy trail is marked by a sign at camp.

FRESH WATER is obtainable from stream 80 feet east of shelter.

Notice the sparkling clear waters of the Ohanapecosh. They flow in stark contrast to the "chocolate milk" streams originating from active glaciers. These waters flow from an inactive glacier and snowfields.

In you still want to do some exploring after reaching camp, you might check out nearby Wauhaukaupauken Falls below camp, whose name means "spouting water." Although not visible from camp, there are actually fourteen waterfalls in Ohanapecosh Park. Most of the "girl" falls, (below Wauhaukaupauken Falls), Marie, Mary Belle, Trixie and Margarete, were named by Ben Longmire for the daughters of E. S. Hall, the first superintendent of the park. (The others are St. John's, Twin and Basaltic). Six unnamed falls are on branches of Boulder Creek above camp.

Ed Walsh Photo

The Wonderland Hilton at Indian Bar

INDIAN BAR TO NICKEL CREEK

This will be one of the favorite sections of those doing the Wonderland, notably for the scenery. All but about the last mile into the Divide Junction could only be described as *spectacular!*

The morning is begun with a brisk climb to the ridge of the Cowlitz Divide (0.7 Miles) only to discover that even ridges, like all God's other creations, are prone to meander. The hiker will also discover he was wrong if he thought this day would be a 6-mile descent. For the first 3-1/2 miles out of camp, he'll swear he's doing more climbing than descending — and he is. He's ridge running and this ridge runs up a little, down a little, with the Wonderland Trail right on top, open to the sights on all sides.

There's an excellent chance of seeing animals this day too, for this is the stomping grounds (literally) of the famed East Side elk herd. (Elk disappeared from Rainier before it was established as a park, but were reintroduced again in 1934 and not only thrived but now threaten to upset the ecological balance because of their ever increasing numbers.) Here are head-on views of the Cowlitz Chimneys, and perhaps the goats — if they're browsing, and, of course, there are also the bears. Where there are huckleberries, there are bound to be bears, and this trail traverses huckleberry heaven — so you stand a good chance of a sharing a berry feast with a bruin.

Just about the time everybody starts to wish for the Cowlitz Divide Junction, there it is.

From there, it's a 2-mile, forested descent to the camp at Nickel Creek. Or, if the objective is to exit at Box Canyon, the party will probably break all speed records in doing the remaining 0.8-mile from Nickel Creek to the Stevens Canyon Road.

That warm feeling felt at the end of this day won't only be from exertion. This time it will be the added satisfaction of having viewed the grand panorama of the East Side.

INDIAN BAR TO NICKEL CREEK

TRAIL CONDITION: The scenery on this section is so engrossing the hiker probably won't even notice the trail except when it rises up to meet him should he stumble or slip.

Much of the ridge trail is trough-like. It's a knee-deep trench running up and down the eight rises of the ridge. At other times, it simply passes unobtrusively through the rolling flower fields. It's a good place to wear your gaiters on dewy mornings.

Tree cover is non-existent, but no complaints from anyone this time, for here the hiker wants nothing between himself and the magnificent scenery. Finally, arrival back in the forest, -4.5 miles out of Indian Bar, is done almost reluctantly, for it marks the end of the grandeur.

From the Divide Junction on, trail markers sprout like orange mushrooms from high on the trees. More for the benefit of winter travelers than the backpacker, they show the snowshoer and cross-country skier the way.

Nickel Creek and the trail beyond will probably be well populated with curious day-hikers up from Box Canyon.

ELEVATION: Gain: 1,285'   Loss: 2,695'

MILEAGE: No sign, but some mileages from here are:

> Summer Land 4.5+
> Sunrise Road 9.7+
> Box Canyon 7.4+

TRAIL BEGINS: Across the **fresh water** creek at Indian Bar. **Fill Canteens!** *There is no water for 6 miles!* Climb the steep pitch past the hillside to the open flower meadows.

0.5-   Enter rocky area. Trail still climbing.

0.6-   The trail ahead looks like a ribbon going over hill and dale

0.7   Look for some very interesting conglomerate and pumice ground cover just preceding the top of ridge. Mount Adams comes into view to the south. Watch for elk and mountain goats from here on. Trail descends slightly before climbing again.

1.0-   Top of second small rise. Look north into a beautiful little enchanted valley dotted with many tiny lakelets and meandering streams. A real storybook setting!

1.1+   First brief forest cover. Still not to top of the third rise. Several small switchbacks.

1.3+   Sign:

> **ELK COUNTRY**
> **Please do not disturb the stakes**
> **where yearly measurements are made**

"THE TOP". (elevation 5,930'). A flat meadow which is the high point of the day's trip. This is one of the most spectacular panoramas on the entire trail, with unobstructed views of Mount Rainier to the west, the Tatoosh Range on the south, with Mount Adams and Mount St. Helens beyond, the Cascades on the east and the Cowlitz Chimneys on the north. If ever a wide-angle lens were needed, it's here. Never will an ordinary lens seem so inadequate.

The mountain goats like this view too. Beth saw about 50 from here one day. The windswept Cowlitz Divide separates the drainages of the Ohanapecosh River on the east, from those of Nickel Creek, Twin Falls Creek, and the Muddy Fork of the Cowlitz River on the west. The Ohanapecosh discharges into the Cowlitz a few miles northeast of Packwood. Nickel Creek (and Twin Falls Creek join the Cowlitz a short distance below the Box Canyon. The Cowlitz flows into the Columbia River at Kelso.

Cowlitz came from the name of an Indian Tribe, the Cow-e-lis-kee or Cow-e-lis-ke.

1.5-   End of descent. Begin climb of fourth rise.

1.6-   Top of fourth rise. (elevation 5,435'). Begin steep descent.

2.0+   Bottom of descent. Begin climb of fifth rise. Watch for area of good sitting rocks amid a natural rockery floral display.

2.3+   Top of sixth rise. (elevation 5,500'). A small open meadow. Begin descent. Mather Memorial Highway visible to the east.

2.7+   Begin short climb of seventh rise. After a short flat meadow, the trail continues to climb. False top on this rise.

3.0+   Actual top of seventh rise. From this point the hiker gets a look straight across to the Cowlitz Chimneys, plus a good view of the Chinook Creek Valley. (Mather Memorial Highway no longer visible.) Begin short descent.

3.4-   **TOP OF EIGHTH RISE**. (elevation 5,485'). There is a spectacular Lupine field in this area. Note the bear damage to the trees (lower bark stripped off). Begin gradual descent. From here, "run the ridge" down the Cowlitz Divide. The trail in this area crosses several open meadows with few trees.

3.5-   Begin switchbacking descent.

3.9-   Steep descent. Good huckleberrying... but remember, the bears here know it is so too.

4.2   Trail enters forest (a mushroom heaven!)

4.4+   Open meadow with young alpine trees. Patches of wild strawberries. Forest cover with heavy snow damage follows.

4.7-   **JUNCTION WITH COWLITZ DIVIDE TRAIL.** (elevation 4,400'). Signs, including a "No Horses" sign:

```
┌─────────────────────────────────────────┐
│        ← WONDERLAND TRAIL →              │
│                                          │
│  ← Indian Bar Camp 4.6mi/7.5 km  (actual 4.6+)  │
│    Nickel Creek 1.9 mi/3 km   (actual 2.0) →    │
└─────────────────────────────────────────┘
```

```
┌─────────────────────────────────────────┐
│        ↑ COWLITZ DIVIDE TRAIL            │
│    ↑ Olallie Creek Camp 1.3 mi/2 km.     │
└─────────────────────────────────────────┘
```

Following here, literally dozens of old orange metal trail markers sprout from the trees along this section. About half a dozen switchbacks, descend you through the forest.

5.4+   Orange trail marker on large dead stump, then more markers and switchbacks.

6.0+   **WATER.** 12-foot bridge over **good water.** (First depend-able water source since shortly after leaving Indian Bar).

6.5+   **WATER.** 14-foot bridge over (fresh) water followed by more trail markers.

6.8-   **NICKEL CREEK.** (elevation 3,350'). 48-foot bridge with hand wire crosses creek. The shelter and comfort station are on the north side of creek.

There are three individual sites (in a nice area beneath old-growth forest.) and one group site here. **Water** from Creek.

The Nickel Creek Shelter cabin has a half floor which would hold five or six, plus another 6-foot wide earth floor. A nice comfortable site.

Signs on south side of bridge read:

```
┌─────────────────────────────────────────┐
│          NICKEL CREEK CAMP               │
│            Camp Stoves only              │
└─────────────────────────────────────────┘
```

```
┌─────────────────────────────────────────┐
│           COMFORT STATION                │
│             across creek                 │
└─────────────────────────────────────────┘
```

NICKEL CREEK TO REFLECTION LAKES

The backpacker's opinion of this section will probably be in direct proportion to when during the trip that he hikes it.

If done first or early in the trip, this will be a fascinating day revealing one surprise after another.

Falling in the middle of the schedule, it may be met with slightly less enthusiasm, but will still be an enjoyable hike.

But if it falls as the last leg of encircling the mountain, the weary backpacker will probably join the throngs of leave-it-till-lasters who don't have a good word to say for it. But it's all in the mind!

Those who have hiked much have no doubt gone on longer hikes to see far less, but this is the Wonderland, and each day is so beautiful, so scenic, and so spectacular, one soon gets spoiled. When a day comes along that the Mountain isn't there to periodically delight the eye with a knock-your-socks-off view or natural phenomenon, the hiker feels disappointed.

The problem lies in comparing this section with the remainder of the Wonderland, when it should be compared with the trails in "the outside world" to get things back into their proper perspective.

To see the beauty of this section for what it really is, do it sometime as a one-day trail trip counter-clockwise (west to east), going from Reflection Lakes to Box Canyon. It will be a delightful hike, as rewarding as any trail anywhere, and one that may even become a family favorite.

Incidentally, this section of trail, probably one of the safest on the Wonderland, was not always considered so. As late as 1920, Joseph Hazard, in his book Glacier *Playfields of Mount Rainier National Park* gave this advice to those considering travel to those considering travel to points east of Reflection Lakes.

> "The more ambitious cheechako can venture even to Panorama Point or to Reflection Lake. Beyond these points it is not safe to go unguided. In fact the ranger at Paradise has placed sign warnings against unattended longer trips."

After those warnings came the Great Depression, then the Second World War. The Stevens Canyon Road was never finished until 1957.

Meanwhile, the hardy Cheechakos were still hiking the Wonderland Trail up the Canyon.

NICKEL CREEK TO REFLECTION LAKES

TRAIL CONDITION: This generally uphill trail is, for the most part, an excellent trail with good forest cover. Rumor has it that it is unshaded, goes right up the canyon, and is directly under the highway, but this is untrue.

While occasionally the highway is seen, it by no means dominates the landscape, nor does it particularly detract from the natural surroundings. It serves instead (or at least it should) as a feature against which to measure progress and elevation gain, on the occasions when it can be seen.

What open stretches exist on the trail are alternated with wooded intermissions. High weeds and flowers will probably provide additional shade in the midst of even completely open stretches. (Gaiters strongly advised here.)

Discomfort from the sun will come (if at all), following the arduous canyon climb. Only after the highway has been reached and crossed, and the final haul to Reflection Lakes begun, does the forest cover thin.

Water is adequate, but take care to bring filled canteens because the streamlets and trickles are all downhill (and down- stream) from the highway.

ELEVATION: Gain: 2,020'   Loss: 460'

MILEAGE: Not shown, but some mileages from Nickel Creek are:

> Cowlitz Box Canyon 0.8-
> Cowlitz Divide Trail 2.0+
> Cougar Rock Campground Junction 11.8
> Longmire 13.5-
> Indian Bar 6.8

TRAIL BEGINS: At the Nickel Creek Camp (elevation 3,350').

0.4-   Trail reenters forest.

0.8-   The rocks above the Box Canyon parking lot (elevation 2,900') followed by trail junction. Signs:

```
WONDERLAND TRAIL

Nickel Creek 1.0    (actual 0.8-)
Cowlitz Divide 3.0    (actual 2.9-)
Indian Bar 7.5    (actual 7.4-)
Paradise 10.5    (not measured)
```

BOX CANYON over Muddy Fork of the Cowlitz River

There are several ways to go here, depending on whether you want to go the scenic or direct route. The trail beyond the restroom is the most direct.

Your objective is to get to west end of the 300-foot canyon bridge. Take the macadam trail going north. Although this appears to be the wrong direction, the trail soon switchbacks up over the highway tunnel and turns to head south again.

To study the canyon, the blacktop trail going north (on the east side) leads to Box Canyon, an interesting natural phenomenon which can be seen by taking about a 10-minute side trip. The water surface is 180 feet below the bridge.

Also take a couple minutes more to see the huge glacially- polished bedrock slab on the south side of the road.

From here the summit looks close enough to touch, but it's 8 miles away as the crow flies. Mount Adams is 40 miles to the south.

Horses must exit the trail and go through the tunnel.

Back on Wonderland, watch for sign:

```
NO PETS
```

Followed shortly by another:

```
WONDERLAND TRAIL

← Paradise
Indian Bar →
```

1.1+ Trail junction with Wonderland Trail. (If coming in from the road on the west side of the Canyon, follow trail north until it meets Wonderland Trail on the left. The Wonderland then climbs up and over the highway bridge.)

Signs:

```
                    WONDERLAND TRAIL
                 Box Canyon 0.2    (actual 0.3-)
              Nickel Creek Camp 1.1   (actual 1.1+)
```

```
                 Stevens Creek Trail 1.1
               Maple Creek Camp 2.1   (actual 2.0+)
```

1.4+ Trail junction on west side of tunnel with short spur trail coming in from Stevens Canyon Highway.

```
              ← STEVENS CANYON ROAD 200'
                     ←All Horses
```

1.5+ Top of the rise. Begin descent to Stevens Creek via quick wooded trail.

1.7- Viewpoint (lookout rock on the left from which Mount Adams is prominent).

2.0- Trail takes 90-degree turn left.

2.3- **STEVENS CREEK BRIDGE** (40 feet) over glacial polished rocks. Take a few minutes to study these unbelievably smooth carved formations. This swift, white water originates from the Stevens Glacier (at the base of Paradise Glacier) far above on Mount Rainier.

Two large boulders (house-size and garage size) to the right. Trail takes a gentle right turn following the smaller rock.

Signs:

```
                 Vista Overlook  0.5 →
                  Picnic Area 1 →
```

```
┌─────────────────────────────────────────────┐
│          ← WONDERLAND TRAIL →                 │
│                                               │
│      Box Canyon 1.6km    (actual 1.5 mi.)     │
│            Paradise 13.6km                    │
└─────────────────────────────────────────────┘
```

Trail climbs immediately after bridge. At top of rise ahead, the river is 100 feet to the right and 50 feet below in elevation. Good forest cover ahead.

2.8+   58' puncheon bridge beside a swift stream. Note the old hollow snag with a deformed tree growing against it at the west end of the bridge.

2.9+   69 foot bridge over creek.

3.1-   **MAPLE CREEK CAMP.** (elevation 2,800'). This camp contains 4 individual sites and one group site. Sign:

```
┌─────────────────────────────────────────────┐
│            MAPLE CREEK CAMP                   │
│                No Fires                       │
│                                               │
│             ← HORSE FORD                      │
│           No Horses on Bridge                 │
└─────────────────────────────────────────────┘
```

WATER from the creek. The trail is very rocky. This is the area of an old burn. Several charred snags are still in evidence.

3.4-   Gradual left turn by the river (which is 70 ft. to the right). Soft needle trail through good forest cover. Soon cross old river bed (gray sand), re-cross same river bed, then pass through cut-out center section of old very decomposed charred tree.

3.9+   **WEST END OF TUNNEL VISIBLE on road above.** (The road on the east end of the tunnel is also visible.) Cross two (dry) streambeds. Large 20-foot high house-size boulder to left.

4.0+   Base of talus to the left. Now at the same elevation as the river bed moraine, 50' to the right.

4.2+   Nice stone wall. Enter forest cover. This point is about opposite the bridge on the highway (above and across the valley).

4.3+   **SYLVIA FALLS TRAIL JUNCTION** with short trail to right. (Unmarked but clear). Easy access for a fine overlook.

4.6- Talus (old sections of andesite columns.) Trail ahead very close to river on the right. A trickle crosses the trail.

4.7- Very nice sturdy bridge, all posts, rails, planks, etc. are BIG. Begin to cross old talus area. Ahead, a steep drop-off to the right at one point.

4.9+ Sign:

```
                        HORSE FORD
                     No Horses on Bridge
```

Horse ford is to the right of the bridge.

5.0- **MARTHA FALLS.** This waterfall (actually a series of falls) was named for Martha Longmire (wife of Elcaine) by her son, Ben Longmire.

5.1+ Stratified rock to the left with log-edged trail at the base. Ahead, road will be visible high above to the right.

5.0+ Rock retaining wall at base of a steep avalanche gully to the left. Ahead cross base of a gully with tree-topped cliffs a hundred feet above.

5.2- Trail rocky and open, directly across the valley from the large fanned-out slide.

5.4- **UNICORN CREEK.** 31' plank bridge with wire handrail. Martha Falls high above (to the south). Horse Ford right beside bridge. Trail switchbacks to the left and is very steep preceding junction with horse ford trail coming in from the left. Soon you will switchback to the right above Unicorn Falls.

5.6- Gradual Climb. Directly across the valley above the highway is an immense gully.

6.0- **STEVENS CANYON HIGHWAY (North Side).** The Wonderland Trail actually crosses the Stevens Canyon Highway at this point.

Signs read:

```
                    WONDERLAND TRAIL

             Maple Creek 2.7      (actual 3.0-)
             Box Canyon 5.0       (actual 5.2-)
             Nickel Creek Camp 6.0    (actual 6.0-)
```

```
← WONDERLAND TRAIL →
```

6.2- Two puncheon bridges followed by slab rock under trail. Beautiful moss-covered rock gully to the left.

6.4- The trail here is just 20 feet off the highway. Ahead, the trail is visible going around the south end of Louise Lake (elevation 4650'). Louise Lake is the first of the two large "Reflection Lakes."

Signs read:

```
← WONDERLAND TRAIL →
```

Another reads "No Pets" and "Trail to Lake".

A duplicate of the "Trail to Lake" sign follows shortly.

Another reads:

```
FRAGILE SHORELINE
No fires, pets, or camping
```

Several small puncheon bridges follow. A pretty little falls to the left.

7.4+ **TRAIL JUNCTION.** Signs read:

```
LAKES TRAIL

Reflection Lakes 0.1
←Paradise 2.0
Paradise 3.3 →
```

```
WONDERLAND TRAIL

Maple Creek Camp 6.4 km    (actual4.3mi)
Westbound 0.8 km
Follow Lakes Trail
```

The Wonderland Trail curves left and up over a short rise.

7.4-   Top of rise. Small lake on the right. Other Reflection Lakes visible beyond
       to the west.

7.4+   Trail meets the road. Sign reads:

LAKES TRAIL
Follows Road 0.3 km

WONDERLAND TRAIL
0.8 km west - east 0.2 km
3.2 km. Paradise 5.4 km

Followed by

REFLECTION LAKES
... Like Mirrors, - Fragile
Fishing, swimming, boating picnicking and
camping
Not permitted because they may
destroy the plants that frame the lakes

A number of identical signs follow.

7.6+   **(WEST) REFLECTION LAKE.** An aluminum sign now replaces a lovely
       old wooden sign that stood here for many, many years. It reads:

THE STORY OF REFLECTION LAKES

"These lakes lie in shallow basins on the surface of a
mudflow deposit that was formed about 5,000 years ago.
The mudflow originated in a landslide of rock from the
summit of Mt. Rainier possibly caused by a volcanic
explosion or earthquake. As it descended the side of the
volcano, the rock broke up, and snow turned the mass into a
wet mudflow. Movement of the mudflow down the steep
mountainside provided enough momentum to carry it across
Mazama Ridge, the wooded ridge in front of you, and into
the Reflection Lakes area. The lakes are fed by streams that
head on Mazama Ridge and on the Northern slope of the
Tatoosh Range behind you. They drain to the West into
Tatoosh Creek, a tributary of the Paradise River."

7.8-   Another sign on the right reads:

> **REFLECTION LAKES**
> **4,861'**

7.9-   West end of lake. Continue on the road about 400 feet (around the bend of the road) for the continuation of the Wonderland Trail to Longmire.

If continuing on to Cougar Rock Campground or Longmire, travel time from this point to Longmire is about 2-1/2 hours, or 2 hours to Cougar Rock, downhill all the way, in either case.

8.0+   Wonderland Trail continues to the west on the south side of the Highway.

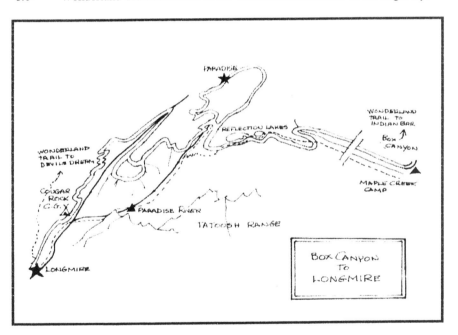

REFLECTION LAKES TO LONGMIRE

This lovely and all too brief section lies close to the most traveled section of highway in the park, and yet is virtually ignored by hikers instead of receiving the attention it deserves.

It's a wonderful hike through beautiful forests, past two mighty glacial rivers, and holding such delights as one of the park's largest waterfalls (Narada), several lesser falls, plus the spectacular merging of the Paradise and Nisqually Rivers.

As if that weren't enough, the backpacker will walk in history when he discovers an old wooden water pipe (such as Seattle and other towns of the old West used in their early days). This one supplied the water to turn the hydroelectric generator for Longmire and Paradise. For those who have read Floyd Schmoe's delightful book *A YEAR IN PARADISE,* they'll be following his snowshoe route between Longmire and Paradise, and his contact with the outside world.

If this is done as the second part of a one-day trip from Nickel Creek to Longmire, time probably won't permit doing justice to this lovely section. By all means, return and bring the family some day to leisurely rehike this interesting segment.

TRAIL CONDITION: A superb trail descending the direct route from Reflection Lakes (and Paradise) to Longmire.

It seems improbable that the foot traveler can descend the ten (road) miles from Narada Falls to Longmire in just a little more time than it takes the automobile, but he can on this trail. While the car and driver must wind and twist around Ricksecker Point and descend the long canyon walls beyond, the hiker is traversing the densely wooded slopes far below the point. He emerges right at the Nisqually Highway, with far less wear and tear — and a great deal more satisfaction than his fellow traveler on wheels.

Water will seldom be out of sight here, for the Paradise River follows the trail for the first part of the trip, and the Nisqually escorts it the remainder of the way.

If supplies are waiting at Longmire, the prudent backpacker must weigh the merits of picking them up _after_ setting up camp at Cougar Rock Campground (and traveling to get them with an empty pack), but adding the extra mileage to the top of an already long day, versus postponing the trip until the following morning when it will be but .3 mile out of the way. (The round trip from the campground to Longmire will add at least 3.4- miles to the trip, 1.7 each way.)

ELEVATION: Gain: 0,   Loss: 1,875'

MILEAGE: According to the sign at west end of Reflection Lakes.

TRAIL BEGINS: On the south side of the road, about 400' west of the west end of Reflection Lake. For the first half mile, the forested trail parallels the road, just slightly below it.

0.5+   Top of rise. Trail turns right and begins the descent via numerous switchbacks.

1.0-   Switchback to the right. Stream to the right. Road visible high above.

1.2-   Trail junction with trail to Narada Falls.

Signs Read:

```
WONDERLAND TRAIL

Reflection Lakes 1.2    (correct)
Longmire 4.5    (actual 4.3+)
```

```
NARADA FALLS TRAIL

Narada Falls 0.3 km
Paradise 2.4 km
Paradise River Camp 1.3 km
```

From this trail junction, it's about a 1,000-foot hike to the top of the falls. (That's distance, not elevation gain.)

BASE OF NARADA FALLS (elevation 4,572 ft.) The Paradise River falls a distance of 168 feet, frequently accompanied by mist or rainbows. The falls got their name in 1893 from the Hindu word meaning "uncontaminated" or "pure."

Puncheon bridges are the most distinguishing characteristics of this section. This trail is well used in the winter by cross-country skiers.

1.9+   **PARADISE RIVER CAMP.** (Elevation 3,750')

```
NO CAMPFIRES
```

The river, named "Glacier Creek" in 1870, by P. B. Van Trump and General Hazard Stevens, was renamed by Mrs. Elcaine Longmire on her first visit in 1885 to the flower fields above, when she likened the sights to Heavenly Paradise.

104-foot elaborate (rustic) bridge over first fork, and 43-foot bridges over the second and third forks of the Paradise River. Huckleberries. More footbridges, more trail markers.

2.2-   Begin rocky steep stretch. More huckleberries.

2.5-   A 3.0 Mileage marker on the right. *The actual mileage to Longmire from this point is 3.0+.* Puncheon bridge precedes a wishing tree over the trail. Watch for junction with a side trail leading to the left that led to the site of the old powerhouse.

2.6+   The remains of old wooden water pipe to the left. (pipe smashed, but wire coil remains.) Falls to the left. A humped 40-foot bridge crosses the water pipe. Short trail to the left to a lookout point.

2.7+   **CARTER FALLS.** Fenced drop off to the left with view.
         Sign:

CARTER FALLS
Elevation 3,660'

These falls are named for the guide who built the first trail to the Paradise Valley. The Longmires used to charge a 50-cent toll to use the trail, a hefty sum in those days.

2.9+   Eagle Peak is visible and prominent to the left across the river.

The wooden water pipe is still to the right and becomes rock covered at the end of the bridge ahead.

3.4+   There used to be an old hydro-electric generator plant and driveway that came this far in (unlikely though it looks today.)

3.7+   Bend to the right. This point is above the junction of the Paradise and Nisqually Rivers. Note the old mine cable crossing above the river.

3.8+   **NISQUALLY RIVER CROSSING.** The river, now with three channels, has a 96' log bridge over the east channel, a 105' log bridge over the west channel and a 60' bridge over the center channel. Signs at both ends of the crossing read:

HORSE FORD
No Horses on Bridge

A sign at the road reads:

WONDERLAND TRAIL

Horse Ford 0.1
Longmire 1.6   (actual 1.7)
Carter Falls 1.1   (actual 1.1)
Paradise 4.1   (not measured)

HORSE FORD
Cougar Rock Camp 0.1 →

The Wonderland Trail cuts west into the forest. It was in this area where the old mining camp was. The mine was across the river, and the (now cemented-over) opening can still be seen high up on the side of Eagle Peak.

NOTE: If camping at Cougar Rock Campground, it is almost diagonally across the road at this point, (to the right about a city block.)The Wonderland Trail continues left into the woods and on to Longmire

4.1-   Junction with trail to the right. Signs read:

WONDERLAND TRAIL

Longmire 1.5   (actual 1.4-)
Carter Falls 1.3   (actual 1.4-)
Narada Falls 2.9   (actual 2.9)
Paradise 4.2   (not measured)

4.2+   Turn right preceding junction with another trail from right. Sign reads:

COUGAR ROCK CAMP   0.1

WONDERLAND TRAIL

Longmire 1.4   (actual 1.3)
Carter Falls 1.3   (actual 1.5-)
Narada Falls 3.0   (actual 3.0+)
Paradise 4.3   (not measured)

Side trail to the river follows.

4.7+   Bottom of hill beside river. Rough plank bridge with big posts, nice trail with hand rails. Side trail to the left to (fresh) **WATER.**

5.4-   Junction with trail to right (Indian Henry Trail). Signs read:

> **WONDERLAND TRAIL**
>
> Longmire 0.2   (actual 0.1+)
> Cougar Rock 1.6   (actual 1.3+)
> Paradise River Camp 3.5   (actual 3.7+)
> Paradise 5.6   (not measured)

> **WONDERLAND TRAIL**
> ← Rampart Ridge 1.4   (actual 1.9+)
> ← Pyramid Creek 3.0   (actual 3.7+)
> ← Devils Dream 5.0   (actual 5.8+)
> ← Indian Henrys 6.0   (actual 7.0+)

5.5+   **LONGMIRE.** Hiker Center to the left.

> **CONGRATULATIONS!**
>
> (Now go treat yourself
> to a piece of wild blackberry pie
> at one of the several fine restaurants
> on the road to the Mountain).

THE WEST SIDE ROAD ACCESS TRAILS
(The West Side Road is Currently Closed)

As of this writing, (Spring 2002) the West Side Road is still closed approximately 3 miles up from the Nisqually Road in the vicinity of Dry Creek. A mudflow in October 1988, washed out three-quarters of a mile of road. It was then redamaged by a 1989 flood. At this time foot and bicycle travel is allowed, but the road is closed to all but Park Service vehicles. There is considerable support in favor of reopening this road, and we keep hearing hopeful reports that Superintendent Jarvis is considering possible options. Primary among those would be a commercial shuttle service that would drive hikers up the West Side Road for a fee. Definitely check on the status of it before attempting to reach the Wonderland Trail via the West Side Road. Otherwise it's a long hike from Dry Creek.

Aside from the access these trails offer to the Wonderland Trail, they were more frequently used as the beginning or end of some marvelous one-day trail trips. They offer numerous possibilities for loop trips or just plain hikes in and back out the same trail.

The Tahoma Creek Trail, for instance, is the shortest (in mileage) and fastest route to Indian Henrys, being only 3.7- miles up this trail versus 7.3- hard miles from Longmire or 5.5 miles from Kautz Creek.

It is also the southern approach to a round trip of Emerald Ridge. Or, a good way to avoid the exposure on the north side of the ridge just beyond the top. (See page 109). Coming back out the same route would also eliminate a transportation problem, since the hiker would end up back at his car. This would result in a nice 8.2- mile round-trip hike.

It's also an interesting 2.3- mile hike to the Wonderland Trail crossing of Tahoma Creek to survey the 1967 and 1989 flood damage.

The South Fork Trail, the second of the West Side Road access trails, is one of the most rewarding short hikes in the park, due mainly to the inspiring andesite column display just preceding its junction with the Wonderland Trail. This is a good, short easy (1.5+) trip on which to take non-mountaineering friends or Eastern relatives to show them some of the rewards the Mountain bestows on those who make even a minimal effort to explore her.

It is also the shortest route to the top of Emerald Ridge. It takes 3.3 miles to gain only 2,000 feet in elevation, as opposed to the 4.2 mile, 2,600 foot gain via the Tahoma Creek route). The exposure mentioned above is not so much of a problem from this direction either. (The trail in the vicinity of the exposure is rumbly pumice and quite steep. It is easier and more stable to go up it rather than to descend it.

The easiest way to do the 7.4- mile Emerald Ridge "loop" is from north to south, — in via the South Fork Trail and out via Tahoma Creek.

The West Side Road Access Trails (to the Wonderland Trail)

When the road is ever again open all the way, transportation possibilities for this loop are just three in number.

. Use two cars. Leaving one at Tahoma Creek, consolidate both parties into the second car which would be left at the beginning of the South Fork Trail Upon exiting, use the first car to drive back and pick up the second vehicle. Or exchange car keys and each party hike separately from opposite ends.

. If you have only one car, drop off 'the party of the first part' as the lawyers would say, at whichever end they're going to hike from, while the driver takes the car to the other end and hikes from there. They meet at the top and hike out together. (A very unpopular choice with many moms responsible for a bunch of kids, and not recommended for the uninitiated). A possible (not recommended) alternate to this plan is to leave the hikers at the entrance trail; the driver then takes the car to the exit trailhead where he leaves it and hikes the road back to the first trail where the rest of the party is (impatiently) waiting.

. The third plan is to hike the road again -- either at the beginning or end of the trip, or leave the car in the middle between both trails and hike half the road before the loop and half after. (Another Not recommended choice.)

The St. Andrews Creek Trail to Klapatche Park is probably the most popular trail of the three. It is lovely in its own right or as a means to another end.

It too, is a good family trail with neither difficulty nor exposure, — just a pleasant hike with a consistent "just right" grade and elevation gain that even small children can navigate and enjoy. This is a good stretch to use as a first hike for two or three year-old children. Given enough time and rest stops, all will eventually reach Klapatche Park. (Bring a backpack kiddie-carrier for the trip down or in case the exertion brings on nap time a little early).

Or, if doing this as the beginning of a loop trip, then the 2.5- mile 1,700-foot elevation gain of the St. Andrews Creek Trail is the best starting route to loop Klapatche Park, either to the north or south.

If coming out at the South Fork Trail, 3,200 feet must be lost, from the St. Andrews Park high point, in the 4.1-mile descent to the road. Or, that much must be climbed and gained if going *to* Klapatche by the South Fork route.

When exiting via the North Puyallup "road", the St. Andrews Creek Trail is again the route of least elevation gain (1,700 feet in 2.5- miles). It loses 2,000 feet in the descent to the river, then gains only another 600 in the 2-1/2 mile hike up the abandoned end segment of the West Side Highway above the North Puyallup River.

Transportation problems remain the same, — the hiker must hike the road back to his car, shuttle two cars, or "divide and conquer" (meet in the middle).

The fourth West Side access to the Wonderland is not a trail at all, but is the above mentioned last 2 1/2 miles of the Road itself. Although since 1932 the road has extended all the way to the North Puyallup River, it has been closed to motor vehicles at the Klapatche Point turn for the last few years due to rockfall.

For many years, it was planned for the road to eventually go all the way around the Mountain and for 104 miles of road to completely encircle the Mountain's south, west and east sides, as "The Wonderland Road." When avalanches took out the massive timber bridge that once crossed the North Puyallup River, plans for encircling the Mountain by road were finally abandoned. It also resulted in a name change. The West Side Highway became the West Side Road.

The danger of rock fall is a hazard which must be considered in hiking this final road section as traveling it carries a certain amount of risk. It may also entail scrambling over a slide or two, but it is another means of access (or retreat) to and from the Wonderland Trail, and is a good hike with an unobstructed view to the north.

It is also a good place to begin the Wonderland Trail if the road ever opens again.

West Side Road Alert:
If you want to see the West Side Road repaired,
relocated or reopened, see the note on page 216

TAHOMA CREEK TRAIL

LOCATION: 4.4 Miles up the West Side Highway.

TRAIL BEGINS: On the north side of Tahoma Creek. Hike or drive north to the trail junction.

ELEVATION GAIN/ LOSS: 1,040'

MILEAGE: According to a sign that used to be at the beginning of the trail.

TAHOMA CREEK TRAIL
Wonderland Trail 2.2   (actual 2.1+)
Indian Henrys 3.6   (actual 3.7-)

This trail is currently closed although trail crews still use it It requires bushwhacking to find the trailhead.

0.3-   A 'chair' cut in the end of a log facing the trail. Ahead is a 15-foot log-edged puncheon bridge. Trail climbing and steepening.

0.6-   Many downed trees. Sparse tree cover because so many are down. Red huckleberry heaven.

0.9-   20-foot puncheon bridge over water (20 feet below). Water comes from stagnant-looking lake to the left beyond the trees.

1.1-   .2 mile marker (?) on 100-foot high snag. Ahead, evidence of where the lahars go through the trees below and to the right. Note the many boulders among the trees.

1.2+   Green and white 5.4 mileage marker on tree to left. Ahead, trail revision due to flood washout area. (These old green and white markers were placed here in 1921 by old-timers Harry Pappajohn and Bert Brouilette.)

1.5-   10-foot log-edged board bridge over run-off stream. Many red huckleberries. River bed about 400 feet wide here. Old flood apparently covered the entire width. Steep climb.

1.6-   Run-off gully. West side of Mt. Ararat (Indian Henrys on top) visible across Tahoma Creek and high above.

1.7+   Trail crosses earth slide area. Steep trail climbs above the broad riverbed, now about 100 feet below.

1.8-   Switchback to the left above the creek. Note the high water mark on the opposite shore. Trail steep. A second switchback to the right. A short segment of rock elevated trail bridges a small dip in the trail.

1.8+   Many huge old cut logs and trees on both sides of trail.

1.9+   Tree-topped cliffs high above to the left.

2.0-   Rock cliffs, and an 80-foot high shoulder of bedrock.

2.1+   **WATER.** immediately preceding **WONDERLAND TRAIL** junction on the north side of Tahoma Creek.

This intersection is described on page 107.

Some additional mileages of interest from this point are:

Klapatche Park	7.8+
Mirror Lakes Trail	1.6+

THE SOUTH FORK TRAIL
(South Puyallup River)

LOCATION: 8.6 Miles up the West Side Highway.

TRAIL BEGINS: By a 90 degree left bend in the road. The trail is at the north end of a steep dirt bank to the right of the road.

ELEVATION: Gain/Loss: 400'

MILEAGES: According to sign at beginning of trail.

SOUTH FORK TRAIL

Wonderland Trail   (actual 1.5+)
Klapatche Park 5.4   (actual 5.6+)

---

200 feet from road: **WATER.** Small stream.

0.1+   Bridge over small stream.

0.2-   Bridge over small stream.

0.3+   **WATER.** 15-foot bridge over (fresh) water.

0.5   16-foot bridge followed by 48-foot bridge.

0.9+   **WATER.** Tiny stream. *Keep a close watch to the right for the beginning of the andesite columns.*

1.5+   **WONDERLAND TRAIL JUNCTION** at South Puyallup River. This intersection is described on page 110.

ST ANDREWS CREEK TRAIL
(To Klapatche Park)

LOCATION: 11.5 miles up the West Side Highway.

TRAIL BEGINS: On the north side of St. Andrews Creek where it crosses the West Side Highway.

ELEVATION GAIN/ LOSS: 1,700'

MILEAGE: According to sign at beginning of trail 2.5 miles (actual 2.5-).

0.3+   First switchback.

0.5-   Second switchback.

0.7-   Third switchback.

0.8-   Fourth switchback.

1.0-   Fifth switchback.

1.2+   Start of the ridge. A good rest spot with several large sitting logs and an interesting large piece of pink pumice in the crook of the turn.

2.1+   **WATER.** A short trail leads 50 feet to the left. This source may be dry in late season. It is the only water between the road and the top.

2.2+   Switchback. Early in the season, the prominent rock at this turn is a wild profusion of flowers growing out of every nook and cranny.

2.5-   **WONDERLAND TRAIL INTERSECTION** in Klapatche Park. This junction is described on page 111.

THE END OF THE WEST SIDE ROAD

LOCATION: Begins 12.8 miles up the West Side Road at Klapatche Point.

ELEVATION: Gain/Loss: 600'

MILEAGE: 2.8 miles

NOTE: At one time the park encouraged use of the road as a "North Puyallup Auto Nature Tour." In case you see one of the old numbered signposts, they were keyed to the following (Park Service) text.

.05   **Signpost #1.** Mount Rainier straight ahead with a superb view of Columbia Crest, the middle summit at 14,411.1 ft. To the right is Point Success, with Liberty Cap on the left. Both points are over 14,000 ft. high. The angle of their ridges gives a graphic demonstration of what the height of the old summit must have been before destroyed by explosions, mudflows and glaciers.

.10   **Signpost #2.** The rock on the right is a typical lava flow, similar to the rock high on Mount Rainier.

.50   **Signpost #3.** The Puyallup Glacier at one time filled the valley below. The present climate is responsible for its receding to where it is now just three miles long.

.75   **Signpost #4.** The North Puyallup River, 700 feet below, flows with a daily "pulse" as do all the mountain's watercourses. As the day warms up, the sun heats the glacier causing more melt, and higher water in the rivers and streams.

.95   **Signpost #5.** 500 years ago, the red sand on the right was carried from high on the mountain by a mudflow and deposited in its present location. The flow, 1,000 feet deep as it flowed past this point, continued down valley for 40 miles, but left only 6 inches to 3 feet of debris on the valley walls.

1.10   **Signpost #6.** These rock formations, and similar columns across the valley, are called Andesite. There were formed by lava that flowed here and crystallized in this manner as it cooled.

1.35   **Signpost #7.** Evidence of another mudflow. Notice the large boulders in this one.

1.70   **Signpost #8.** This slide occurred in the winter of 1944. The forces of nature are at work trying to convert man's road back into a wild natural slope.

1.85   **Signpost #9.** A typical avalanche gully. All winter and spring, avalanches of snow, mud and rock thunder down this natural chute, wiping it clean of everything and anything in their path.

2.10   **Signpost #10.** The talus slope below the road is a good example of the action of freezing and thawing on rocks. Such slopes are the natural homes of hoary marmots and conies (pikas).

2.30   **Signpost #11.** The small waterfall located 100 feet above the road, has its source at the 5,000 foot elevation in Klapatche Park, high above.

2.50   **Signpost #12.** Junction with the **WONDERLAND TRAIL** and bridge over the North Puyallup River. In the early days of the park (1922-23) a road was planned to run all the way up the west side of the mountain as part of an "around the mountain" plan. This section, which was to run to Mowich Lake, could not be completed for lack of funds.

The mighty North Puyallup River was bridged, and the roadwork began on the other side of the river, extending for 1/4 mile before the funds gave out.

Horrendous avalanches in 1947, 1948 and 1952 smashed not only the bridge, but hopes of ever completing the "Wonderland Road."

This junction is described on page 114.

GLOSSARY

Since this adventure will take place on a major volcanic mountain, and you may be seeing formations unique to such a peak for the first time, or be unfamiliar with the names of the phenomenon you're seeing, this glossary is a brief overview of mountain terminology.

Andesite: Dark grayish rock Of volcanic origin derived from magma. Several times around the mountain, spectacular displays of Andesite columns will be seen. They are multiple towering columns of six-sided rock formed as flowing molten lava cooled rapidly when hitting ice or cold water. The rapid cooling causes an effect similar to a mass of pillars.

Avalanche: A sudden overwhelming rush of snow, ice, earth, or rock. Avalanche Gully: A descending chute below an avalanche course. These steep gullys are identified by the freshly scoured earth, and the small or grotesquely twisted trees and ground cover in the gully.

Basalt: a rock formed during a volcanic eruption when lava flows from a fissure. Cairn: An distinctive and obviously man-made pile of rocks which marks the trail.

Cirque: A high semi-circular basin formed by a glacier.

Crevasse: A deep crevice or fissure on the face of a glacier caused by stresses of the ice moving over the contours of the land. Many crevasses are visible on the mountain, and range in depth from a few feet to over 300 feet deep.

Erosion: The continual on-going process of the mountain "coming down" and being transported elsewhere, by way of gravity, glaciers, glacial scouring, rockfall, landslides, weather, water, and wind. Mount Rainier is already considerably smaller than it's original estimated height of well over 16,000 ft.

Stream Erosion: The rivers and steams emanating from the mountain methodically work days and night to grind and carry away pebble and grain of sand toward the sea.

Erratics: Large boulders left perched on foreign soil by past glaciers.

Glacier: A large body of accumulated ice and compressed snow moving slowly down the slopes of the mountain. There are 28 named glaciers on Mount Rainier.

Glissade: A controlled standing or sitting descent on steep snow. Skiing sans skis.

Hanging Glacier: One which originates on a steep cliff.

Ice Axe: A functional tool with a pick and adz on one end and a spike on the other, designed for use in mountaineering applications ranging from chopping steps, to arresting oneself in a fall.

Moraine: The accumulation of rocky debris deposited by a glacier. The types of moraine you will cross are:

Lateral Moraine: The accumulations of rock left along the sides of the glacier. terminal moraine: The deposits left at the bottom or end of a glacier.

Rock Flour: Ground rock pulverized to small particles by the milling action of rock against rock. Rock flour gives glacier streams a characteristic opaque chocolate milk color.

Serac: A giant ice tower in the upper reaches, "broken-up" portion of a glacier.

Snout: The lowest reach of the glacial front or terminus. As a glacier advances or retreats, the terminus moves up and down the mountain.

Snowfield: A non-moving expanse of perennial snow.

Switchback: A zigzag in the trail.

Talus (talus slopes): A slope formed by an accumulation of rock debris, or rock debris at the base of a cliff.

Tarn: A small shallow lake in a depression carved by a glacier.

**ALL ART IN
FULL COLOR**

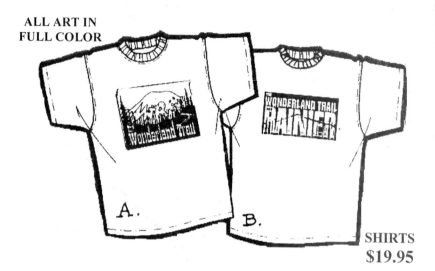

A.

B.

**SHIRTS
$19.95**

WONDERLAND T's

All T-shirts are 50/50 heavyweight poly cotton blend.
Adult sizes S:(34-36) Medium (38-40) Large 42-44 XL (46-48)

MOUNT RAINIER NATIONAL PARK
WASHINGTON

MOLENAAR MAP (left)
Acclaimed as the most
accurate artistic portrayal of
the Mountain. An oblique
view, incredibly detailed.

$7.50 (folded)

**Earthwalk Press
Hiking Map & Guide
Mt. Rainier National Park**

EARTHWALK MAP (right)
5-color topographic waterproof
map perfect for trail use.

(folded) $8.95

**WATERPROOF
NEW EDITION**

Features:
Topographic Map (1:50,000) of Mt. Rainier National Park
Backcountry, Climbing and Winter Information
Map Locator Coordinates, Trail Mileages, Safety

Latest Edition

Discovering the Wonders of the Wonderland Trail encircling Mount Rainier

Share this wonderful adventure with all who love the great mountain. A great gift, only

$13.95 + shipping and sales tax (WA res. only)

Send order to: Dunamis House
Box 321, Issaquah, WA 98027

NAME _____ PHONE _____

STREET _____

CITY/STATE/ZIP _____

Qty	Item	Size	Price	Total
			Subtotal	
			WA Tax 8.6%	
			Shipping	
			Total	

Date trail completed: _____
For those ordering certificates, list trip

Shipping: Up to $15.00 = $2.50, 16.00 - $25.00 = $4.00, $26.00 - $99.00 = $5.50
$100 or more, shipping FREE

Mount Rainier Merchandise

Wonderland Trail Video

Planning on doing the trail? Here's a chance to see what it's really like in the beaut-iful backcountry. Relive the rigors of the ridges from your armchair.

$24.95

Wonderland Trail Patch

Celebrate your accomplishment with this beautiful patch for use on your pack or jacket. These are sold only to those who have completed the trail.

$12.95

Certificate of Completion

A beautiful full-color certifticate personalized with your name and the highlights of your trip. They're laminated, suitable for framing. Those who have bought them, *love* them!

$12.95

The Big Fact Book About Mount Rainier

Bette Filley's big companion book of fascinating facts, figures, characters, stories, records, statistics, legends and more. A must-read for Mount Rainier fans.

$17.95

RESERVING CAMPSITES

An in-park Wilderness Reservation System is now available for backpackers planning trips during the May 1 to September 30 period. The reservations office is staffed and maintained at the Longmire Wilderness Information Center beginning the first Monday in April. Reservations can be made by completing a Reservation Request Form at http://www.nps.gov/mora/recreation/rsvpform.htm and faxing it to (360) 569-3131 or mailing it to: Wilderness Reservations Office, Tahoma Woods Star Route, Ashford, WA 98304. Phone reservations can be made by calling (360) 569-HIKE. There is a $20 reservation fee for advance reservations. Reservations can be made up to two months in advance of the day you start your trip (i.e., a reservation for July 4 may be made no earlier than May 4) and are for trips between May 1 and September 30 only.

It can be difficult getting through on the reservation phone line. Rangers assist callers between 8 a.m. and 5 p.m. daily. It may be easier to fax your completed reservation request as soon as you know the dates of your planned trip (at least 7 days in advance of your trip). Be sure to include accurate day, evening, and fax numbers on your request.

All trailside campsites and crosscountry zones along the Wonderland can be reserved no earlier than two months in advance of the first day of one's backpacking trip. Sites are available on a first-come, first-served basis. Reservations are available during the use limit season of May 1 through September 30 only, and are not available for other times of the year. The $20 fee per party per trip covers the cost of operating the reservation system. One itinerary change or readjustment before and during one's trip is permitted without additional charge. The $20 fee is non-refundable.

Reservations are required on the Wonderland Trail. Though often early and late in the summer and on some weekdays during mid summer, you may get every choice you want, be prepared to make some alterations. Such factors as poor weather radically affects demand. Out-of-state visitors especially should make advance reservations to avoid interruptions in their trip plans.

Reservations may be requested no earlier than April 2 for trips starting June 2. If, for example, your hike doesn't begin until July 15th, don't request a reservation before May 15th. Reservations may be requested as late as 24 hours before a trip is to begin but chances are slim you'll get the itinerary you desire. Reservations are not confirmed until your payment has been received (Visa or Mastercard by phone, mailed check, or in-person payment).

The Longmire Wilderness Information Center will be open daily for in-person hiking and backpacking information, wilderness permits, and wilderness reservations beginning around the end of May each year.

Mount Rainier National Park

Wonderland Trail Permit Reservation Request
(for trips between May 1 and September 30)

Reservations may be made up to two months prior to start date of your trip. Reservation requests submitted more than two months in advance of a trip will not be accepted. Please print clearly in dark ink. Use a separate form for each reservation you wish to make. Fax it (360) 569-3131 or mail it to: Wilderness Information Center, Mount Rainier National Park, Tahoma Woods, Start Route, Ashford, WA 98304-9751. For trips longer than eight nights, complex itineraries, or reservation information, call (360) 569-HIKE (4453).

CONTACT INFORMATION		REQUESTED ITINERARY	
Name:		**Date**	**Camp or Zone Name**
Address:		/	
City:		/	
State: Zip:		/	
Fax #:	**1st Choice**	/	
Home Tel.:		/	
Work Tel.:		/	
# of People:		/	
Vehicle 1 State & Plate #:		/	
Vehicle 2 State & Plate #:		/	
PAYMENT INFORMATION		**Date**	**Camp or Zone Name**
Check One: ☐ Visa ☐ Master Card		/	
# _ _ _ _ _ _ _ _ _ _ _ _ _ _ _	**2nd Choice**	/	
Expiration Date:		/	
Cardholder Name:		/	
Signature:		/	
		/	
Date:		/	

Authorized Amount: $ 20* * Per Reservation — Covers up to 12 people in a single group for up to 14 consecutive nights. **Reservation Fees are NON-REFUNDABLE.**	If the above choices are not available, are you willing to accept variations? Yes ☐ No ☐ Alternate start dates between: _____ & _____ Will you accept alternate sites? ☐ Yes ☐ No

Beginning the first Monday in April, you can make advance reservations for Wonderland Trail trip from May through September. While there is no fee for a permit, there is a $20 fee if you wish to reserve your permit in advance. Reservations may be made for up to 12 people (in the same group) for a maximum of 14 consecutive nights.

ENLARGE THIS FORM ON A COPY MACHINE FOR EASIER READABILITY. SEND IN THE ENLARGED FORM.

INDEX

Discovering the Wonders of the Wonderland Trail

Please let us hear from you

In preparing this book for publication, it soon became evident that this will have to be an ongoing project. In order to keep it up to date and accurate, we're going to need a continuous flow of current information of what's going on (trail and sign changes, etc.) in the Mount Rainier backcountry.

Let us hear about your adventures on the trail, animal stories, problems encountered and ingenius solutions. Got any pictures that would be a good additon to future editions? Want to be a volunteer wheel pusher? Give us suggestions on how to improve the book.

Drop us a note. Thanks.

Dunamis House
Box 321
Issaquah, WA 98027

Phone: 425-255-52   FAX: 425-277-8780

e-mail: rainierbooks@wahoo.com
rainierbooks@hotmail.com